Young Lust

Kathy Acker is the author of *Blood and Guts in Highschool* (Picador 1984); *Great Expectations* (Picador 1984); *Don Quixote* (Paladin 1986) and *Empire of the Senseless* (Picador 1988). She has also worked with Richard Foreman on a play version of *My Death My Life* presented at the Théâtre de la Bastille in Paris and on an opera, *The Birth of a Poet* which was shown in New York. She wrote the film *Variety* for director Bette Gordon.

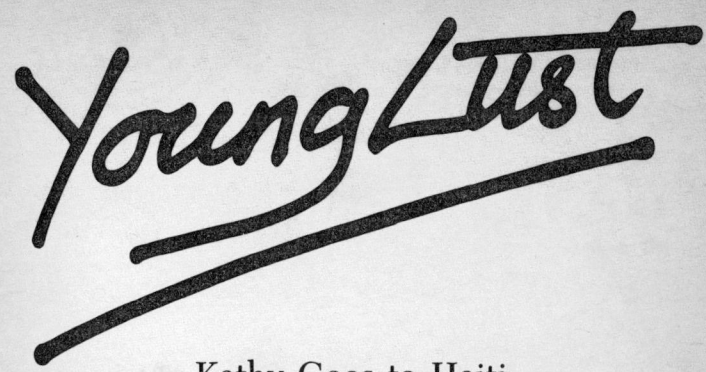

Young Lust

Kathy Goes to Haiti

The Adult Life of Toulouse Lautrec by Henri
Toulouse Lautrec

Florida

KATHY ACKER

PANDORA

LONDON SYDNEY WELLINGTON

First published by Pandora Press, an imprint of the Trade Division of
Unwin Hyman in 1989.

PANDORA PRESS
Unwin Hyman Ltd
15/17 Broadwick Street, London W1V 1FP

Unwin Hyman Inc
8 Winchester Place, Winchester, MA 01890, USA

Allen & Unwin Australian Pty Ltd
P.O. Box 764, 8 Napier Street, North Sydney, NSW 2060, Australia

Allen & Unwin NZ Ltd (in association with the Port Nicholson Press)
Compusates Building, 75 Ghunzee Street, Wellington, New Zealand

ISBN 0 04 440349 6

British Library Cataloguing in Publication Data
Acker, Kathy
   Young Lust.
   1. Fiction in English. American writers,
   1945– —Critical studies
   I. Title
   813'.54'09
   ISBN 0-04-440349-6

Phototypeset by Input Typesetting Ltd., London
Printed in Great Britain by Cox & Wyman Ltd, Reading

CONTENTS

Kathy Goes to Haiti   5
The Adult Life of Toulouse Lautrec   171
Florida   291

INTRODUCTION TO MY EARLY LUST TO WRITE

I CAME out of the poetry world of America. Specifically, I was taught by the second generation of the Black Mountain poets and by Jackson MacLow who was a crossover between that group and Fluxus. Among the many lessons I had learned by the time I was in my early twenties was a practical one: poets never make money and are, as both Rimbaud and Patti Smith said, the white niggers of this earth.

All the pieces included in this collection are early works. *Kathy Goes to Haiti*, which came right after the trilogy which included *The Adult Life of Toulouse Lautrec*, was written with two purposes. The first, to make money. In my early twenties I knew that I would never make a living through writing; I was broke and was working at a succession of varied and mainly disgusting jobs. The most disgusting being a file clerk for Texaco, Inc. I filed that company's employees' insurance claims while doing my best to forget the alphabet. *Kathy Goes to Haiti* was my attempt to make money through writing by writing a porn novel. In those days, a porn novel was any loosely-plotted collection of at least a hundred and twenty pages in which a sex scene occurred at least every twenty pages. It was the anarchic days of American porn. Poets including Diane Di Prima and David Meltzer had been commissioned by a fly-by-night company named Venice Books to write quality porn, for which a flat fee of eight hundred dollars was paid.

So I decided to write a novel in which a sex scene occurred at least every twenty pages.

This rule wasn't interesting enough. I needed more rules in order to write. Having been trained as a poet, I was, and still am, interested in verbal architecture, in language and how language works, rather than in telling a story. There seemed to be many stories in the world, some of them quite complex, and I saw no need to add to them. A novel, I had been taught, was composed of a plot and believable or well-rounded characters. I decided to write a novel that, while seeming to have a story, had none and whose characters were so deprived of psychology as to almost not exist. I wanted to stick a knife, a little one, up the ass of the novel.

Kathy Goes to Haiti was mathematically composed: every other chapter is a porn chapter; each chapter, except for the central one, mirrors its facing chapter. Mirrors are a significant part of the Voodoo cosmogony. *Kathy Goes to Haiti* was also my version both of a Nancy Drew book (an American girls' book) and of a travel journal. Thus, the rather black humor use of my own name. Using mathematical structure and genre parodies were my final two jokes—stabs into the form of the novel.

I never considered *Kathy Goes to Haiti* important. I just wanted to show—someone—I could write a 'real' novel.

The Adult Life of Toulouse Lautrec is the final part of the trilogy including *The Childlike Life of the Black Tarantula* (by the Black Tarantula) and *I Dreamt I was a Nymphomaniac: Imagining!* (also by the Black Tarantula). *The Adult Life of Toulouse Lautrec* was by Toulouse himself. In those days, I liked to change my identity. I still do. This trilogy was my first real novel: my first book, *Politics*, mainly a description of my life when I had worked in a sex-show on Forty-second street, is more poetry than prose.

When I began writing this trilogy, I gave myself numerous rules, too numerous to enumerate fully. Here are a few. I was to write as badly as possible, to never rewrite. To ensure

I did so, I sent out a sixth of each novel every month to whoever wanted it, a sort of serial mail-order novel. Why did I hate the academic rules of good writing? Because these rules were and are arbitrary, and writing cannot be arbitrary: writing always has a purpose, is communcative. For instance, in *Tarantula*, I wanted to examine the word 'I'. What is identity? I placed 'real' autobiography next to 'fake' autobiography. Nothing else mattered but the examination of this word 'I'; any other writing rules pointed the finger away from the moon.

By the time of *Nymphomanic*, I realized that my investigation of identity was too naive. I had not been taking account of how language works, of the medium of language. So I began to investigate language in terms of memory.

By the time of *Toulouse*, the problem of identity had become too complex and, at the same time, had resolved itself. I realized that identity is made, the legend of Daedalus is true, and perhaps of Icarus, that when one writes, one doesn't express true or false identity, truth or falsity, one makes identity. So I moved on to *Great Expectations* in which I was no longer interested in truth or falsehood, but in text. I began, simply, to plagiarize.

Florida is a short story, written between the trilogy and *Haiti*. I used to have a severe, chronic infection. During one bout of the infection, the usual three weeks in bed, I had a strong, undeniable urge to read the script for *Key Largo*. Such a script was not to be found, at least by me in my bed. So I did the next best thing, I wrote this script according to my memory. A memory of holes, like those landscapes I love the most. Landscapes of identity. Some of my friends and I performed this story or script at The Kitchen in New York City. I remember that Laurie Anderson played the Lauren Bacall role, by candlelight, and she was superb . . .

Kathy Acker, 1988

KATHY GOES TO HAITI

"THE LORD GIVETH AND THE LORD TAKETH AWAY;
BLESSED BE THE NAME OF THE LORD."

FIRST DAYS IN PORT-AU-PRINCE

KATHY is a middle-class, though she has no money, American white girl, twenty-nine years of age, no lovers and no prospects of money, who doesn't believe in anyone or anything. One summer she goes down to Haiti. She steps out of the American Airlines plane and on to the cement runway, her first example of Haitian soil. She's scared to death because she doesn't know anybody, she doesn't know where to go in Haiti, and she can't speak the language.

Kathy has her small duffel bag strapped to her shoulder and is going through Customs. The Customs man asks Kathy where she's going to stay in Port-au-Prince. "I don't know," Kathy replies. "Most tourists stay at the _____ or the _____ " The Customs man says two indistinguishable names. "Oh," says Kathy. "I'm sure you'll be very comfortable there. We just want to make sure that you know where you're going." "Thank you," says Kathy. "I'll be sure to take your advice."

Kathy takes up her bag and continues traveling through the airport. A man comes over to her.

"Would you like a taxi?"

"No, thank you. I prefer to travel more cheaply."

"Do you know anyone in Port-au-Prince?"

"No."

"You'll have to take a taxi to get into the city."

"OK I'll take a taxi."

The man introduces Kathy to another man. The second man is fat. Kathy and the fat man shake hands.

"OK," she says. "Where's the taxi?"

"It's outside."

Kathy and the fat man walk out of the Jean-Claude Duvalier airport to a small parking lot. The light from a big white sun is beating down on the cement. The man opens the door of a light blue Plymouth.

"This is a nice car."

"I decorated it myself."

Kathy and the fat man climb into the car.

The fat man starts the car.

Everywhere she sees the combinations of things she's never seen before. The land is very flat and dry. Shoeless women with huge baskets balanced on their heads walk on the sides of the road. Sometimes these women walk past small brick and cement motel and cocktail lounges. Nothing surrounds these motel and cocktail lounges. There are no trees. No brush. Suddenly there's a bridge and a huge cement bank which is tall enough to look like an American bank. It says THE BANK OF NOVA SCOTIA.

"Where am I going?" the driver asks the woman.

"I don't know. I've never been to Haiti before I know nothing about Haiti. I guess to a hotel."

"Which hotel?"

"I don't know. Which one do you recommend? I don't have much money."

"It all depends on how much you want to spend. How much do you want to spend?"

"I don't have any idea. It depends on how much I have to spend. Do you understand?"

"Do you want to spend twelve a night? Fifteen? Twenty? You can spend as much as you want."

"Twelve, fifteen would be OK. I'd like to get cheaper. I want a bathroom."

"Do you want a pool? Most Americans like a pool."

"I don't care much about a pool. You know what I'd really love? I'd love to be next to the ocean. Can I go swimming in the ocean?"

"Not around here."

"I mean can I find a place that's near the ocean?"

"I know a place you'll like. It won't cost you much."

"Is it near the ocean?"

"It's right on the ocean."

"Oh goody. I'm so happy. This is the first time I've ever been out of New York. Everything is so strange to me." She watches the children in torn dresses, the men in cut-off sandals shirtless lead the yoked cows and mules. The doorless stores set on wooden platforms. "How much will it cost for you to take me there?"

"That depends."

"What does it depend on?"

"Do you like me?"

"Yes."

"I'll take you for nothing. You'll be my girlfriend."

"I don't know."

"Why not?"

"I don't want to stay in Port-au-Prince more than one night. I want to go to Jacmel."

"To be my girlfriend you'll have to stay in Port-au-Prince a week. I can tell. You're going to like it in Port-au-Prince a lot."

"I don't know. I don't think I'm going to stay here."

"Do you speak French?"

"A little."

"Speak French."

From now on Kathy speaks only French in Port-au-Prince. Her French stinks.

"I'll stay in Port-au-Prince two days."

"A week."

"We're arguing already."

The fat man smiles. His right hand covers her left hand. Kathy and the taxi-driver hold hands.

Haiti is a mountainous country. Mountains rise from the sea-coasts and cover most of the inland part of the country. There are almost no roads in Haiti and many of the people who live inland have not and cannot leave the acres that are their village of birth. The city of Port-au-Prince lies between the beginning of the mountains and the ocean. Because hot winds sweep dust and then pollution down from the mountains into the lower lands and because the heat collects in the lower regions, the rich Port-au-Prince inhabitants—the tourists and the Haitian multimillionaires—live in the mountains: at the edge of Port-au-Prince in the suburb of Petionville and even farther west into the mountains. Port-au-Prince is a city that descends. One moves from the mansions hidden in the mountainous luxuriant foliage down to the tourist hotels and government offices of the wide city streets down, as it gets hotter and hotter, to the block-large markets, the Iron Market, where all the Haitians buy their necessities, down to the slums where shacks are piled on shacks, where twenty people live in one room, down to the edge of the water, the docks, where there are no breezes, only hot dust, and where the United States Navy waits a mile away in the ocean.

This is what Kathy sees: First paper-thin paper-like-wall shacks on thin wooden platforms. Walls are dirty pink, dirty pale green, dirty tan. Some of these shacks are stores because they have no doors and bear signs like EPICERIE and BOUTIQUE DE PARIS. There are more and more people everywhere. Soon there's at least one person per square foot. Men and women and girls and boys and babies sit and argue and sell and buy and stand around and eat and walk. No animals in sight. A few thin mangy green-leafed trees. The shacks move closer and closer together until they form a solid row that walls in the road. So there's this road with lots of cars running up and down it and long eight-feet-high paper strips on each side of it. The paper strips contain small paper doors. As they grow larger, the paper strips separate from each other and become individual buildings. Partly rotting two-and three-story houses surrounded by weeds and high concrete white fences. Larger semi-decaying mansions. Some of the buildings are stone and there are one or two rectangular cement office buildings. The buildings lie far apart from each other. The roads are wide. All the people here are walking. Some of the people wear clothes which aren't torn. There's a park. To the left and right of the road there are quasi-triangular ten-acre sections of low-cut grass, trimmed hedges, and here and there small circles of red flowers in the low-cut grass. To the right, below the grass, there's another few acres of plain dirt. Across the road from the dirt, still descending, there're a strip of joined yellow concrete houses which form a fence around a large dirt square.

"That's the army barracks," the taxi-driver says. The light blue Plymouth keeps moving. "To your left's a mausoleum."

On the left, the park continues. Low-cut grass and occasional small white and yellow flowers surround white steps and the large white building the white steps lead up to. Below the park there's a huge oval strip of land. A black metal fence surrounds this strip. Within the fence is a huge totally clean whiter-than-the-sun mansion. The mansion looks like an American government mansion. White white steps lead up to the mansion. There are no trees. There are no people. The shacks begin again and all the people walk and sit and talk and carry baskets and have dogs and quarrel. The road's a hard dirt road. It winds around, goes up and down, basically it moves north-south. There's dust everywhere. Dust on the road, dust in the air, dust on the skin, dust on the straw and wood shacks. The distance is a light tan haze. The shacks are light tan and grey. They're about two feet apart from each other. Dogs and chickens run from the shacks into the street. The sides of the road are ruts. Women and a few children walk in these ruts. There are almost no men. The women wear brightly colored scarves around their heads and closefitting dresses or blouses and skirts ending at their knees. Some of the dresses and skirts are torn. Sometimes they wear aprons over their skirts. The road's flat and runs directly north and south. On the right the dry land rises and on the left it slopes down and can't be seen again. Eight-feet-high paper walls line the road. There are so many men and women walking in front of the walls, there's a closer wall of black flesh. Cars pass on top of each other. Honk.

Honk. The people thin out. To the right, on the sloping dirt's a small cement house. The sign on the wood fence that surrounds this house says MARIE'S VOODOO. NIGHTLY. There are lots of similar houses surrounded by fences that are nightclubs and voodoo places. The sun is hot and bright. There are fewer and fewer houses. Just a long strip of road and more trees.

Kathy hasn't seen any white people.

The light blue Plymouth pulls into a driveway. On one side of the driveway there's a white stucco rectangular building. The other side is a patio: a round thatched roof reaches upward to a point over a raised cement floor. There are about ten rough wood chairs and tables and then a clear space around the jukebox which says WURLITZER.

"You stay in the car," the taxi-driver says to his new girlfriend. "I'm going to talk to somebody."

When the fat man returns to the taxicab, he tells Kathy she can stay here for nine dollars a night. That includes two meals a day. Kathy thinks that's cheap. "Is this a motel or your friend's house?" she asks the taxi-driver.

"A motel. Lots of tourists stay here."

The proprietor of the motel, a tall elegant Haitian who speaks French rather than Creole walks with the taxi-driver and the girl through the rubble and stones in back of the white building. From the rubble a hill made up of stone pebbles and a bit of dirt rises sharply upward toward inland Haiti. The sun beats down on the broken glass and rubbish under the girl's feet. Small white concrete rooms stick together and form the two rows of buildings behind the large white building. The last room is about a foot from the paved highway.

"How long will you be staying here?"

"I don't know. Probably three days."

"She'll be staying longer," the taxi-driver says.

"No, I won't."

"Well, we can have this room fixed up for you tomorrow." The proprietor shows Kathy the last room, a ten foot by eight foot room containing a rocking chair and a large window. The room has no floor.

"I like the room," the girl says. "I like the rocking chair."

"You also have your own bathroom here and you can come and leave without anyone bothering you."

The proprietor, the taxi-driver, and the girl walk around the building, through the hot rubble, to the first row of stuck-together rooms. The proprietor opens the door of the first room on the right. The room is ten feet by seven feet, has a cot, a small window, a table with a fan on it, and a straw mat. It looks like a cell.

"You can take this room for tonight. The other will be ready tomorrow."

"This is fine. This is perfect. I'm very happy." The taxi-driver goes to bring the girl her bag. The proprietor leaves. The taxi-driver brings the girl her bag and she starts unpacking.

"I'm going to go swimming. That's what I want to do most of all. I haven't been swimming in two years." The taxi-driver leaves the girl alone.

There's a knocking at the door.

"Who's there?"

"It's Sammy."

Kathy opens the door and sees the taxi-driver.

"I went to the car to get my bathing suit." He walks into the room. "Close the door."

Kathy closes the door and puts her arms around him and hugs him. He kisses her. Their tongues touch. Their tongues touch for a long time.

"Put on your suit. I'll put mine on," says the taxi-driver. She watches the taxi-driver and takes off her blue shirt. Her blue jeans. She's taking off her underpants. The taxi-driver walks into the bathroom. He comes back wearing a tiny yellow and orange flower bikini. His stomach sticks out over the bikini.

"Would you like a drink?"

"Sure."

A tall rather handsome young man's leaning against a stone wall. On the top of the stone wall's a bottle of rum, a tin bowl of ice, and two plastic cups. He pours rum into one of the cups and hands it to Kathy.

The taxi-driver puts his arm around Kathy. A small girl in a green bathing suit leans against the handsome young man's front.

"Where are you from?" the handsome man asks Kathy.

"I'm from New York City."

"Oh. How old are you?"

"I'm twenty-nine."

"I'm twenty-four. Sammy is twenty-nine."

"You are my age," she says to the fat man. "How old are you?" she asks the girl.

"Twenty-two."

"Uh."

Sammy and the two other people talk for a while in Creole.

"I want to talk to you," the handsome man says to Kathy and takes her hand in his.

"Is something the matter?"

"My brother tells me he loves you very much. There is a great deal of love in his heart for you. He says to me that he's very glad he has met you."

"Uh. That's nice."

"When are you going to get married?"

"Married? Wait a minute. Who's your brother?"

"Sammy. He's your driver."

"But we were just holding hands. You know. I don't even know him. Even if I did know him, I don't want to get married."

"Maybe you're married already."

"No, I'm not married."

"You're not going to marry him? He tells me he loves you very much."

"I don't want to get married. No. No way."

The handsome man leads Kathy to the right, on to the empty porch of a deserted white stucco house. "I want to talk to you very openly. I want you to tell me the truth. My brother says he feels a lot of love for you in his heart. Do you love him?"

"I don't love him or don't not love him. I don't know your brother."

"I want you to understand. My brother has been very lonely. He has had no girlfriend for a long time. His girlfriend left him and went away to the north last year. He needs to go with someone. Are you going with anyone?"

"No."

"Then he'll go with you. And we'll see what happens."

"I'm not staying. I'm going away tomorrow."

"Why? You could stay here for awhile."

"I want to go to Jacmel."

"Do you have some friends in Jacmel?"

"No. I just want to go to Jacmel."

"You could stay here for a few days and we could see what happens."

"No. I'm going to go to Jacmel."

"You like my brother?"

"Yes. Your brother seems like a nice person."

"When you go away, you'll write my brother?"

"Look. You have to tell me what's going on. I don't want to hurt your brother. You understand? I don't want to do anything to hurt anyone. I'm in a foreign land and I don't know quite how to act, what the customs are here. In my country people take a long time to get married. They have to know each other very well."

"My brother's alone and you are alone."

"I don't want to do anything to hurt your brother. I think he's a nice person, but I want to be free. I know it's hard being lonely so I don't want to do anything to hurt him. I don't know what to do in this situation."

"You like him?"

"I think he's a nice person."

"When you go away, you'll write him?"

"Yes. I'll write him some letters."

"You'll write him, he'll answer, maybe you'll fall in love. That'll be good."

They walk back to the other two people. Everyone but Kathy drinks some more rum. The three Haitians talk to each other. "I'm going swimming," says the white girl.

At a break in the concrete wall some rough stone steps lead down to the ocean. Kathy walks down the rough steps and into the ocean. Swims out in the cold gray wetness. Gray and gray-green with late sun looking more like a sheath of white diamond light than a fiery ball. Through tiny gray waves on the surface of this moving shifting air. Outward as far as she wants to go. Lays on her back and kicks water into the air. A three-seat wood rowboat moves by her. To her left's a small dirt beach. Skinny kids play on the beach. Time is slow here. The taxi-driver swims out to her. She swims to the stone steps. The rowboat turns around and comes to the stone steps. The man in the rowboat gives Sammy's younger brother a heavy straw bag. The younger brother's sitting on the steps. He opens the ugly black, white, and gray shells. Gives half a shell to the white girl. Remembers. Give her a slice of lime. She squeezes the lime over the oyster and swallows. He gives half a shell to Sammy. Sammy doesn't like to eat these things. He eats a few oysters. He and the white girl eat three rounds of tiny oysters. The girl goes back to swimming. She returns and they eat two more rounds of oysters. The man hands the straw bag and twenty cents to the fisherman. The rowboat goes back into the ocean. The air's turning gray and cold. The ocean's warmer and warmer. The white girl rises out of the water and shivers.

"Why don't you eat now?" the taxi-driver tells the white girl.

"Are you going to eat?"

"I'll eat."

The taxi-driver puts his arm around the girl and kisses her neck. The motel proprietor appears.

"We have chicken tonight. Is that OK?"

The fat man says something in Creole.

"That's fine," says the girl. "I'm starving." The girl turns to the handsome man and his girlfriend. "Aren't you going to eat?"

They look at her.

"I don't want to eat if you're not going to eat."

"We'll eat later."

A young girl places a large plate containing fried plantains, tomatoes, lettuce, and half-a-chicken roasted dry in front of Kathy. Kathy turns to the fat man. "Aren't you going to eat?"

"I'll help you eat." The fat man cuts up the chicken and places pieces of chicken in Kathy's mouth. When he's not putting pieces of chicken in her mouth, he's placing slobbering kisses on her neck. She finishes her dinner.

It's too dark outside to see the three Haitians and the white girl sitting on the patio under the thatched roof. To the left ten teenagers dance to American music on the jukebox.

"We'll go dancing tonight," the fat man tells Kathy. "I want to please you."

"I'd love to go dancing."

He orders a bottle of rum and pours a glass of rum for Kathy. The three Haitians talk to each other and drink rum. Kathy can't speak Creole.

"Come here," the fat man whispers. She leans her head on his shoulder. "It'll cost us to go dancing."

"How much?"

"Ten dollars."

"Ten dollars? That's ridiculous. I can't afford to pay that much money."

"We have to pay to get in and then we have to drink rum. It costs."

"OK." She gives the fat man ten dollars.

"Drink your rum."

She doesn't drink any rum. The three Haitians talk desultorily. "I'm too tired," she says. "I'm sorry. We'll go dancing tomorrow night. I want to go to my room."

"You don't want to go dancing? I thought you wanted to dance."

"Tomorrow night. I'm too tired now."

"I'll go to your room with you."

The fat man keeps his arm closely around Kathy. They say goodnight to his younger brother and the girl.

"I'm kind of weird," Kathy says to him as they step into her room.

"Close the door."

She closes the door. "I like to sleep alone. I mean, I like to be with guys, but I never spend the whole night with anyone."

"I understand."

She smiles. "That's wonderful. I mean, I know I'm weird." She turns around and kisses the guy as passionately as she can since she doesn't feel anything. He leads her to the bed, lays her down, and kisses her lightly. He doesn't want to take her clothes off, he just wants to kiss her slowly and lightly. She can't stand this. She reaches into his bathing suit and finds a long, thin cock. He doesn't react. After a while she takes her hand out of the bathing suit.

"In Haiti time is very very slow," the taxi-driver says.

The girl sighs. The man and the girl kiss some more. They take off their bathing suits. The girl leans down and gently places the man's cock in her mouth. It gets semi-hard. She turns her hand around the cock and opens and closes her hand. Her tongue moves fast up and down along the ridge of the head. Her mouth opens and closes. Softly. The cock is long and hard. She presses and rubs and licks. Nothing else happens no matter what she does.

"Since we're not going dancing, why don't you give me the money back?"

"No. I bought you rum."

"I didn't ask you for rum. And the rum couldn't have cost ten dollars."

"I don't want to give you the money."

"It's my money."

"Do you really need it?"

"OK. Keep it."

The girl and the man go back to kissing. Kathy grabs the man's cock. As soon as it's hard, she sticks it in her cunt. She pulls away, reaches for her purse, opens a blue plastic case, and sticks her diaphragm in her. "What's that?" asks the man.

"A diaphragm."

"I don't like it."

"I have to use it. I can't afford to get pregnant."

"I don't like it." The man refuses to fuck the girl. She takes her diaphragm out. She's scared he's going to hit her. They kiss for a while. "I'm going to drink," says the man. "Do you mind?"

"Do you get violent when you're drunk?"

"What do you mean?"

"Do you smash chairs and beat up people?"

"No."

"Why should I mind?"

"I'm going to go now."

"Where are you going?"

"I'm going to drink."

Kathy locks the door of her cell after the man and starts to meditate.

There's a knocking at the door. "Put this on the table," the taxi-driver tells Kathy as he enters the room. "I brought it for you."

"I don't like rum." She puts the bottle on the table.

"C'mon baby. Do you like me?"

She puts her lips up to his.

"Oh. Mon amour. Mon amour."

They take off their clothes and lie in the hot room on the narrow cot. She tries to put his cock in her cunt. It's too soft. She touches him and tries to put the cock in again. It's still too soft.

"I can't fuck you cause of that thing."

"The diaphragm."

"I don't like it." He turns her around and sticks his cock in her ass. Kathy's so happy to get laid at last she immediately comes. "Mon amour. Mon amour," says the man. "Je t'aime. Je t'aime. Do you know what that means?"

"Yes."

"Mon amour. Mon amour." The man comes. They sit in the middle of the bed and stare at the door. "I'm very tired," she says. "I'd like to go to sleep." The man looks at his watch and keeps sitting on the bed.

Around eleven o'clock the man tells her he loves her, she's his girlfriend, and leaves. Kathy can't sleep cause it's hot and the bed is strange.

It's hot and dry. Kathy sits on the patio porch, doing nothing. There's no one around. After a while some young boys show up. They sit down by her and stare at her. The white girl walks into the large building of the motel to get a beer. A boy who's sixteen, older than the boys outside, asks her where's she from.

"New York City."

"I have a relative in New York City."

She goes back outside. The fat man drives his light blue Plymouth into the driveway. He gets out of the car. When he puts his arm around Kathy, she shies away. He asks her when he should pick her up. She tells him she wants to be alone today. He should pick her up at six. He tells her he's very jealous and he'll be by at six. She kisses his cheek. Eight or nine young boys are sitting on the patio, talking, drinking beer, smoking. The girl walks across the black highway to the concrete wall.

The tall thin sixteen-year-old boy who was sitting inside the large motel building walks up to her.

"Are you a student?"

"No. I'm not."

"Do you have any babies?"

"No."

"You don't have any babies? Why not?"

"I never wanted any babies."

"Are you married?"

"No."

"Why don't you marry me?"

"What?"

"You could marry me and stay in Haiti."

"I don't want to get married. I like being alone."

"Don't you like Haiti?"

"Yes. It's beautiful here. Everything is very slow here. There's no tension."

"There is no time in Haiti. No one has to do anything here."

"Yes," says Kathy. "That's true."

They watch the green ocean for awhile. Another young boy walks up to Kathy and the tall thin boy. "This is Kathy," the tall thin boy says. "She's from New York City."

"Hello," says the shorter boy. "How long have you been here?"

"A day."

"You act like you've been here longer."

Kathy smiles.

"How long are you going to stay here?"

"I don't know," says Kathy. She smiles. "I'll be in Haiti for a month, two months. I'm going to Jacmel today."

"Today? How are you going today?"

"The motel proprietor told I don't know who the jeep to stop by the motel for me. The jeep'll come by about four o'clock."

"Why are you going to Jacmel?"

"Friends of mine told me it was very beautiful. They told me to stay at Pension Kraft."

"Don't go there. You won't like it there. Nothing ever happens in Jacmel. Stay in Port-au-Prince." He puts his hand over her hand.

"The car's coming for me today. Since I found a ride I have to go."

"No. You'll stay with me tonight. In Port-au-Prince. I'll take you to the bus tomorrow."

"I want to go to Jacmel today."

"Please. If you don't stay with me, I'll become very sick." The boy sings to her a Haitian rock-n-roll song. "You'll stay with me tonight." His brown eyes look pleading into hers.

"I'm going swimming now. It's too hot." Kathy swims in the cold green waters. The boys walk away. She sits on one of the lowest concrete steps. Every now and then the waves fall over this step. She swims some more. A man's sitting on the concrete wall that connects to the porch of the deserted house. Kathy gets out of the ocean and sits on another part of the wall.

"It's hot, isn't it?" the older man says.

"Yes," says the girl.

A strange boy walks up to Kathy. "Hello." He takes off his shirt. A friend of his joins him.

"Hello," says Kathy.

"Where are you from?" the first boy asks Kathy.

"New York City."

The boy's friend jumps up and sits down on the concrete wall. A copy of *Les Freres Karamazov* lies in his hand.

"Oh. Dostoyevsky. He's one of my favorite authors." She's happy she can talk about books.

"We're reading him in school."

"What school do you go to?"

"I study biology at the college."

"Oh," says Kathy. "Are these your notes?" She's looking at a small pink notebook.

"These are my biology notes. I'm studying to be a doctor."

"Can I look at them?"

"Sure."

Kathy looks at the green and red pen drawings of plants. Some of them look familiar.

"Why did you come to Haiti?" asks the medical student.

"I don't know. I wanted to. For the last two years I've wanted to come to Haiti."

"That's not that long."

"I guess not."

"You are very beautiful."

"Thank you."

"It's not usual for a young beautiful girl to travel alone."

"I'm not that young. I'm twenty-nine."

"You're not twenty-nine. I don't believe it."

"I am twenty-nine."

"You're younger than that. You're about twenty-two or twenty-three. Do you have a boyfriend?"

"No."

"You don't have a boyfriend. How can that be? You don't like love?"

"Well, I have several boyfriends. Kind of. Back in the States. You know how it is."

"When I come to the United States to study, I'll come visit you. Give me your name and address."

"OK."

"Tonight we'll go dancing together."

"We can't go dancing. I'm going to Jacmel at four o'clock."

"Do you have any babies?" the first boy asks.

"No."

"You've never had any babies?"

"Never."

"That's very strange. How come?"

"A woman can't have babies in New York City unless she's got money or a husband. Everything's too expensive in New York City."

"Do you want a baby?"

"Yes. Sometimes. When I can afford it."

"I'd like to have a baby with you."

"I can't have your baby. I don't know you."

"That way you'd get to know me. We'd have a beautiful baby."

"We can't have a baby." A dark blue car honks. "I'm going to Jacmel today." The car honks again. Kathy turns around. A hand's waving from the car. She walks over to the car.

"Hello. How are you this morning?" asks the taxi-driver's brother.

"This is Kathy." The brother introduces her to three gorgeous men. "This is Robert. Malcolm. Henri. You'n Sammy're going dancing with us tonight. Right?"

"Yeah. Sammy already dropped by this morning to see me. He's going to pick me up around six."

"I'll see you then. How'd you and my brother get along last night?"

"OK. He tells me he loves me, but I don't know him."

"I'll see you at six. Stay good until then."

"I'll try, but it'll be hard."

"Are those your friends in the car?" the medical student's friend asks the girl.

"He's the brother of the guy who drove me yesterday from the airport to the motel."

"Is he your husband?"

"Oh. I see what you mean by 'husband.' "

"Is he your husband?"

"No. I don't have a husband."

"Listen. You don't understand how things are in Haiti. Women in Haiti don't go around alone."

"What about the women who aren't married? Are there any woman who aren't married?"

"They live with their families."

"It's not like that in the United States."

"You can't go to Jacmel alone. You have to have a boyfriend."

"But I don't want a boyfriend. I want to be alone."

"If you don't go with a boyfriend, the driver of the jeep'll become your boyfriend."

"You mean he'll rape me?"

"No. No. There's no violence in Haiti. Anybody can do anything they want in Haiti."

"What'm I supposed to do?"

"I'll be your boyfriend in Jacmel."

"But you're in Port-au-Prince."

"I'll go to Jacmel with you. You'll stay over at my house tonight and we'll go together tomorrow."

"I want to go to Jacmel today."

"It's no good today. I'll put my name and address in Port-au-Prince in your book and you'll come to my house in Port-au-Prince this afternoon. Around four o'clock. I'll take you to the museum and all the art galleries. Are you interested in Haitian art?"

"Yes."

The boy writes his name and address on the first page of *Desolation Angels*. "You take a tap-tap and tell the driver to let you off here. I'll see you at four o'clock and tomorrow we'll go to Jacmel."

"At four o'clock. I'm going in swimming now." She walks down the concrete steps, across the sharp stones about two feet below the water, and dives. No one's around the concrete wall and the white porch. She gets out of the water and sits on the highest stone step. A strange thin boy walks up to her.

"Do you go swimming here a lot?"

"This is my first time. I just got to Port-au-Prince."

"How do you like Port-au-Prince?"

"I don't know." She sighs. "There are too many men here. They're always following me around."

The thin boy's silent.

"Are there very few women in Haiti? Am I acting in a funny way?"

"There are more women in Haiti than men. The women usually chase the men. But it's unusual for someone so young and beautiful to be alone. Everyone's curious about you."

"Oh. But they all want me to be their girlfriend."

"Don't you have a boyfriend?"

"No. I like being alone."

"I'll be your boyfriend if you want."

The medical student and his friend walk up to Kathy and the thin boy. She nods hello to them and turns back to the thin boy. "I like you very much but I don't want a boyfriend."

"She's going to Jacmel with me," says the medical student's friend.

"Well," she says, "I don't know."

"You're coming to my house today at four o'clock and we'll go to Jacmel tomorrow."

"Why're you going to Jacmel?" the thin boy questions her. "There's nothing in Jacmel."

"Friends of mine back in New York City told me I should stay at this pension in Jacmel. They said it's very beautiful there."

"Why don't you stay in Port-au-Prince?" the thin boy says. "You can stay with me."

"I don't want to stay in Port-au-Prince. I want to go somewhere where I can be alone. In New York City everything's always crazy and I want somewhere it's not crazy. Where it's very peaceful."

"You should go to Cap Haitian."

"Where's Cap Haitian?"

"It's up north. It's a tourist city. You'd like it there."

"I don't want to be a tourist. I just want to go somewhere where I can lie on a beach and not be hassled."

"I'm from Cap Haitian," the thin boy says. "I love it there. I love Port-au-Prince. This is also my homeland but even more I love Cap Haitian. It's very very peaceful there and very small. You can walk anywhere. No one will bother you. It's not big and noisy like Port-au-Prince. If you want nightlife, you stay in Port-au-Prince."

"I don't want nightlife. I got all the nightlife I wanted in New York."

"You should stay at L'Ouverture pension."

"I stayed there when I was in Cap Haitian," says the medical student's friend. "That's a really good place."

"Is it like the motel here?" asks Kathy. "I feel like I'm staying in a dumpy prison."

"Which motel?"

"The one right across the street."

"No no. L'Ouverture is really nice. Everyone who goes to Cap Haitian stays there. All the Haitians stay there."

"That's true," says the medical student's friend.

"I think I'll go to Jacmel and then to Cap Haitian."

"Where are you going now?"

"I'm going to the motel to see whether the jeep that's going to Jacmel came yet."

"I thought you were going to come to my house today and go to Jacmel with me tomorrow," says the medical student's friend.

"I really want to go to Jacmel today. I already had the motel proprietor send someone just so I could get this ride. I'll meet you in Jacmel tomorrow."

"The car won't come today," says the medical student's friend.

"Why do you say that?"

"It won't."

"Well, if it doesn't come, I'll go to your house at four o'clock and then we'll go to Jacmel tomorrow. Either way I'll see you in Jacmel tomorrow. OK?"

"No problem."

The thin boy grabs her arm. "If you leave me like this, I'm going to die."

"C'mon," says Kathy. "That's not true."

"It is true." The boy cries. "I love you."

"I'm just going to the motel," says Kathy. "I'm not leaving yet."

"You'll be at the motel?"

"I'll be at the motel."

"OK. I'll join you there."

The sun's at its hottest. Against the stucco white wall by the highway a woman sits by a small black pig. Another woman peels a mango for a young boy. Across the highway everything's white. White motel walls. White cement underneath. The patio's crowded. Women with full short torn skirts and homemade bandanas, huge baskets filled with clean laundry, walk in the ruts.

"Has the jeep that goes to Jacmel come by yet?"

"No."

There are men everywhere. Men talk to men. Ten-year-old men. Forty-year-old men. Most of all twenty-year-old men. Men lounge around and do nothing. Men drink rum and coke. Men play the jukebox. Kathy sits down at an empty table on the patio.

"Would you like to join us?"

Kathy says no, then yes. She sits next to a semi-gray-haired man and a short-haired robust woman.

"My name's Walter," says the man. He pours her some rum.

"Mine's Kathy. What's your name?"

"I'm Marguerite."

The thin boy who was talking to Kathy asks her to dance. She dances with him. A slightly older and heavier boy cuts in. The older boy holds Kathy close and grinds his cock against her. The medical student and his friend show up. Kathy walks away from the older boy to the medical student.

"You're still here? I thought you were going to Jacmel."

"The jeep hasn't shown up. I guess it isn't going to come."

Seven boys crowd around Kathy. One of them sticks his hand under her bathing suit top and strokes her breast. She walks back to Walter and Marguerite.

"Walter's my boyfriend," says Marguerite. "I spend the days with him and the nights with my husband."

"Does your husband know about this?"

"My husband and Walter are best friends. It's wonderful. I like everything to be out in the open. You know, in Haiti a woman has to be married."

"What do you mean?"

"If a woman's married, she can do anything she wants. She's protected. If she's not married, no man'll respect her."

"You're the first woman here I've been able to talk with. I'm confused about what's happening. How do the women in Haiti act? Everyone here tells me that women never go anywhere alone. Is that true? Am I going to be unable to travel here?"

"That's not true. There are career women here." Marguerite laughs. "But there is a problem in Haiti. A woman has no freedom unless she's married. She needs a man who'll take care of her. Then she can do anything. I have a man who takes care of me, my husband, and then I have as many boyfriends as I want. I don't love my husband."

"But I don't want a husband."

"You need to have a man who'll protect you. So men will respect you. The men here don't respect you."

"You're too young for this place," Walter says to Kathy. "How d'you get here?"

"The driver brought me here from the airport. I didn't know where I was going."

"You know what?" says Marguerite. "Tonight Walter and I'll take you back to my place. You'll eat dinner with us. I want you to understand: I don't know if you'll like it: my place is very small, but you can stay at my place. Did your driver take you around Port-au-Prince?"

"I haven't been anywhere. Just here."

"Tomorrow we'll go around Port-au-Prince and you'll see how beautiful my city is. I want you to have a good impression of my city. Would you like that?"

"That would be incredibly wonderful. I'm very happy now."

The taxi-driver and his brother sit down at the table. Everyone says hello. Sammy tries to put his arm around Kathy, and Kathy moves away.

"I don't want to be your girlfriend."

"OK. No problem."

The Haitians talk Creole to each other. Sammy asks Kathy where she's going. She's going to Marguerite's house.

The sky's growing dark. A $6,000 light tan car. Almost all consumer goods are imports from the US. If a Haitian wants to produce cars or TV's in Haiti, he has to make the items in Haiti, export them to the US, import them to Haiti. That's the only way the Haitian government can make the luxury taxes they so desperately need. Light tan leather seats.

"Sammy told us he's your boyfriend. You have to be back by six o'clock so you can go dancing with him."

"He's not my boyfriend. Sure we kissed a little and you know but that doesn't make him my boyfriend. He's crazy. He picks me up at the airport yesterday, he's my driver, and takes me to this godforsaken motel. I don't even know how to get out of it and get back to Port-au-Prince. Then he tells me I can't speak to any other men cause he's very jealous. Then he asks me if I want to go dancing. 'OK,' I tell him, 'sure.' He asks me for ten bucks. We don't go dancing, but he keeps the ten bucks. Some boyfriend."

"I want to explain something to you. Sammy's a driver. I know all the drivers in this town and they're all the same. They only see money. Tourists to them, first of all, mean money."

"Then you understand. I don't see why I have to keep the date with him tonight. When I left the motel just now, I told him he wasn't my boyfriend. He acts like he doesn't hear. I don't want to make trouble, understand; I'm in a foreign country."

"When Sammy was your driver, did he take you on a tour of Port-au-Prince?"

"Huh? No . . . He just drove straight to the motel. As far as I can tell cause I don't know the place."

"He should have taken you on a tour. Sammy's an evil man. All he cares about is money. Most Haitians are gentle and good. I want you to see the other side of Haiti."

The gray sky turns purples. Layers of roses and lavenders. Top layers of blues and dark purples. Everything in front of the sky has become forms of dark blues and black. The sky is dark blue. Now and then there are tiny lights. Carrefour, the town or stretch of land and swamp on the ocean between the motel and Port-au-Prince. Paper walls are black. Black shapes pass each other in front of these black walls.

The air's hot. The drums are beating.

"If you want, you can stay at my house for as long as you're in Port-au-Prince," Marguerite says to the white girl.

"I'd love to stay at your house. But I'm going to Jacmel tomorrow morning."

"Why are you going to Jacmel? If you want to go somewhere,

you should go to Cap Haitian. Cap Haitian is my hometown. It's the most beautiful place in Haiti. The people there are all gentle and good. No one will harm you there. Sometimes the people in Port-au-Prince are no good."

"If you want," Walter says, "I can drive you there. I'm a driver for tourists." He shows Kathy his card.

"How far is it to Cap Haitian?"

"Six hours. Four hours."

"How much will you charge me?"

"I don't charge you anything. I don't want your money. I do it for friendship."

"Walter will take care of you. He'll be very good to you."

"I don't understand. Why will you do this? Are you going to Cap Haitian on your own?"

"No. I'll drive you there and then I'll come back. It won't take me long."

"Will I have to be your girlfriend?"

"Well. Yes."

"But Marguerite's your girlfriend. I don't want to come between you and Marguerite."

"It's OK," says Marguerite.

"No. I'll go to Cap Haitian by plane."

"You don't have to be my girlfriend. We'll just see what happens."

Port-au-Prince is a mass of decaying white and yellow houses. The sky grows blacker and blacker. The black road between Port-au-Prince and the motel stretches out into the blackness. Trees, walls, huts are indistinct shapes. Walter, Marguerite, and Kathy are drinking rum on the motel patio. Walter's wearing pale yellow pants and a pale yellow shirt.

"I dressed up especially for you. Because you're my girl."

"Oh," says Kathy. She's extremely tired since she hasn't slept in two days. "I'm going to sleep."

"I'll pick you up early tomorrow morning and take you all around Port-au-Prince so you can see how beautiful my city is.

I want you to go home with a good impression of Haiti. Then you stay at my house and the next day you can go to Jacmel."

"That'd be great," says Kathy, "goodnight." She locks herself in her cell and immediately falls asleep.

The small black-and-white goats bleat. The rooster crows, stops, crows again. Footsteps outside the window. Sound of water dripping on the rubble. Outside there's no one except for two young girls short tight skirts with slips showing under skirts T-shirts and bras plastic sandals who're cleaning up last night's debris. One girl disappears into the large room. The other girl sweeps the patio, straightens the chairs, sweeps the cement driveway, sweeps the rocks on the sides of the driveway. Men without shirts leading two yoked oxen or two yoked mules start to walk down the road south to the market.

Kathy, Marguerite, and Marguerite's husband climb into the tan Buick.

"Did you pay your bill?"

"Yes." Actually Kathy didn't pay for the last night.

"I've got to be at work at eight o'clock," says Marguerite. "But I don't have to stay. You'll go to my house now, and I'll come back for you at nine o'clock and I'll take you around Port-au-Prince. When are you going to Jacmel?"

"I think I'm going to Cap Haitian today."

"I thought you were going to Jacmel."

"I changed my mind. You made Cap Haitian sound so terrific. I can do whatever I want."

"Are you going with Walter?"

"No. Walter wants me to be his girlfriend and I'm just not attracted to him."

"Does he know this?"

"Yes. We discussed it last night."

"We'll go around Port-au-Prince today and then I'll take you to the airport. You know what I'll do for you because you're alone and you don't know anyone in Cap Haitian? I want you to be happy. Cap Haitian is my hometown: I love Port-au-Prince, but

I love Cap Haitian most of all. It's the most beautiful place in Haiti. I'll write a note for you to Api. He's a driver there so he'll take you around. He'll respect you."

"He won't want to fuck me?"

"No. That's why I tell you about him. He's what-do-you-call-it? a lesbian."

"A homosexual."

"Yes. I'll write you a note introducing you to him."

The Buick swerves up a thin winding street in the center of Port-au-Prince and stops in front of a wooden fence. Beyond the fence there's an old decaying mansion. Soil mixed with inches of grass, a few stone steps, then a dark room containing a cuttingboard and a sink. This must be the kitchen. There seems to be no ceiling. To the left, up a huge staircase half of whose stairs are missing. Huge wide open windows with gray shutters. Lots of light. No air and what air there is, is hot. A wide white and gray hall. Five rooms all of whose doors are open or broken lie off this hall. Different kinds of beds, curtains, cabinets fill each room. Each room contains a different family. Half-dressed men and women lounge around.

Kathy and Marguerite are lying on a huge double bed in the corner of one of these rooms. Over the bed there's a large open shuttered window. The window frame's falling down. The room contains three beds and one huge wooden antique cabinet dominating the middle of the room. Hand-hung ropes and large pieces of silver cloth separate the beds. There's almost no visible floor. A table covered with a red-and-white checkered cloth situated against the door wall holds all the dishes silverware bottles of gingerale different kinds of cola mineral water and beer. A dressing table against the wall between the double bed and one of the cots holds lots of makeup bottles and a bottle of Barbancourt rum. Kathy has her clothes on; Marguerite wears a bra and underpants. Kathy and Marguerite hold hands. Marguerite's sister and her child sit on the cot behind the dressing table. A male cousin sits in a wood chair by the double bed. Another young woman's standing. Everyone's watching "Hogan's Heroes" on TV. Another boy's sleeping on the cot in back of the cabinet. Three families who are all interrelated live in this room. A program in French about a Haitian woman who murders her child comes on the TV.

"What's your life like? Are you able to do what you want?"

"I have a good life. I don't have to work too much: I only go to work three days a week I only work in the mornings. I only want to work as much as I have to. I would rather do what I want and be poor, than work."

"I'm the same way. Work's the worst thing that can happen to someone."

"I don't live this way all the time. In Cap Haitian I have a big beautiful house. But here I don't want to spend all my money on rent. It's too expensive here. I'd rather spend my money on other things."

"Do you have many girlfriends?"

"A woman can't have girlfriends. Not the way things are in Haiti. I tell you something. I have a good husband who protects me. If I have a girlfriend, immediately she steals my husband or my boyfriend. I've never really had a girlfriend."

"That's terrible. Is that the way things are for all Haitian women?"

"There's some influx of American ideas, some of the women are starting to have careers, but I tell you, things are very slow. Women still don't have their freedom here. I tell you something. If I ever stop being married, I'm not going to get married again. I want my freedom."

The sun coming through the window is growing hotter and hotter. There's no breeze. Children run in and out of the room. The two women drink rum, beer and lay around. Then they go to the airport. The airport contains hundreds and hundreds of people. Kathy gives Marguerite a fan and some money for the taxis. Marguerite gives Kathy the letter for Api the driver. They drink some more beer.

LOVE AT FIRST SIGHT

I T's rapidly turning dark. The winds are blowing. Water hits
the stone wall and leaps straight up into the air, thirty feet.
Forty feet. Behind the stone wall there's a black road behind
that a high white stucco wall. Stucco wall, overgrown garden,
terrace.

There are musicians playing in the dark night.

Kathy looks up and sees a good-looking man.

"Gee, he must be an American. He looks like an American.
And he's not even looking at me, much less chasing after me
like all the Haitian men. I haven't spoken English in four days
and I haven't talked to any man like a friend cause all the men
here think about is sex and marriage and I'm confused and I want
to ask someone what's going on, but I can't walk over to a strange
man. I'd be picking him up."

Breezes blow through the coconut trees and musicians wiggle
their long-cock hips.

The white girl walks over to the man. "Are you an American?"

"No," he says in a thick Southern accent.

He has light brown curly hair. His nose and his face are as fat
and snub as a beautiful hard red cock. "Oh, I'm sorry. I didn't
mean to interrupt you. I just haven't seen an American in four
days, much less anyone who speaks English."

"Sit down anyway. Take a load off your feet."

"I don't want to interrupt you. I just thought . . . Are you sure
it's OK?" She doesn't want the man to think she's trying to pick
him up.

"My name's Gerard. What's yours?"

"Kathy. How come you've got a Southern accent?"

He takes off his light brown-tinted glasses. "I went to school in the States. In Nashville."

"Did you like it there?"

"It was real nice. The people there were all nice, real friendly."

"Just like here. But I get confused. Listen. I mean you're the first person I've been able to talk with, you know, really talk with in the last four days and I don't understand what's going on. There's been nobody I've been able to ask."

"Where have you been?"

"Port-au-Prince. I just got to the Cap a few hours ago."

"You can ask me anything you want. I'm just a nice, friendly person."

"I don't understand what the relations are between men and women in this country."

"What don't you understand?"

"Are the men desperately horny all the time?"

"There are lots more women than men in Haiti. I think that can hardly be true."

"Well why are these men following me all the time? I don't understand. When I was in Port-au-Prince, all the time, these guys would follow me. At least twenty guys. I could never be alone. Every time I went somewhere, there was another guy. The first day I was in Port-au-Prince, I got seven marriage proposals, not to mention the other propositions. I don't even know anyone."

"Well, I'm not going to ask you to marry me."

"Thank God."

"I'm going to get married myself. In September."

"That's wonderful. Who to?"

"I don't know yet."

"Oh. How the hell can you get married if you don't know who to?"

"I work in the mountains. I only come down here on the

weekend. And when I finally get down here, I'm so goddamn tired all I can do is grab a book I fall asleep before I know it. I don't have the time to go looking for a girl. I'm real lonely. I want to come off that goddamn mountain and find someone waiting for me. I want a hot meal cause I'm sick of eating out of cans and I want someone in my bed."

"I see your point. I wouldn't mind shacking up with someone myself, I don't know, I like my freedom. It's hard to find someone I can bear to stay with for a while."

A young Fidel Castro in a filthy Donald Duck T-shirt walks past Gerard and Kathy. "Hey Roger, don't go away. Sit down at the table with us. This here is Kathy. She just came to the Cap today."

Fidel Castro doesn't say hello to Kathy. "We were talking about you getting married," she says to Gerard.

"Oh yeah I'm getting married in September. All I need to do is find the girl. But I tell you, girls are scarce around here."

"I thought you said there are more Haitian women than men."

"Sure there are, but they're dogs. Most of them you can't even look at. Either they're after you all the time cause they're so desperate for men, or they're the type their mothers keep them at home and won't let them dance closer than two feet to a man and watch every little thing they do."

"Oh brother," says Fidel Castro. "Women. When I was in school in Florida, I was involved with this woman. Or rather she was involved with me. She was my teacher."

" 'I remember when I was a teacher,' " she says, " 'Jesus Christ I couldn't keep my hands off those young boys. They were so cute. I knew I shouldn't, being a teacher and all that ethics or something but I couldn't resist.' "

"She chased me all over the place. Oh brother. First she wants me to stay after class. Says I need help with my work or something. I know what she wants. I stay after class and she's always pulling up her skirt or shoving her breasts in my face or something."

"Was she pretty?"

"She was alright. She was, I don't know how to say it, too sweet. She was all over the place. She was a big woman, her blonde hair tied up in a bun, but she acted like she was real small and cute. All the time she was too sweet."

"I know the type. Blabblabblabblabblab. All over the place." The girl's hands wave in the air. "I don't like women like that. You can't trust them."

"I don't like sweet women either. One time I take her out. Boy, was that a mistake. Immediately, she's all over me. Dancing real close to me laying her head on my shoulder."

"So did you sleep with her?"

"Yeah but I didn't want to have anything to do with her after that. She wore all this stuff in her hair you know? I didn't really like her. Then she was after me even more. She said she'd make trouble for me if I didn't see her again."

"Why didn't you tell her to go to hell?"

"She knew I was smoking in the bathroom during class. You know, pot."

"Yeah."

"She threatened to tell the principal about me. I had to be very careful because I'm a foreigner."

"But everybody smokes in college."

"This was high school."

"High school! Oh my God. Now I understand."

"But she was so hot for me, you know, she couldn't do anything. Finally, she'd do anything for me."

"Well, I hope you got As out of it."

"I did."

Kathy and Gerard laugh.

"Do you take a lot of drugs?" Roger asks Kathy.

"No," Kathy says. "Certainly not as many as my friends take. I'm pretty puritanical. I never buy pot though I take it if someone offers it to me. Well, you know. The only drugs I like are psychedelics. I used to take a lot of acid, well, not a lot, not like some people would take it, every fucking day, that was really crazy, I took it about once a month for a year, when I was in college. I just stopped. Now and then I still take some peyote and psilocybin. I mean I use them. Oh I love opium. Opium's my one big habit. I've never eaten it goddamnit I hear it's wonderful I've only smoked it. It's not expensive but it's real impossible to get. So you can't get hooked on it, cause it really only comes through once a year."

"Everyone in America takes drugs," says Roger, "that's why Americans are so crazy. Drugs are ruining everything about America."

"It's true," Kathy says. "Not psychedelics or shit like that, but those damn pills. Everyone pops them. When I first went to California, the first thing I saw was a newspaper article saying that nine-year-old kids were shooting stuff into the undersides of their tongues."

"Oh brother. California. Everyone there is somewhere else. When I first rode in there, I saw a sign saying THE GRASS IS FREE. I don't like it there everyone's too much in the clouds."

"I like San Francisco. I lived there for two years. The people are real gentle and open. Just like the people here. LA's a horror show."

"The people in San Francisco take those new things, what are they?"

"Quaaludes?"

"Yeah, Quaaludes. The kids here are even beginning to take them: reds, whites, Quaaludes. Here it's worse because the Haitians don't know anything about drugs. They don't know what they're doing. Like Ally, Henry's son. He takes everything he can put his hands on and he keeps wanting more. He's acting hyper and strung-out."

"If he doesn't know about drugs, he could end up poisoning himself. Like he could take downs on top of liquor."

"What's worse here is that if you get caught, even if you get caught just smoking a joint, oh brother, that's it for you. A year in jail or maybe a lifetime. The jails here are deathpits. So everyone's very cool. You don't talk about drugs."

Gerard, Roger, and Kathy leave Pension L'Ouverture and go

to the Imperial. The Imperial is a small motel and cocktail lounge with food in the outskirts of Cap Haitian. Stretch of road over flat empty soil, a semicircle of white stucco rooms, flat empty land until the mountains begin. The center room is the cocktail lounge, a dark red-light room full of empty tables covered with white cloths, a New York City 1950s cocktail lounge.

"Where's your wife?" Gerard asks Roger.

"You're married?"

"I'm married," Roger says. "Oh brother."

"What's your wife like?"

"If you're interested, I can show you pictures of her."

"She's very pretty. I like her better with the short hair."

"That's what she had when I first met her in Oklahoma. But she's let it grow since then."

"You should have seen him," Gerard says, "when he was getting married. He comes to me and says, 'Gerard, what'm I supposed to do with her? I can't treat her like any other girl.' I say, 'Roger, buddy, look. Marriage is very simple. You come home from the wedding, you know, and you're madly in love, you can't keep your hands off each other, and you don't. Well, you calm down from that a little, maybe you drink a little, you talk a little, it's your wedding night, you know, so you do it three, four times. You fall asleep. Then maybe, about two o'clock in the morning, you're both a little nervous, you don't really know each other, you wake up and you're surprised: you feel a warm body next to you and you're not used to feeling a warm body next to you. So you feel around a little, you know, just to check out who's next to you and before you know it, you're doing it again. Then about four in the morning, maybe one of you has a bad dream. You know, all that champagne and wedding cake and crap you've eaten in the past day, it's probable that one of you's going to have a bad dream. There's a scream; both of you wake up; one of you's going to have to comfort the other. You do it again.' "

"And the next day you get divorced," says Kathy. "How else can you handle all that fucking?"

" 'Well you wake up around five cause you have to go to work and you kiss sweetie goodbye. But she's so sorry to see you go, she doesn't want to see you go and after all, she's your wife, you've got to help her out. You do it again. Now about twelve o'clock you come home for your lunch. You've got to have lunch. Your wife's been waiting for you all day; she's been worried about you; you're so happy to see her you've missed her so much you can't help yourselves you just do it again.' "

"I should have listened to you. I never would have gotten married."

" 'Then about two o'clock, well, you're getting a little nervous. You know you're wondering what she's doing all alone in that big house. So you decide to take a little peek, just to be sure she's not with some other man. You go home and take a little peek, and there she is, her dress pulled up over her legs, her hand up there, well you just have to help her out. She loves you so much.' "

"I don't even want to fuck that much. I wouldn't have the time to do anything else."

"I agree," says Roger.

Kathy and Roger stare at each other.

"No. You've got to realize what marriage is. 'Well, about five o'clock you get home and you're exhausted. Just plumb tired. You just open that door and fall down on that soft bed. She comes over to you and rubs your feet and your calves and the insides of your knees and your thighs and by the time she goes up a little farther, you just can't help yourself. After all, she's been sitting in the house all day, alone, just waiting for your return. Then she serves you this hot meal and you feel terrific. All your energy returns. So you look at this woman you've married who's doing everything possible to make you feel terrific and you grab her, just to show how much you love her. You do it again. By now it's dark and the stars are shining, it's time to go to bed. So it begins all over again.' "

"So that's what your marriage's like," the girl says to Roger.

"I never see my wife. She stays shut up in the house and does what I tell her to do."

"You're weird, Roger."

Roger reacts as if she said something horrible. "I'm just an ordinary person. I'm like anyone else. It's bad to be unlike everybody else. You stick out and people pick on you. My goal in life is to be an ordinary person. That's why I wear these filthy clothes."

"I used to think I was a freak all the time, but I don't think so anymore."

Next stop: three huge bronze statues overlook the deserted road. Roger's huge white truck clambers to a halt.

"Can you see that bronze thing through the trees?"

"No," says Kathy. "Yes. I can see it. Who is it?"

"Toussaint L'Ouverture. There are some others with him, but I don't know who they are."

"What happened to him? Did he die in battle?"

"The French took him prisoner and brought him back to France. They imprisoned him in the Jura Mountains because they knew his body couldn't adjust to the cold. He spent a winter in an unheated cell—he had never before known the cold—without blankets, no doctor, so by the end of the winter he died."

Gerard leaves to buy some beers.

Kathy and Roger sit in the silence and don't speak to each other and don't look at each other.

Gerard gives them two beers and leaves.

Kathy and Roger sit in the silence and don't speak to each other and don't look at each other.

"Don't look at me like that," Roger says.

"How'm I looking at you?"

"I don't know. You're looking at me strangely. You're making me unable to drink my beer."

"That's funny. This guy I uh knew in New York used to tell me I looked at him strangely. I never knew I was doing anything. I guess there's something in the way I look."

The two of them don't speak.

"I'm not looking at you now, so drink your beer."

They don't speak.

"Hey folks," Gerard says, "I've brought us all some cigarettes."

They stop in front of a place where they can dance.

The first room of The Fish contains a small bar and a low black couch. A Jimi Hendrix poster, a hippy fuck poster, a Black Satan female poster, a Janis Joplin poster, words such as REVO-LUTION and LOVE written in orange and green day-glo cover the walls of this room.

The next room is empty and dark.

The third room is black. Low black couches hug the walls of this room. A few indistinguishable couples sit and lie on the couches.

"Let's dance," Roger says.

They walk into the next room.

"How do Haitians dance?" Kathy asks.

Roger puts his arms around Kathy and holds her body lightly against his. His thighs move slightly from side to side. Sometimes his feet move slightly. She tries to follow him. It feels easy to her.

"This is how my friends in New York dance." She pulls away from him and leaps on her toes and turns in circles. "This is what we do at parties."

Roger pulls her to him. They move together so that inch by inch they're slowly traversing the floor, their genitals are lightly grinding against each other.

The jukebox plays another song. This one's an old American rock tune. His face falls so that his lips brush across Kathy's forehead.

"You're so small," Roger says.

"I know."

She lifts her face and his lips touch her lips. Kathy thinks they both feel slightly embarrassed.

"You're not dancing like a Haitian."

"Oh. How do Haitians dance?"

"You're twisting too much to one side. We move from side to side. Like this."

"I see. Like this. The weight's mainly in your knees."

"Let's go back."

They go back to the other room and sit down next to each other on the couch. For a while they don't touch. Roger takes Kathy's left hand in his right hand.

"I don't understand what's happening."

"I don't either."

"I mean, I . . . I mean, I . . . Where did Gerard go to?"

"He's in the front room. I think he's with a girlfriend."

They're both silent for a long time.

"You're very shy."

"Yes. I am. How do you know that? Most people don't realize that."

"I don't know. It's obvious. I'm very shy too."

"I'm just like everybody else."

"You keep saying that," she says. "Why? You're obviously not."

"You're too smart."

Gerard appears. "Do you want to dance?" he asks the girl.

"Well," she hesitates, "OK."

Gerard and Kathy walk into the next room. He puts his arms around her and holds her lightly against him. His left leg falls between her thighs so that as they dance, her cunt and inner thighs rub against his leg. Her body gets hot. She moves away from him and starts dancing American style. Gerard pulls Kathy close to him. The music stops. He wants to dance another dance, but she says no.

They walk back to the couches and sit down next to Roger. Nobody says anything. Nobody does anything.

"Let's dance."

As soon as they get to the dance floor, Roger's and Kathy's arms slide around each other's bodies. They kiss and their tongues enter each other's mouth. They remain this way for several minutes. Hot spasms are shooting up and down Kathy's spine. She's scared because she feels so turned on. She moves her face down and to the side so that her face sleeps in the hollow of Roger's chest under his head and in from his armpit. His muscled arms hold her tightly enough that she feels protected. Roger and Kathy alternately kiss and dance with Kathy's head under Roger's head. Roger and Kathy, as far as they know, are the only people left in the bar. They keep on dancing.

"Let's go," Roger tells Kathy.

Roger and Kathy walk by the high white pension wall. Across the street, the ocean.

They sit down on the grass and begin to kiss.

"What do you want to do?" Roger asks.

"What do y'mean, 'what do I want to do'?"

"What do you want to do?" He smiles.

Kathy kisses Roger.

"Well, what do you want to do?"

Kathy buries her head to the side in Roger's lap and giggles. "For God's sakes Roger you know what . . ." She can't finish her statement.

"I want you to be sure."

"Good God I am sure."

Roger and Kathy kiss for a while.

"Look at that couple over there," says Roger. "They're really in love. They're quarreling. Oh brother. Once two people who are really in love start quarreling, they can't turn back. Their love's starting to end."

"That isn't always true. I think for love to last you have to learn to survive the quarrels. I mean it's possible to survive the quarrels, but you have to be real smart and know how to compromise. I don't know. I've never had any love that lasted."

"I know. Once two people start quarreling, that's it. There's no way they can patch it up. Things just keep getting worse and worse."

"Is that the way it is between you and your wife?"

Roger and Kathy start walking back on the sidewalk to Kathy's pension.

"We don't get along." Silence. "My wife. Oh brother. We don't understand each other at all. I like to go out at night and boogie, and she doesn't go out of the house at all. You know most people in this town don't even know I'm married."

"Well, there's no reason you and she have to do the same things."

"She keeps trying to leave me. Last year she went back to the United States three times to visit her parents. She said she was homesick. And I had to give her a thousand dollars plus plane fare every time she went."

"It must be hard for an American girl to adjust to the life here. Haitian women live real differently than American women."

"We almost got divorced. The last time she went back to the States she wanted to leave me for good. We had the papers signed and everything. She's calling me up collect every day in Haiti always bothering me and crying oh brother. So just as we're about to sign the final papers she tells the American ambassador to Haiti she doesn't want to do it and he tells my lawyer. My lawyer stops everything. So we're still married."

Kathy opens the white door and walks in. She turns around and sees Roger about six inches away from her. They kiss passionately. Tongues slither down throats. Roger pushes Kathy they topple on the bed.

"Draw your curtains."

Kathy tries to draw the curtains and fails.

Kathy lies down next to Roger so their faces are only a few inches apart. Kathy and Roger look at each other for a long time. They reach out to each other and Roger moves down on her.

They start doing the same things at the same time without thinking about it.

Roger kisses Kathy's lips and eyes. His tongue sticks up her nostrils. His hand reaches down, under her halter, and rubs her nipples.

"Do you ever come from this?" Roger asks.

"From what?"

"From having your titties played with?"

"Once I did."

Roger bends his head, lifts the halter, and places his mouth on the brown aureole. While he licks and sucks this nipple, his hand rubs the other breast.

Kathy's so open she can't believe it.

Roger and Kathy take off their clothes. They're glad to get their clothes off cause now they can touch each other all over.

They lie on their sides so all of their front presses, and rub, and slip, shove against each other. They're constantly kissing.

Roger's upper legs thrust down between Kathy's thighs so that Roger's lying partially on top of Kathy. Kathy's dying to fuck.

Kathy's in agony. She knows this is going to be a good fuck. Roger rubs his cock-head up and down Kathy's clit and the skin around her clit. Kathy knows that Roger's playing with her but she's too hot to care.

She opens her legs wider and thrusts upward. The right part of her body rises higher than her left. Roger moves slightly backward so the back part of his cock rubs roughly against the skin at the back of Kathy's cunt. Then he moves forward so he's lying fully on top of Kathy. Kathy wants to come so badly she's thrusting and shoving and bouncing too much every which way.

Roger and Kathy roll to their sides and Kathy's left leg bends so her knee's near Roger's face. He's using his hands to push her back and forth. Kathy swings her left leg over Roger's thigh so his cock presses against the back and left side of her cunt. They begin to fuck a little bit faster.

Kathy's about to come.

Roger slips on top of Kathy. He continues fucking at the same pace. Kathy feels spasms run up and down his cock and at the same time she feels all her muscles relax, a force like a warm fire an exploding bomb and all the wants in the world, these three things together rise up her cunt muscles and then slowly into her whole body. She shakes and relaxes in Roger's arms.

"That fuck was good, but it wasn't as terrific as the buildup had promised. I've got to try harder the second time so that the fuck'll be as good as we've kind of promised each other."

He slides down her body with his face upraised so she watches his large brown eyes. When his face reaches her cunt, he stops and his fingers open her nether lips.

"You don't have to do that."

"I love to suck women. Sometimes I come in my pants when I'm sucking a woman I like it so much."

Roger opens Kathy's lips and sticks his tongue into her. Kathy wants to tell Roger he's hurting her, but she doesn't because she's scared she'll hurt his feelings and he'll stop sucking her. She tries to relax to him and open herself up to him. "If Roger likes to suck, I don't have to worry about making myself come as soon as possible. I must taste terrible cause of the dysentery."

Kathy feels Roger's tongue move up to the extra-sensitive spot where her cunt lips meet. Roger's tonguing hurts and makes Kathy feel good. The hurt increases the pleasure. The hurt disappears. Kathy feels the beginning of the rising that always comes when she relaxes.

Kathy's amazed that the rising's beginning so fast. All of her cunt skin begins to tingle. The trick is your cunt membrane has to get more and more sensitive but not so fast that you tense up cause the more you relax the more you feel. You want to feel everything. Roger touches Kathy's clit with his tongue and her clit swells. The tingling increases strength and speed. Then Roger blows on her cunt so Kathy feels almost nothing. Instantaneously she wants him to touch her even harder. By the time his tongue returns to her clit, her clit feels like a three inch long raw desirous nerve.

"Follow Roger's tongue, follow Roger's tongue. Don't let the feeling carry you away. Don't go too fast."

The vibrations move around Kathy's cunt like a snake. Are what Roger's doing. As the vibrations run up and down, they grow fiercer and sharper so at the extreme there are these peaks of fire, tiny explosions everywhere, and nothing.

Kathy's cunt is silent, ready, nothing. Roger's tongue is the explosions, the fires, the desire. The explosions the fires the desire come faster and harder they become simultaneous and infinite.

Roger's tongue draws Kathy out of herself, makes her quiver, and puts her back, slightly changed, into herself.

"Oh my God," Kathy says. She's in love with Roger.

Roger rises up and sticks his cock in Kathy. As soon as he moves back and forth about three times, she comes. She spreads her legs as wide as possible. She feels like she's ready for anything. He continues moving his cock slowly back and forth in her cunt. Her cunt is sensitive to feel his cock. She can feel every inch of that cock it's going into her.

He pulls out of her so that only his cock-head is lying in her cunt. He presses and rubs the upper ridge of his cock back and forth past the tight uterine opening.

Kathy can't come again because Roger's cock isn't in her. She's desperate. She begins to flex her cunt muscles. Soft. Tight. Around and around. Soft. Tight. He sticks his cock back in her and begins to fuck her good and hard. She comes again. She keeps on tensing her cunt muscles.

They're both a little crazy. They roll around so she's sitting on top of him.

She leans down over him so her breasts dangle in his eyes. His hands hold her breasts for dear life. Her clit catches against the edge of the bones above his cock. She arches her back so his cock razes the sides of her cunt. She bends back as far as she can, now she can move freely, and

Roger and Kathy begin fucking like maniacs. They crash against each other. They throw themselves against each other as hard as they can. They rub their genitals against each other like they're trying to grind each other to bits. They're too out of it to do anything but want more. Kathy comes again but she hardly knows what she's doing any more. The cheap pension double bed is bumping against the back wall and banging in time to the fucking movements. Roger rolls over Kathy so he's partially on his side and partially over Kathy. His hands hold Kathy's thighs. He moves his cock in and out of Kathy and his thighs up and down on Kathy steadily and hard. Kathy comes so much she no longer knows what coming means. Roger's body stops moving. Only his cock moves. Kathy's cunt clearly feels his cock grow smaller and larger like an accordion and hot liquid shooting out of the end of his cock.

"I get crazy when I come too much."

"I thought women could come indefinitely."

"I can't. When I come too hard and too much, I can't stop anymore. My body gets out of control. I shiver and shake and go crazy cause I'm so oversensitive."

"Do you fuck a lot of men?"

"No. Not a lot. I'm alone, you know, and I've got to get laid. I've changed a lot in the past few years though. I used to fuck around all the time just fuck anyone. I can't do that. I guess fucking's getting too important to me or too serious. I can only fuck people I really go for now, and I only go for about three or four different men a year. And sometimes these men don't go for me."

"The only person I've slept with since I started living with my wife," Roger says, "was this French teacher. She was staying here at L'Ouverture. And she really wanted it oh boy. She came after me."

"But you fucked her?"

"I spent the night with her. But it didn't mean anything."

"What do you do when you go out at night?"

"I drink so much you wouldn't believe it. Last month I really drank too much."

"That's no good. Why don't you take your wife out now and then?"

"She doesn't want to go. She wants to stay shut up in the house. You know she doesn't even like to fuck. She won't let me do anything to her but fuck her how-do-you-call-it?"

"Missionary style?"

"Yes. She's from Kansas and she's very young. She stays all alone in that house and never sees anyone."

"I'd love to meet her. I'd love to be able to talk to an American who's been in Haiti for a while."

"Why don't you come to Le Roi tomorrow?"

"What's Le Roi?"

"It's where all of us live. Betty, me, my two brothers and their families. It's one of my father's factories."

"What does your father do?"

"Oh, he's into lots of things. He's got lumber rubber sugar cocoa and coffee factories and plantations. He owns Cap Haitian."

"Oh."

"Last year the government tried to arrest him cause they wanted to take over his money. They sent some troops up here to arrest him. All the people around here stood up for my father and protected him. My father's nice to his peasants so the peasants'll protect him. The troops had to go back to Port-au-Prince. All of us are always in danger of being arrested."

"That's why Gerard said you're 'retired.' "

"I'm not retired. I work at the factory as hard as Gerard works on the mountain. But I earn much more for my work than he does for his and he resents that. Everyone in this town knows who I am and resents me cause I'm my father's son."

"Everyone watches what you do. You have no privacy."

"Whatever I'm doing, I have to be very careful. I live out in the country where no one can spy on me. Sometimes I can relax out there."

He gets up to go to the bathroom. Kathy hears him piss. "Come here."

She walks into the bathroom and sees him sitting on the toilet. "Sit on me."

She sits down slowly, her back facing him. His cock slides up her asshole. His hands grab her tits.

She wonders if he's still going to the bathroom. "Shit and piss," she thinks to herself, "Fuck and suck what and not."

Everything's everything else. Kathy's crouching behind the window, watching the gray cat stalk someone she can't see. "Let's go to bed," Roger says.

He takes Kathy's hand and leads her to the bed.

Lays her back down on the bed. "This bed makes too much noise."

"It's just a lousy bed."

"Let's move it away from the wall."

"Do I have to get up?"

"No." He pulls the bed away from the wall so the wood head-board doesn't bang against the wall and lies down. His head is on Kathy's cunt. He sticks his tongue in Kathy's cunt and licks. Then he raises his head. His dark brown beard hairs are rubbing the lighter brown wet cunt hairs. Roger's beard hairs are partly white from sucking Kathy.

She moans.

"Now do you like my beard?" Roger asks.

"I always liked your beard."

"But now you see why my beard's so special."

"Oh shit." Kathy's heat's rising. She's about to come again. Roger doesn't want her to come again from his tongue. He rises over Kathy and sticks his cock into her cunt.

Kathy doesn't exactly know what's happening. Roger and Kathy fuck and then stop fuck and then stop fuck and then stop. They're actually fucking slowly and in a steady rhythm. Kathy's cunt is so sore that Kathy comes whenever Roger's cock is inside her. Yet they're fucking slowly enough that she's not becoming hysterical. Fucking is not fucking and not fucking is fucking. No one can tell who's coming or who's not coming. No one knows and forgets anything.

"Will you really come to Le Roi tomorrow?"

"I said I would," laughing.

"What haven't you done in bed?"

"I don't know. If I knew, I'd do it. Oh, I've never really gotten tied up and beaten or tied up and beaten someone, though I've thought about it a lot. Have you?"

"Oh yes. I once went with a girl the only way she could get off was if I tied her up and hit her. Otherwise she didn't want it, no way. I tied her wrists behind her back. I hit her hard. When she was ready she'd be writhing and shaking and then she'd want it so bad."

"You didn't like it?"

"It was OK. I didn't care for it that much. Did you ever ass fuck?"

"Jesus Christ we were ass fucking when we were on the toilet. Couldn't you tell?"

"I was so hot, all I could think about was getting my own. I don't even know if you've been coming."

"I've been coming enough. I'm satisfied."

"I want to fuck you up the ass when I know it."

"I like to fuck women. I don't do it much anymore though I used to."

"I like when women make love with women."

"Have you ever made it with a man?"

"I wouldn't let a man near me. I know what I want," Roger says.

"What do you want?"

"Are you really going to come to Le Roi?"

"I said I was going to. Jesus Christ, I'm here cause I want to see as much of Haiti as possible."

"I'd love to have you make love to my wife. That's why I want you to come to Le Roi."

"Waaiit a minute. I don't go for women all that much and I definitely only go for women I want. I don't even know Betty. I'd like to meet Betty cause she's an American and cause she sounds pretty damn lonely, but that's it."

"Maybe you and her will get something together. I want to find a woman who'll make love to my wife. That's what Betty needs."

"Roger, even if Betty and I do do anything, that's between me and Betty. It's none of your business. What goes on between you and Betty doesn't concern me. Jesus Christ I don't even know Betty yet."

"I don't believe you're going to come to Le Roi tomorrow."

"How do I get to Le Roi?"

"Everyone in town knows where Le Roi is. You can ask anyone. There's a bridge and there's a big red chimney. The big red chimney's Le Roi."

"On the way to the airport?"

"Yes."

"I guess I'll find it."

"What time will you come?"

"About one o'clock."

"I'll wait for you. My father's rebuilding the factory. He has three new rum tanks. I'll show you the rum tanks, and then I'll take you in to meet Betty."

"Are you sure it'll be OK with Betty? I don't know if she wants to meet me."

"The only way Betty ever meets people is when I introduce them to her."

Roger and Kathy look at each other. Their lips meet. Roger sticks his cock into Kathy's overfucked cunt. Roger comes. Kathy feels every inch of his cock spasm back and forth as clearly as she sees the white ceiling above her. Roger's orgasm makes Kathy hot.

They stop fucking. Roger's cock is hard again. Roger wets his finger and sticks it into Kathy's ass. His finger moves around easily. He sloshes some saliva on the asshole and eases his cock into Kathy's ass. Kathy doesn't feel any pain at all.

Roger's moving his cock back and forth rapidly. Kathy's coming like a maniac. All of her ass and intestinal muscles are shaking. "Oh oh oh," Kathy cries. Kathy stops coming. Roger's still shaking away. Kathy feels a little pain. Kathy and Roger both come again.

THE Mysteres are a family of mulatto robber barons. The grandfather of the present M. Mystere made and lost a million dollars. The grandfather's son made a million and lost a million two times and then went crazy. The present M. Mystere started out life with this heritage and nothing else. Like his grandfather and father, he made and lost a million. Presently he is working on his second million or, at this point, multimillion.

M. Mystere or le Mystere, nobody in town calls him anything else probably nobody even knows his first name, has a wife, three sons, and a daughter. The three sons are married and the oldest two have children. The daughter, although twenty-seven years old, is a virgin. The three sons work for their father and, like the daughter, live where their father tells them to live. The youngest son's name is Roger.

Of the several lumber, cocoa, coffee, rum and bottling plantations and factories le Mystere owns, Le Roi is his baby. He is currently rebuilding Le Roi. The decaying wood scarecrow building with its rusted metal ceiling, old dead machines surrounded by dust, is abandoned. Giant new brick cylinders filled with new rum rise into the sky. Sweating men construct massive orange metal frames. There are no more buildings here. Only metal skeletons, huge machines, and dust.

Like the American robber barons of early this century, le Mystere wants to depend on no one but himself. All the profits he makes are immediately turned into new business. His baby, Le

Roi, was built and is being rebuilt from cash, the cash profits which his other factories and plantations made last year. Le Roi is part of a giant rum concern, a concern which will rival Barbancourt, a Haitian rum monopoly which so far has no competitor. Rum is one of Haiti's main products. If the rum concern succeeds, by this spring as soon as the rum's distributed for the first time, le Mystere will make three million dollars above costs. And then more.

The sugar grows and the rum is aged at Le Roi. Miles and miles of sugar cane, tall strong green plants, lie mixed with weeds. Machines that extract a syrup from the sugar cane. Machines for fermenting and flavoring the syrup. The pride of Le Roi is the three giant red brick tanks which hold the syrup plus at least sixty per cent water for the fermentation period. In Haiti it's hard to get decent machines, the government tries to get everything, so these tanks might explode at any second. The cheap raw white rum can be packaged almost immediately. Le Mystere's cheapest rum is aging a year. His most expensive rum has already aged three years. When all this rum is ready, in March, it will be shipped to le Mystere's bottling factory in Port-au-Prince, bottled, and there exported and distributed throughout Haiti.

The road to Le Roi, after it leaves the bridge and the overhead arch announcing the town of Cap Haitian, under which women in torn filthy short skirts sit and stand beside their baskets filled with mangoes of all varieties, plantains, figs or bananas, breadfruit, meat-filled pastries, dried fish, whole fishes, canaps, cashews, sit and stand and talk in the dust, the road curves around a small bay and then reaches straight, like an extended arm, into the Haitian countryside. At this point the road's mostly though badly paved. Deep ruts line both sides of the road. Men leading mules or women in the same short full skirts with huge filled straw baskets balanced on their heads every now and then walk in the deep ruts. A truck filled with rocks or bananas and people packed together like rocks or bananas sitting on top of the rocks or bananas passes them by.

To the sides of the road, the country is flat and the soil is dry. Bare earth now and then covered with low-lying bush. At first there are no houses. Then a few rectangular thatch houses lie a few feet away from the road. There's usually a mango or some kind of palm tree next to each of these huts.

The road gets dustier and dustier. It passes by the small Cap Haitian airport. Twice a day for twenty minutes a six-seater plane lands here. Otherwise the airport's empty. Now the bush at the sides of the road is thicker and there are more trees. There's more green. But one can still see the dry dusty brown through the areas of shiny light and darkening greens.

Weeds rise up everywhere. Birds and crickets are making noise. The endless sun. The weeds and trees are becoming a tangle. About ten minutes inland from the airport, it's necessary to turn off the almost-paved road on to a path of dirt and stones to get to Le Roi. There are no signs on the road. As is true everywhere in Haiti, you have to know what you're doing. Or not care what you're doing.

Here the weeds and sparsely-leafed trees and tall grasses and small wild yellow flowers choke the dirt path. Tangle. The car gets through slowly. Finally it stops.

"I drove down to L'Ouverture to pick you up at eleven o'clock but you weren't there."

The girl looks around and sees a small black man walking toward her. "Oh shit. I was out playing with the little beggar boys. We sat in the park."

"Yeah, they told me that."

"I wish I had known you were going to pick me up. I could hardly find this place and the taxi-driver charged me a fortune."

"How much did he charge you?"

"Six bucks."

"Shee-it." Kathy and Roger hold hands. "First, I'm going to show you my factory. This part of my father's business is the part that's mine."

"I'd like to see it. I want to see as much of Haiti as possible."

"This is the new factory. The old wood structure over there is where the factory used to be. That was no good. It used to leak a lot. We've got to get all this up by the beginning of September cause that's when the sugar cane comes in."

"Will you be able to do it by then?"

"It'll have to be finished. That's how things are around here. We work as hard as we have to and, then, when we don't have to work, sometimes we don't work at all. My father works all the time; he never thinks about anything but his work. Oh brother. He's sharp too. If you say or do one thing wrong, he'll remember it, and three days later he'll ask you why you said or did exactly what you said or did. He remembers every little detail where you don't remember anything. He doesn't care about nobody."

"Does he do anything besides work?"

"Sometimes he reads a book at night. My mother and he live quietly. They hardly see anyone."

"Huh. What's your mother like?"

"My mother? She's just a mother."

"Oh. What are these?"

"That's sugar cane. Haven't you seen sugar cane before?"

"No."

"Here. Eat one." Roger hands her the top part of the sugar cane stalk, a thick woody cylinder. She gnaws at it. "Sometimes about six o'clock when nobody's here, I come here and sit down. I just sit down. I love it here. This is my home. I sit here against this white wall and watch the plants. This is the only time I really rest. No one bothers me here."

A slim bearded man walks up to them. "Hello."

"Kathy, this is my older brother Nicolas. Nicolas, Kathy."

"Hello."

"Nicolas is the chemist of the family. He went to college for two years in the States." She sits down against the white wall of the building that holds the rum tanks. "I'm going back to work now and you wait here. I'll come get you when I'm finished. Are you going to be OK?"

"I like being alone."

She stares at the orange metal skeletons, the welding equipment, the half-naked workers, huge yellow tractors plastered against a solid wall of green. A few minutes later he returns.

"Will you be OK here?"

"Of course I'll be alright." To her left's the small empty dirt field that's the end of the road and a low white fence. The stucco fence surrounds a huge pink rectangular building. To her right are miles and miles of sugar cane plants. Flat land as far as the eye can see. Clear light blue sky. Burning white sun.

When her ass starts to hurt, she moves to her right and back, into the sugar cane plants. Lies down among the tall rough green plants. The sun can only reach small sections of her body. Thousands of different kinds of insects crawl over her. Wasps the size of bumblebees and small red ants large red ants and small black ants and thin-bodied fliers translucent green wings and grasshoppers and big black beetles. When the ants start crawling under her clothes, into her nostrils, and biting her, she moves back to the concrete step in front of the white building.

At first, she can't see anything. She sees men climbing up the orange shafts and men hammering men sticking stakes in the ground men wiping their hands on their dark pants. She sees Roger on top of a big yellow tractor. He's circling the tractor around the periphery of welding, hammering, and building. He doesn't see her. He sees her and waves.

Five minutes later he stops the tractor and walks over to her. Sweat runs down his face and arms. Muscles cover his body. "Come on. I'm ready."

"You can't be ready. It's only early afternoon. Go back and work."

"I want to take time off now. I can take off when I want. I'm going to take you in to meet Betty. I'll have a beer, and then I'll come back here."

They're walking.

"Does Betty live in that pink house over there?"

"Yes. She never leaves the house. Her skin's allergic to the sun down here so she can't go out of the house during the day unless she's totally covered up. All this summer she kept begging me to buy her an air-conditioner. 'Roger,' she kept saying, 'I can't live without an air-conditioner. I've got to have an air-conditioner.' Finally I gave in and bought her this air-conditioner that was designed to air-condition a factory. She made me put the air-conditioner in the bedroom and now she stays in the bedroom all the time."

"But it's not even hot here."

"Betty's very delicate. She can't take the heat."

They walk in silence for a while. "I feel upset," Kathy says to herself. "Every time this year I fucked someone I liked, I fell in love. I'd want to see the person again in the next few days. Every time I wanted this, the guy'd start hating me. Either he wouldn't see me or he'd kick me in the guts. I spent all my time trying to figure out if everyone who fucked me hated me. I knew I was obsessing. I hated myself. I decided I was going to get rid of all my thoughts. No more love. I don't love anyone I fuck with and no one loves me. And I thought I had succeeded Jesus Christ I've been so proud of myself. So here I am again. I want to tell Roger I love him. That's insane. I want to tell him I love him and I can't. Does he love me? I know he doesn't care about me I'm a cunt he hates me. He hates me cause I love him. Jesus Christ I'm going to cry. I've got to tell him I love him and I absolutely must not. I have to control myself or I'll never be able to do anything."

They've reached the archway in the white wall. A few feet away're the steps of the pink house.

"Roger I think I'm falling in love with you." She starts crying.

"I think about it too."

She can't say anything. Her tears dry.

"C'mon. We've got to see Betty. Betty!" he yells at a large barred window. Kathy follows him as he walks through a small white door, up some narrow steps, through a large stainless steel kitchen, through a hall, into an empty white room. The only things in this room are two pushed-together beds and a large air-conditioner. "Kathy, this is Betty."

Betty's skinny and there's no blood in her face. She looks like she has no blood. She's not albino. Even though her hair is so blonde it's almost white, it's dingy. Straggly. She looks as if she's been totally permanently frightened. Otherwise she's pretty in a midwestern American way. Her eyes are pale pale blue. She's wearing an obviously new dark cotton dress which chokes her neck, droops at her waist and ruffles again and again around her nonexistent hips. She doesn't want to look at Kathy.

"Hello, Betty. Do you uh have a bathroom?"

"Of course," says Roger. He points to the left.

A huge clean bathroom with a bathtub and a shower. Kathy throws herself on the toilet as wave after wave of dysentery hits her. Shit pours out of her.

"Roger, why don't you get some lunch? You haven't eaten lunch today."

"I don't want any."

"But I've kept it in the oven waiting for you. It's probably burnt to a crisp by now."

"I'm not hungry."

"You have to eat, Roger. You can't work all day and not eat. If you're not going to eat, you have to get back to work. You can't take off from work like this. You know what your father said."

"I can stop working whenever I want to."

Kathy gets off the toilet, though she doesn't want to, and walks back to the bedroom. "I've been traveling through Haiti for the past week and I haven't seen any Americans much less spoken English the whole time. It's a treat for me to meet an American here."

"There are lots of Americans in Haiti."

She sits down on the bed next to Betty. "There are? I haven't met any. Last night I met Gerard. You know Gerard. He introduced me to Roger and Roger invited me to visit you two. I thought it'd be nice to talk with you cause you're an American who's lived in Haiti for a while. I hope I'm not disturbing you."

"You're not disturbing me. I don't do anything. I don't like Haiti very much. I don't go out of the house much and now that I don't have a car . . ."

"What happened to your car?"

Roger's watching the two women. "It's getting fixed," he says to Kathy. "It just takes a while."

"It's been broken for two weeks now and Roger won't get it fixed."

"You see how she is," Roger says to his girlfriend.

"It must be lonely here," Kathy says to Betty. "Why don't you get a small cycle or a motorbike so at least you can get into town?"

"What I really want is a horse. I've always adored horses. I was really scared of them when I was younger, but even then I couldn't stay away from them. I know I'm not scared anymore. If I had a horse, I could go anywhere around here."

"Why don't you get a horse?"

"She doesn't know how to ride," says Roger.

"You know Roger, if I had a horse, I could keep it here real cheap. It wouldn't cost anything. We could feed the horse the scrap sugar cane plants. We could stable the horse right here in the yard. I know your father wouldn't mind."

He doesn't reply.

"And there are horse-trails all over the country."

"We've talked about this before. There are no horses around here."

"I know where I could get a horse. Mr. Palero's bringing two palominos here from Port-au-Prince. Even if I couldn't buy one, I know he'd let me stable one here."

"She talks all the time about horses," he says. "If she tried riding one, she'd get so scared, she'd run away yelling 'Eek, eek.' "

"I would not Roger. I know I wouldn't be scared now."

"Why don't you try riding one of the horses I saw out there?"

asks Kathy. "You would get more confident and then you could get a bigger horse."

"What horses are you talking about?"

"Weren't those horses I saw," she asks Roger, "when we were walking from the factory to this house?"

"Oh, those old things," Betty says. "They're not really horses, they're like mules."

"If they're so old, they'd be good to learn to ride on. They wouldn't hurt you."

"I don't want to," says Betty.

"Betty's crazy about animals. She wanted to bring her dog here from the United States the last time she was in the United States, but I wouldn't let her do it. It would cost a fortune. She really loves that dog. Betty, show Kathy pictures of your dog."

"I'd love to see them."

"No. They're boring."

"It's too bad you can't ship your dog here. I know how you feel. Every time I've had a pet, it's killed me, not killed me but you know what I mean, to abandon it. You always have to leave a pet and it hurts so much, I'm scared to have a pet again. I think pets are babies."

"We couldn't bring the dog into Haiti. You can't bring anything into Haiti. It's like being in prison here. When I first moved here my mother sent me a carton of books, just some old books I had at home, and it cost me seventy-five dollars to take these books out of the post office."

"Seventy-five dollars?"

"The government calls it the luxury tax. Whenever anyone takes anything in or out of Haiti, that person has to pay a huge luxury tax. It's one of the only ways the Haitian government makes money."

"She keeps going back to her parents in the United States. Last year she went back to the United States three times. And then when she's back there the last time, she wanted to return here with her dog."

"He's really a beautiful dog. You should see him. He's so big he's as big as Roger but he wouldn't hurt anybody. You should see him around people he doesn't like. He never growls. He just goes 'rrrrrrr.' Low and steady. The people take one look at him and run. He's never even bitten anyone. Once he bit the postman. He's really very gentle. Would you like to see pictures of him?"

"I'd love to."

Betty shows Kathy a picture of a huge mutt standing in front of an empty rectangular wood-frame house. Bare flat soil surrounds the mutt and the house.

"He's a really beautiful dog," Kathy says to Betty. "Why don't you get another kind of pet here? One you don't have to import. You won't feel so bad and you can see your dog when you go back home."

"I once kept a cat here, but Roger kicked him out of the house. Roger says animals don't belong in a house."

"Animals don't belong in a house," he says. "Animals belong outside a house. That's how things are in Haiti."

"He doesn't understand. In Kansas we have animals running around all over the place."

"I love animals. When I had cats, I slept with them every night. Pickle Paul, that was the male one's name, used to place his back against me and just rub into me. Then he'd look up at me with his big blue eyes and take his paw and put it on my hand. His paw pushed my hand to his nipple. He loved having his nipples rubbed. That's what he liked most in the world. Lizzie, she was his sister and wife, would sit on things and claim them. She especially loved leather. She was incredibly beautiful: green eyes lined in black, black tongue, a calico. In San Francisco I had these wonderful parakeets."

"The only pets I really like are dogs."

"I don't want Betty to have any pets. Animals belong outside the house. There are lots of animals outside the house she can play with."

Kathy can't answer because she's about to shit in her pants.

She barely makes it to the toilet when the gook starts flowing out of her. She looks down and sees a beautiful calico long-hair cat skin. "Shit. What's this?"

"What are you talking about?"

"This cat."

"Oh," Betty replies, "that's a cat."

"You mean I'm stepping on your pet cat? Did he die naturally?"

"We killed him," Roger says.

"You killed him? Oh. I'm not being sentimental or anything isn't it weird to kill your pet and stick him in the toilet?"

"Do you want a beer?" Betty asks her husband.

"No."

"Well, at least take something to eat. Your lunch is still in the oven. You've got to eat your lunch."

"I told you. I'm not hungry. Ask Kathy if she wants a beer."

"That cat wasn't a pet," she yells to Kathy. "It was just a stray cat."

"I thought it was your pet. I got scared for a moment. I thought you were horrible people."

Roger's girlfriend is lying down on the huge double bed. His wife's sitting upright, almost touching her. He watches the two women.

"Ask Kathy if she wants a beer."

"Do you want a beer?"

"No. Yes, I'll split one with you if you want."

"I'll also have a beer," says Roger.

"Roger, go down to the kitchen and get two beers."

"I don't want to move. You go down."

"I don't want to move either. Please, Roger, do me a favor."

"I'll go get the beers," says the girlfriend. "I love to walk. You two have to stop fighting."

Roger goes to get the beers.

The girlfriend and the wife are alone in the huge air-conditioned bedroom. They feel embarrassed.

"Would you like to see the rest of our house?"

"I'd love to."

Through a narrow gray hall to the kitchen. All the latest stain-less steel tools and no food. One can of peaches. The refrigerator holds sixteen packages of Kraft cream cheese. The servants do all the work. Down the stairs. Through the narrow white door. Mowed green lawns. Through another white door. A long empty dark gray hall. The doors stuck in the walls of this hall are closed. Turn right. The same gray hall. Turn left. The same gray hall only light gray. "Roger's brother Nicolas and his family live here. We're not allowed to enter." Turn left again. A shorter light gray hall. Ends in a huge light yellow room. The yellow makes you want to puke. Two Holiday Inn chairs one Holiday Inn couch in the center of this room. White polyester curtains cover the windows. Turn left. This part of the yellow room's empty. The yellow room ends. Through a light yellow door. A long dark gray hall. A darker gray room just big enough to contain an ironing board and a maid. A narrow white door. Green lawn. Through the other white door. Up the steps. The modern kitchen. Two long light gray halls.

"You've got a really nice house. How come all the doors are locked?"

"Roger's brothers' wives don't want us coming into their parts of the house. They're scared something might get stolen."

"Jesus Christ. What are these women like?"

"Nicolas, he's the second oldest, is married to a Chinese girl. The oldest brother married a Haitian girl. They're both real pretty. They don't pay much attention to me. They act like typical upper-class Haitian women, you know, they go out every day and buy clothes, they have servants who do everything for them and they don't do anything for themselves, even though they were born real poor. I'm not like that. I don't get along with them."

"So you're here alone most of the time?"

"I don't go out of the house anymore. I like to read. I read a lot. It's really hard to get books in Haiti. There's nowhere to buy books and the only person I can get them from is papa."

"Papa?"

"Peter. The old guy at L'Ouverture."

"I haven't met him."

"He's probably still down in Port-au-Prince. You'll meet him when he comes back. Everyone knows papa."

"That's horrible that you can't get hold of books. I'd die if I couldn't get hold of the books I wanted to read. Much less any books." She turns around and sees a pile of dusty paperbacks lying in the corner. "What books do you have here?"

"Have you ever read John Fowles' book?"

"That one? I've never read any of John Fowles' books. I hear he's a good writer."

"You should read him. He's a great writer. You know what book I like the best? You must have read it. *Future Shock*. I think that book really says what's happening."

"I know everyone was reading it last year."

"I think that guy what's his name?"

"Toffler."

"Toffler puts his finger on it when he says the world's going to end."

"Uh."

"Have you read any E. Eddison? I love his writing."

"Do you know any books about Haiti? About what's happening now?"

"No. I like to read books about imaginary places. Do you? You know who else I think's a great writer? Irving Wallace."

"I don't know. I just like to read. What's this book about?"

"Oh, Thurber. That's just a funny book. Do you want to borrow it?"

"I've got enough to read. You can have the Dostoyevsky book I'm reading when I'm finished if you want it. What do you do when you're not reading?"

"Sometimes Roger takes me out. Last Saturday night he took me to the voodoo dances in the country. They hold them every Saturday night."

"Oh wow what are those like? I want to go to them."

"They're nothing special. I didn't see anything exciting happen like they say happens like people breathing fire and walking over hot coals. I didn't even see anyone go into a trance. Roger and I might not have stayed there long enough to see the good part. We got there around eleven o'clock. There were some women turning in circles. That was all. They turned in circles for a long time. At the end just before we left, it wasn't the end of the ceremony, this man started to stick needles into his skin. Maybe he was in a trance. I don't know. I didn't like it. He stuck these long needles into his skin, all over his body and then he went around the perimeter of the circle and asked other people to stick needles into him."

"Did he ask you?"

"Yes. I couldn't do it. I wanted to vomit. I felt I was watching him torture himself."

"Maybe he wasn't torturing himself. Maybe he was using the pain to bring himself, I don't know how to explain it, into a new consciousness."

"Right after he asked me to stick needles into him, Roger and I left. I didn't feel good."

"I think I'd like it. What was Roger's reaction?"

"Roger didn't like it. Roger has trouble with that stuff."

"What do you mean?"

Betty looks through the bars over the air-conditioner, out the window. "Roger's great-grandfather, grandfather Mystere, made a fortune and lost it. His son, Roger's grandfather, made his fortune, lost that, made a second fortune and lost it. After he lost his second fortune, he went crazy. Roger's father felt he had to make money. He made a million dollars and, like his father and grandfather, lost that million. Now he's working on his second fortune. He's very scared he's going to lose the money he now has. All he does is work. All he cares about is work. All the money he makes goes back into the business. He has no real money. He doesn't want to depend on banks or on other partners. Whenever he does work like the rebuilding he's doing at Le Roi now, it's all done out of cash. He has to keep expanding the business, cause if he loses this money, he thinks he'll go crazy like his father did. Roger's father is a very powerful man."

"I still don't understand why he's scared of going crazy."

"Roger's uncle went to some business school and came back and started working. He was doing OK but he wasn't making a lot of money. He kept working harder and harder. He didn't take a vacation for two years, not one day off, and then he started working nights. Finally one month he tried to go without sleep. He sees things and he gets very nervous if anyone's even around him with a pencil. They keep him locked up in their house in Port-au-Prince. He says he needs peace and quiet. He sits in an empty cool white room. The doctor says if he gets constant peace and rest, he might be OK in a year or two. No one wants to talk about him."

"Maybe he just got overworked and overstrained. That doesn't mean there's insanity in the family. Rich people often go crazy, but they're so rich, the other rich people protect them."

"Roger's sister lives with her parents. She never leaves the house unless they tell her to. She's twenty-seven. She's sick all the time: she has these special allergies. The only thing she likes to do is eat. She eats all the time. She can cook anything you ask her to cook: Spanish, Chinese, American. You'd really like her. Two years ago she got this incurable liver disease so she's not allowed to eat anymore."

"She doesn't sound so crazy. Does she fuck?"

"She's never had any boyfriends."

"Never? Jesus Christ I didn't think there was a virgin in Haiti. Except for the zero to three year olds. She must be a case. What are Roger's brothers like?"

"I don't see them much. The oldest one runs the lumber plant. Nicolas is the chemist, he went to some college in the States for two years. He likes to tell people what to do. I see their wives more, but I don't like them. They're very mean to me. I'm pretty lonely here."

"You and Roger should have a house of your own."

"Roger's his father's right-hand man. Roger has to go wherever his father tells him to. Sometimes we live here and sometimes we live in Port-au-Prince."

"But couldn't you live somewhere else besides right here in this building when you're in Cap Haitian?"

"Roger says he's going to build us a house with the money that comes in from the rum factory this spring. His father expects to net a few million immediately which he's going to split among his sons to avoid taxes. I don't know if Roger'll build a house. He loves living here."

"It must be hard for you. Do you have anyone you can talk to around here?"

"There's this girl named Suzy. She lives in the hills in the back of Mont Joli pension. Do you know where Mont Joli is?"

"Yes."

"She and her boyfriend came here from Port-au-Prince three years ago when there were no roads. They rode on horseback through the inland mountains and swamps. They met tribes in the mountains who had never seen white men before. I don't see her anymore cause I don't have a car."

"I'd love to meet her."

"You'd really like her. She does macramé. Her house is incredibly beautiful. It's covered with macramé and weaving. She and her boyfriend and Oliver run a pottery factory just outside of town. Roger and I used to visit them all the time but lately we've stopped. I don't see them anymore. If I could borrow Nicolas' car one day, we could visit them."

"I'd like that. I'd love to find out more about their trip through the inland. You should get your car fixed."

"Roger says it takes a long time. It's hard to get machine parts in Haiti."

"Then why don't you buy yourself a small scooter or motorbike? You have enough money to do that."

"Roger says they're dangerous. He doesn't want me to ride a

bicycle cause the natives might bother me because of who we are."

"Roger's crazy. Nobody's going to hurt you. I go everywhere around here night and day by myself and nobody even bothers me. Everyone thinks I'm crazy cause I'm always alone they're real curious, but so what? You've got to do what you want."

"Roger doesn't even want me to walk through the town. He says there are a lot of poor people around and I might get syphilis."

"How are you going to get syphilis?"

"Most of those poor people have large sores. If I touch one of them or one of them grabs me, I might brush against the sore and pick up his germs. That's how I'd get syphilis."

"You can't get syphilis by touching someone. You can only get it by fucking. Oh you can get syphilis of the mouth, but even that has to be genital contact. I know."

"Roger says I'll get syphilis if I walk through the poor parts of town."

"Then Roger doesn't know. It's absolutely impossible for you to get syphilis if you don't fuck."

"Well, I might pick up some other germs. Those people are crowded closely together."

"What are you going to do with your life?"

"I had a job at Mont Joli pension earlier this year. I really liked that job. I was working from nine to twelve five days a week and earning fifty dollars a week."

"That's a lot of money here."

"The maids at L'Ouverture work twelve hours a day every day and earn thirty dollars a month. They're allowed to eat rice once a day. That's high pay for Haiti."

"So why aren't you working now?"

"The people at Mont Joli told me to leave. They were able to get the woman they wanted who had lots and lots of experience. I couldn't keep the job anyway cause I had to follow Roger down to Port-au-Prince."

"You could hold down a job. When Roger goes to Port-au-Prince, you could stay here."

"I don't get along with Roger's brothers' wives. I don't want to stay here alone."

"Then you could stay in town at L'Ouverture. You've got to have your own life."

"It doesn't matter. I lost the job at Mont Joli and there are no other jobs in Cap Haitian."

"But you don't need money. Roger's rich. You could teach some of the beggar kids how to read, you could help the doctors, there are thousands of things that need to be done in this town."

"If I mix with the poor kids, I might get syphilis." Betty looks through the bars over the air-conditioner, out the window.

"Roger says you do art. You're very good. Do you have anything around I could see?"

"Do you really want to see my work?"

"Sure."

Betty walks into a large empty boiling-hot room. She moves part of a wall, climbs up on a chair, and starts piling huge boxes, hidden behind the sliding wall, on the floor. Box after box. "I'm not really good. I took art in school and all the teachers said I was their best student, but I haven't shown anyone my work in two years." She lugs a thin tan portfolio out of the back of the closet, steps over the piles of cartons, and opens it up. "This is a Japanese print I did. I drew some of it myself, traced some pictures I found, cut out some things."

"This is my favorite."

"This is just an abstract color thing. I was starting to use colors."

"The rest are just drawings. I like to draw. These are drawings of Roger."

"This is a drawing of a cat."

"These are two self-portraits. I don't like the rest of the drawings. I can't work anymore cause I can't get the right kind of pencils and paper down here."

"Why don't you show these to some Haitian artist as long as you're down here? There are lots of terrific artists in Haiti. You could show your work and maybe you could study with someone.

That'd be terrific: you'd get all this off your hands you'd be able to learn you'd meet people."

"We don't know any Haitian artists."

"There's a real famous one who lives right in Cap Haitian. His name begins with U. What the hell is it? Just go and introduce yourself to him. You can't lose. Lots of artists take on students. Even if the artist isn't that great you're studying with, you still learn a whole lot about how an artist creates."

"I don't think I'm into art that much anymore. I want a job like the one I had at Mont Joli."

"You've got to do something. You're as pale as a ghost."

"That's cause I can't go out into the sun. I'm allergic to the Haitian sun. I'm allergic to most Haitian foods."

"Betty's very very delicate," Roger says. Both the women turn around.

"Roger, why don't you get some lunch? You haven't eaten lunch today."

"I don't want any."

"But I've kept it in the oven waiting for you. It's probably burnt to a crisp by now."

"I'm not hungry."

"At least change your pants. Those pants are filthy. We should throw them away."

"I'm comfortable in these pants." Roger turns to his girlfriend. "She always wants me to wear clothes that make me feel uncomfortable. She doesn't understand that I'm a workman. I want to dress like a workman."

"I'm going out to the garden," she replies.

"You should try a canap," says Betty. "Those little round green fruits on that tree. I don't know if they're ripe yet. They make you high."

"I'm going to try a canap."

The garden between the back of the pink rectangular house and the part of the white wall which faces the factory part of Le Roi, unlike the smooth green lawn in front of the pink house,

is wild and overgrown. Some of the grass is short; some, long.
Grass mingles with dirt. Occasional patches of dirt and strips of
dirt hide in the welter of grass or hug the white stucco wall. Three
small black-and-white goats nibble at the grass and weeds. A
wood picnic bench and a half-rotting wood picnic table. Behind
and on both sides of this table grow two gnarled-branched trees.
A low round wood platform surrounds one of the tree trunks.

Kathy leaps on this platform. She's able to stick her foot into
a depression between the tree's two main branches. But she's not
tall enough to get her right leg up there. Shit. She brings her
left leg back down. She's standing on the platform. She jumps
up her hands grab a thick low branch her feet hit the trunk
monkey-style and stick. Her arms pull her legs up into the depression. She kneels, stands upright in the depression.

Wants to climb upward but can't reach any of the branches.

Tries to crawl out on a wood stick, part of a square wood frame
for hanging laundry or just plain hanging, that's sticking out of
the tree trunk. The entire wood frame starts shaking.

Slowly climbs out of the hunchback tree, and steps off the
wood platform down to the grass. Thick weeds everywhere rose
bushes with dark heavy open roses a stone fountain that has no
water. Sky is white light. Heating beating down except for one
cool breeze slithers in and out of the heat like a little lizard. Blue
blue sky. The garden's incredibly beautiful and silent. Goats are
munching by the hunchback tree. Tries to pet the goats, but they
don't want anything to do with her.

Sees some beautiful large white flowers. Walks over to the
beautiful large white flowers. Beyond the flowers there's a chicken
coop. A wood frame, a wood shelf, and lots of chicken wire form
the square coop. Three roosters and six hens run around inside
the coop and two hens run around outside. "You see what I mean
about Betty. She's still a baby."

"She's very unhappy," Kathy says to Roger. "She can't stay
shut up here. She has to be doing some kind of work."

"You can't do anything with her. You can't tell her anything.

If you try to say anything, she says 'Just leave me alone.' She's like a child and you can't tell her what the world's like. Now do you see why I act the way I do? Now do you see what I'm up against?"

"She's very scared, Roger. She's so scared she almost can't function any more. She doesn't have any blood in her. No one has to be as pale as she is. It's unhealthy. You've got to let her get a job or at least have transportation so she can get out of here now and then."

"She had a job. She couldn't keep it."

Kathy sees her standing almost next to her and Roger. "Shut up," she whispers to Roger.

"Now do you see what I'm up against? I'll never be able to leave her."

"We'll talk about this later, Roger. Shut up." She walks over to Betty. "This is a beautiful garden."

Betty doesn't reply.

"This is a beautiful garden."

"I don't like it."

"You're just in it too much. You can't see it anymore. After being in a city for two years, this place is paradise."

"I guess so."

"Do you ever come here and play with the chickens and the goats?"

"I don't like chickens. I think they're horrible."

"I like chickens," says Roger.

"I play with the goats sometimes. This one's my favorite. Isn't he beautiful?" Exactly half of the little goat's face is white and half is black.

"He is beautiful. Look at that goat there. He's got a gray spot. Can I pet him?"

"Sure you can. He's tied to the tree."

"I don't want to torture him. That's no way to love an animal."

"Look. The servants are bringing the cows in for the night."

"Cows!"

"I used to wrestle that one when I was a kid. He was a mean one. I would win though."

"Jesus, he's huge. How the hell could you wrestle with him?"

"Not the brown one. The one with the black stripe over his eye behind him."

"He's smaller. You must love him."

"I do."

"Do you still wrestle him?"

Roger walks over to the bull and makes faces. The bull ignores him. "Not anymore. Why don't you go inside now? You're getting too much sun and you're going to get sick."

"OK."

"Roger," says Betty, "stop it. You're treating her like you're her father."

"It's OK." Kathy smiles at Roger.

The three people walk around to the front of the house where the grass is short. Roger and his wife go inside the house while Kathy stays on the lawn. She dances and knows that Roger's watching her.

She goes through one of the white doors. She finds herself in a light gray hall. At the end of the hall a maid's ironing in a small gray room. She walks down this hall and turns left down a white hall. All the doors in this hall have huge brass bolts bolted shut. At the end of this hall's a large empty living room, the yellow room she had seen before. The door from the living room to the front lawn's bolted. The servant who's cleaning the living room stares at her. She turns back down the white hall. The maid who's ironing stares at her and doesn't reply to her hello. She walks through the white door to the green-gray lawn. She tries another white door. She walks up the narrow white steps into Betty's and Roger's kitchen. "I got lost."

"We were wondering where you were," Roger says to Kathy.

"I want to go soon. I want to get back to the pension for dinner."

"You can get a ride back with my father's engineer. He'll be leaving about now. I'll ride into town with you. I'll go see where he is." Roger goes back downstairs.

The two women follow him. "I loved being able to meet you," Kathy says to Betty. "Why don't you visit me at the pension and we can go swimming and sunbathing together?"

"Roger'll have to drive me there. I have no other way of getting there."

"Come visit me. I can give you the books I've finished reading so you'll have some new books to read."

"OK. I'll come tomorrow or the next day. You're getting a bad burn. Here's some good suntan oil and here are some Haitian matches."

"Oh, they're beautiful."

"The engineer's waiting," says Roger.

Roger's girlfriend climbs into a huge gray jeep. "Aren't you going to come with me, Roger? I thought you were going into town with me."

"I'm not going tonight. I'll see you tomorrow night."

She wanted to fuck all day, and now she's not going to be able to. "Goodbye Roger."

Roger throws her a kiss.

PASSIONS

YOUR past comes back and hooks you. Your insane search for affection because your mother didn't want you, disliked you, and she wouldn't tell you who your father was. You kept looking for someone to turn to. You kept looking for a home. Your need gathers. Passion collects. You're in it now, baby . . . passions, just as they are . . .

You're going to bang your head against that wall again. No affection. You. Where are you going to find love? How can you run away from yourself? Last year you banged your head against a wall so hard you were sure it had to break, but it didn't. The only difference this time is you know you can't break down that wall. You're going to hit your head so hard against it this time, you're going to bust in your head. What a pleasure it'll be when your head breaks . . .

You've got to get love. You've lost your sense of propriety. Your social so-called graces. You're running around a cunt without a head. You could fuck anybody anytime any place you don't give a damn who the person is except you really don't want to get murdered any number of people except when the sex situations happen you have this idea lingering from the past maybe you shouldn't fuck so much and so openly other people are looking down on you other people are thinking you're shit. People misunderstand why you act the ways you do so they might harm you. You've already gotten beaten up once even though you kind of liked it. You've got to use your intellect to keep you in line, no insane sexual behavior no pleading and groveling for love, you don't know the difference between friends and strangers, cause if you don't use your arbitrary, it feels arbitrary, intellect to keep you in line, you're going to go too far out, you're beyond the limits of decent human behavior, pleading and groveling on the ground, every time you get a bit a scrap of love wanting twice as much more more, you've got to have more cause you know no one could love you cause no one's ever loved you, and home is secure love you've got to get enough love all the love in the world to make it secure. You step on the people you meet. You use them for your insane desires. You don't know the difference between friends and strangers and you're unable to give anyone, especially the people who say they want to fuck you, ordinary human affection. You're beyond the bounds of being human. You're inhuman. You're now out of control and you're showing only the slightest pretense that it's otherwise. "I love you," Roger says to Kathy. "I love you so much I think I'm going to die."

Someday there'll have to be a new world. A new kind of woman. Or a new world for women because the world we perceive, what we perceive, causes our characteristics. In that future time a woman will be a strong warrior: free, stern, proud, able to control her own destiny, able to kick anyone in the guts, able to punch out any goddamn son-of-a-bitch who tells her he loves her she's the most beautiful thing on earth she's the greatest artist going fucks her beats her up a little then refuses to talk to her, and able to fuck (love and get love) as much as she wants. In that future time the woman will be beautiful and be the hottest number whose eyes breathe fire, who works hard, who's honest and blunt, who demands total honesty. Greta Garbo in *Queen Christina*. Meanwhile things stink, Kathy thinks to herself. I have to be two different people if I want to be a woman. I'm me: I'm lonely I'm miserable I'm crazy I'm hard and tough I work so much I'm determined to see reality I don't compromise I use people especially men to get money to keep surviving I juggle reality (thoughts of reality) I feel sorry for myself I love to hurt myself and to get hurt etc. i.e., I'm a person like any goddamn man's a person. I have to make my way in this world like any man makes his way and I'm as tough as any man. I earned that respect. But unlike most other goddamn men, I don't want a woman. I tried wanting women but it was no go. I want a man. I want to be a woman to a man. I'm usually not a woman so it's a little weird. Two types of men come on to me. One type thinks I'm a little sweetheart cause I'm small, pretty, and I'm shy. As soon as he talks to me he finds out I'm a brassy maniacal Jew. I have to keep acting out the shy baby number to keep this one. The second type knows I'm loud hard together. He wants to fuck me cause he wants someone who won't jellyfish all over him. This type is butch. I love butch men. The minute he says "I love you" boom I'm a woman. I'm creaming all over him. So to keep this type I have to act out the tough role. Not too tough cause everyone wants affection even though he doesn't want to give any. This is all so cold and academic. I'm in constant pain cause I want a lover and I don't have a lover. I don't know how anymore. I can't be polite I can barely manage to mutter "Let's fuck." Most of the time when I want to fuck, I stumble over to the guy and stare at him. Real feminine. I can't tell anyone how lonely I am and I can't show any feeling. Just this blunt shit. I don't show any feeling and then when the tough guy leaves me call him up and say "Please take me back, please tell me why you're leaving me, are you leaving me? I don't understand what reality is, please I'll do anything become anyone please I need love." The guy who wants me to be the tough girl he desires and expects and who has his own goddamn problems, panics and leaves I'm alone all the time I want to throw everything out the windows I want to bust up the windows the jibberjabbers are getting me again and mad whirling energy I've got to get away from myself I've got to get away from myself. "I love you too."

He rolls over Kathy and rubs his naked body against hers and the cold floor. "I've never told any girl before I love her. Not like this. I feel scared."

"I don't understand what's happening."

Roger rolls on top of her and lays his throbbing cock in her cunt. The moment she feels him enter her, she moans and cries out. She loves to have his cock in her.

They don't move. She moves the muscles of her vaginal walls very softly. No other part of her body moves. They go crazy and tear at each other, naked, on that cold motel floor, abdomen battering abdomen, hands grab at shoulders bite, bite hard through the skin, they're wild beasts, they find the rhythm. Fast strong hard steady rhythm. Boom boom boom. Bone at the base of the cock smashes against bone immediately above the clit.

"I don't know how I'm going to exist when you're not in Haiti. I can't stand being away from you for even a day right now."

"Shh. Roger."

"I don't want to know you. I don't want you to go away. I know you're going to go away and leave me."

"I'm here right now. Shh, baby. I have to go away, but I won't be going away for a long time, and then, if I want, I can come back here in a month. We don't need to talk about this now."

"Will you come back? I don't think you'll come back. Everyone always goes away and leaves me."

"If you want me to, I'll come back. I love Haiti. New York is hell you don't know how horrible it is. I hate living there. I just have to be there sometimes cause at this point that's the only place I can get money for my writing. I'm not rich: if I don't make money I'm going to die. I don't have to be in New York all the time. I can be here whenever you want."

"I love you too much. It's no good. Will you really come back to Haiti?"

"Would, would you want me to come back?"

"I hate you because you're going to leave." He pulls his dripping cock out of her.

"Roger, oh Roger, look Roger this is totally ridiculous because I'm not going to be leaving for two months, but I'll discuss it anyway. I'm not the one who's married. You are. I can do whatever I want."

"She doesn't matter. I tell you already: I try to get away from her, but she won't let me go. I don't know what to do."

"I know I know. But look, as it stands right now, between your work and your wife, I hardly get to see you. You know this' true."

"You're right." He lays his curly-haired head on her cunt.

"I'm the one who's on shaky ground. This is your country and you've got a wife. I'll stay here for you, darling, but I want to know you want me."

His tongue's lapping the insides of her cunt lips. Liquid drips out of her. His cock grows hard. For a moment he stops.

"Don't stop," she moans. "I'm about to come."

"How do I know you'll come back to Haiti? I'll wait around for you, already I dream of you every night last night I lay on my bed I thought of fucking you and I masturbated."

"Didn't you fuck Betty?"

"No, I never fuck Betty anymore. I don't like to. I masturbated as I saw your body and then I fell asleep and dreamt all night about you, I was always with you . . ."

You don't want to steal, but you don't know how to get along if you don't steal. You make seven dollars a night you work an average of two to three nights a week. However you can always borrow money from a guy you used to fuck who still loves you, he may have gotten wise and doesn't anymore, or you can make a porn film. Even if you don't need the money, you get off on stealing. You steal from your friends; if they every caught you, you'd be out. Totally out. You get off on the danger. The only guy you keep fucking is a guy who doesn't give a shit whether you live or die, who tells you he loves you only when you decide to stop fucking him, and who beats you up when you have sex.

You wonder why you're getting sick all the time . . .

Writing these things down doesn't alleviate your suffering. You don't want to steal. You steal. There's a sharp constant pain in you running from ovary to ovary. When this pain hits you, you think you're going to die. You're a stupid bitch. At least half your thoughts are about the men you've fucked or want to fuck: you're desperate for affection, you don't want any affection because you're selfish and egotistical and insecure, so you get sick. For the past year you've had a lousy medical history: four abortions, four PID attacks, five flu cases, one breast cancer (now almost gone). Maybe you're in a bind.

"I want to buy you a yacht," Roger murmurs. "What color yacht do you want?"

"What do you mean?"

Roger's sperm's dripping out of her cunt. His hand cups and presses her left breast. "When you come back to Haiti, there'll be a yacht waiting for you. What color do you like?"

"Roger, when I'm in the United States, sometimes I don't even have enough money to buy food. I don't even know what I'd do with a yacht. Sure, I'd like a yacht. If you really want to help me out, you can help pay for the ticket so I can come back to Haiti to see you."

"How much did it cost you to come here?"

"Two hundred and forty dollars round trip. If I stay more than three weeks, which I'm going to, I'll have to plunk down another hundred dollars. Three hundred and forty dollars."

"That's not any money. I spend more than that amount of money on my bar drinking every month."

"It's a lot of money to me."

"If I send you a ticket, will you come back to me?"

"I said I would."

"I want you to tell me again."

They're lying on the cold floor and looking up at the white ceiling. "You work for your father and you're going to keep working for him. You have to do what your father tells you. Plus you're married. As it is I only get to see you once every few days."

"You're not going to come back to Haiti. I'm never going to see you again."

"I'm trying to be straight Roger. It's silly for me to spend all this money to come see you and never get to see you. I want to come back to Haiti when I'll be able to spend a lot of time with you. As it is I spend most of my time daydreaming about you sucking my cunt."

"Do you like that?"

"I love it."

"I'm going to do it now." Their flesh's so wet, it squeaks as it separates, recloses, she moans her nerves are sprung up like thousands of open wounds. He wiggles two fingers up her asshole.

About a minute later she starts to come.

"I can't stop shaking."

"I want to get rid of Betty and marry you."

"Oh my God Roger not again. I can't take anymore. I'm so sore the moment you touch me I come. I just want you more and more. I'm going to go crazy."

"I'm coming too. I'm going to come inside you."

Roger looks into Kathy's eyes while his cock grows larger and harder.

His right hand strokes her tenderized cunt. "I'm going to be with you all the time from now on."

"You can't be with me all the time. I have to go back to the States now and then cause that's where my money is. I have a career. I couldn't stand staying in Haiti all the time. There's not enough for me to do here. For me, the women here live in prison."

"People can't stay together the way we are. This isn't going to last."

"Does that make you sad? Roger, this is right now. You're tormenting yourself with your thoughts. You've got lots of money, or you're going to have lots of money, so you can do exactly what you want. Don't be a fool. You're not going to find another American woman so easily who can stand the life down here, being cooped up all the time. Keep Betty, I mean if you want to I don't know what you want. Betty's not so bad. She's a little scared, but all you have to do is treat her gently. She could use some gentle treatment. You don't have to love her. She adores you, and she'll stick with you, and that's the main thing if you want to have kids. Then you can fall in love with whoever you want. You've got enough money. You can keep as many mistresses as you want buy them all houses. As long as you're fortunate enough to be rich, fuck, why don't you set things up exactly the way you want them?

"I'm going to build a mansion near Gonaives, in the inland, where I'll be all alone. No one will ever be allowed to come there. I won't have any mistresses, nothing. I won't let any of my family in. I'm going to build tennis courts and swimming pools and a golf course."

"Golf? Golf's disgusting."

"Golf's my favorite sport. I learned to play golf in the United States when I went to this school for ambassadors' kids. I'm going to let you come there."

"I'll come if you have some books there."

"No. I don't like to read."

"Don't your parents ever read?"

"Sometimes my father picks up a book after work's over. He doesn't care what he reads."

"You've got to have some books for me. Otherwise I'll go crazy and I won't be able to stay there."

"You'll play golf with me and tennis. I'll have the tennis courts for you."

"I could stay there at least half the year and then hit New York for the height of the art season. I have to be in New York sometime during the art season."

Maybe your body will forget about being fucked. You forget about being fucked. For a moment. Tra la la la la la la. A layer of not caring if you're fucked over desperate to get fucked.

But it seems so weird to get fucked. This huge red hard object pointed at you. You're supposed to do something with it? It's warm. It moves when you touch it. The rest of the skin is cold and clammy and it smells and it's too close to you. Go away.

Go away. I don't want the ground pulled out from under my feet. I don't want to lose consciousness.

I'm nauseous. I know what this territory's like. I've been here before. Terror horror the red means. I can sit it out. I know my own strength.

All around me buildings are crumbling strange vibrations are going about people are so miserable they're doing everything they can to escape everything. I should tell them the only thing I know: there's no fire escape.

He sinks his cock into her and pulls it back and forth. The membrane inside her cunt sticks to his cock.

"I don't want you to come back to Haiti."

"You don't?"

"In September we'll harvest the sugar cane. After that, I'll take my vacation. You'll take my vacation with me. You're going to go to Puerto Rico."

"OK. I don't care where I go."

"You'll stay with me in my hotel and we'll do everything together. We'll go out drinking and gambling and eating all the expensive food. The only thing is you can't get upset when I go with other women."

"I don't care if you go with other women. It's so hard these days for a man and woman to stay together for more than two days, jealousy's the least of all the problems. I don't get jealous anymore. But I don't want to be left alone in some strange hotel room for days. I have to have the same freedom you have."

"What do you mean?"

"If you fuck around, I fuck around."

"I don't like that."

"Tough shitty. I'm not the kind of woman you can keep locked up in a hotel room. If you want that kind of woman, you can get anyone. I'm as tough as you are."

"I like that. You can do what you want as long as I don't find out about it. If I find out about it . . . watch out. I beat you up."

"I like being beat up."

"You do?" He smiles. His eyes are soft and gentle. "When I send you a ticket, you come down there."

"You'll have to send me a round-trip ticket. I don't trust you and I don't want to get stuck without any money in some god-forsaken hotel room."

He smiles again. "I shouldn't love you. I love you too much."

"Roger . . . There's something I don't understand." Her big brown eyes look up at him.

"What?"

"Not exactly 'don't understand.' I think I'm in a bit of trouble. You know Ally's always bugging me to sleep with him."

"Ally's always trying to compete with me. He knows damn well you're going with me."

"I don't know if I should tell you this. Yesterday afternoon I was smoking with Duval and that nice Spanish sailor, I was totally stoned and the Spanish guy left the room. I didn't know he was going to leave the room. Duval wanted to fuck me. I told him I couldn't cause I was going with you."

"Duval told me he didn't have any more grass. Where did he get that grass from?"

"I was real stoned. Duval didn't listen to me: he grabbed me and almost raped me. When I got the chance, I pushed him away and ran out of the room. I think he's very angry. You know how close he and Ally are and how they talk. I hope there isn't any trouble."

"Did he kiss you?"

"Yeah, he kissed me. So what? That isn't the point."

"Did you like him kissing you?"

"Look, Roger, I'm scared. Last night there was this knocking on my door. Not on the front door to the room which is always locked, on the back door. I was asleep the knocking woke me up I couldn't tell what was happening I thought it was you. I yelled, 'Qui est la?' Someone said, I think, 'Alfred.' I don't know: I was asleep. I don't know any Alfred. I said 'Go away.' Then the doorknob started turning. He was trying to break in. The doorknob turned for about ten minutes. I freaked. I mean in New York City women get raped all the time. I didn't think. I screamed. I ran to the front door, opened it, saw that little twerp who runs around the motel. He looked at me like I was crazy. I slammed the door in his face. I was really scared. Scared out of my mind. I didn't know what to do. Finally I was able to get to sleep. Who do you think it was?"

"It was Ally. He has the hots for you and he's pissed because you're fucking me and not him. He usually gets all the women who come here. You better watch out he doesn't rape you. Now that you've kissed Duval, you're fair game."

"I didn't kiss Duval because I wanted to. I was stoned and he grabbed me. I got out of there as soon as I could."

"You let him kiss you. C'mon. Put your clothes on. Let's go."

"But Roger, what can I do? I'm really scared."

Disgusting putrid horror-face no one wants to fuck you you make a fool of yourself you always make a fool of yourself everyone's always laughing at you everywhere you go you don't belong anywhere nowhere nowhere you're worse than a bum cause a bum can take care of himself he can stand sleeping on the streetcorners at night he can travel from place to place without worrying about his five thousand books how he's going to drag the right dresses with him you can't do anything for yourself you're a demented abortion on God's earth you don't do anything useful you hate to work all of you is one mass of squirming and totally disgusting worms that squirm against each other hate each other.

Gotta run. Gotta get out. Gotta get moving. Get out. Escape. Escape. Burst open. Stop. Get the fuck out of here anyway I can. Dig my way out. Break all these goddamn windows. Bust the world open. Beat up everyone until someone pounds me into a pulp. Stick more razor blades in my wrists. Fuck up my life. Destroy.

I want to go home, mommy. I thought this was a passion, but

it's not. Emotions are like thoughts. They come and go. They're not me. I can play at being in one, being one, but it's not me, it's just playing, and after a while it makes me sick. I don't know what to do anymore, mommy. Mommy mommy mommy mommy mommy mommy mommy mommy mommy mommy mommy mommy mommy mommy mommy mommy mommy mommy mommy

Middle finger of left hand presses down cunt lips above clit. See hand with ring. See bluejean jumpsuit and scarf twisted black yellow red blue orange. Have to stop to say colors. Don't stop when see. Feel finger pressing down lips. Lips feel. I feel. I can see. Mind (perceptions, thoughts, emotions) swirling. I can perceive mind swirling.

You can't rely on those passions . . . you don't know where to go . . .

The gray sportscar races down the boulevard, the main road in Cap Haitian, which separates the ocean and the houses.

"Is something the matter? Are you angry with me?"

"I'm not angry about nothing."

She thinks for a minute. "You are angry. I don't know what I did wrong."

"I said 'I'm not angry.' "

"Why are you acting so queer? You won't notice me or nothing. You must be upset."

The sportscar moves faster and faster. "Where do you want to go?"

"I don't know anything about this place. Where do you want to go?"

"Where do you want me to take you?"

"Is it Duval? Are you angry cause that thing happened with Duval?"

The car races around the poor people who are walking.

"It wasn't my fault that thing happened with Duval. He grabbed me. I didn't know what to do. I was scared if I fought back, he'd murder me. I don't know karate: I have to use my wits. I got away as soon as I could. Nothing happened Roger. I didn't even take my clothes off."

"Did he touch your titty?"

"His hand might have brushed it when we were struggling."

"I see. You're in a lot of trouble. He's going to tell Ally he's had you and Ally's going to tell everyone. That's how those two are. All the men are going to want you to go with them."

"Is everyone in this town crazy?" She starts to cry. "Duval attacked me. I didn't want him to attack me. If one guy attacks me, does that mean every guy here has the right to attack me?"

"He wouldn't have attacked you if you didn't want him to. You liked it when he touched your breast. Did he touch it nicely?"

"No, he didn't touch it nicely. Do you want me to go with Duval?"

"I don't care what you do."

"Goddamnit. I was smoking and I was stoned. Totally stoned. When I get stoned, I get horny and also, when I have great sex and I've been having the best sex with you I've ever had, I'm horny all the time. I can't help it. That's the way I am. I just don't know what I'm doing sometimes and I get turned on. But I didn't want to sleep with Duval I'm sleeping with you. I even told Duval I couldn't sleep with him cause I'm sleeping with you. I can't handle two boyfriends." She puts her hand on his hard cock. "All I want is you."

"What did Duval say when you told him that?"

"He said all the girls here have more than one boyfriend."

"He's lying to you. Duval, Ally, and I are a threesome and sometimes we trade girls around, but those girls aren't worth anything. You can do what you want. I don't want to tell you to do anything."

Her hand rubs his cock through his pants material. "I've slept with a lot of men. I just don't want another man right now. I couldn't see another man right now if he stood naked in front of me and raped me. You're satisfying me completely."

"You like me?"

"I love you. I don't give a shit about Duval or anybody. You're happy now? I love it when you're happy."

"I love you too much."

"Roger, this is serious. Do you think it was Ally who tried to break into my room? If it was Ally and Duval tells him what happened today."

"Unzip my pants and put your hand on my cock. I love that. I love when a girl sucks me in the car. I know Ally. He's going crazy from all the drugs he's been taking. When he hears Duval had you today, he's going to rape you."

"What am I going to do?"

"Suck my cock. Lean down and put your mouth around my cock."

She leans down and places her mouth around his distended cock.

The car pulls up in front of a small white building. A woman leans against the wood bar in the large empty room of a brothel that has Dominican Republic girls. The woman's wearing a bright green dress. When Roger and Kathy walk into the room, the woman walks over to Kathy and smiles at her.

Roger tells one of the girls to bring him some cigarettes. When she returns with the cigarettes, he refuses to pay her. The girls think Kathy's Roger's wife because she's white. They crowd around her and giggle. Heat flashes through her body. She walks over to Roger and sits next to him.

The gray car speeds down the empty road away from Cap Haitian. "Do you realize you're a very powerful person here? You're going to get more powerful as you get older and older. It's not only that you're rich: everyone here knows who you are and looks up to you. Everybody knows every little thing you do."

"I know this."

"I'm not being clear what I mean to say . . . Do you realize most of the people here are poor?"

"I think about it."

"It's not just that they're poor. There are a lot of poor people in the world. These people don't have a chance to be anything else. Your father's business is going to come to you and you're going to have a chance to do something for these people. If nothing else, you're an example for these people."

"I've told you that. That's why I live out in the country. There nobody can see me. Even the servants we have out there take advantage of us, they spy on us, and they steal everything. Last week one of our workers stole two black cows. My father dismissed him."

"Maybe he was hungry. You've got to think about who you are. That's what I'm trying to say. These people follow you. If you have love in your heart and live for other people, these people will have love in their hearts. I know I'm sounding soppy, but it's what I believe."

"That's why I don't hang around with Ally and Duval anymore. We three used to be like one person, I told you this, we split our women and shared our dope. But now I'm a man. They're still boys. I have a lot of responsibilities. The only men I can talk to are thirty and forty years old."

"You have to show people who act like babies the way. In one way you're lucky cause you were born rich, you have every opportunity anyone could want, but in another way it's really hard for you: you can't be a private person. You have to think in terms of other people."

"I have no friends. Everyone in this town will do anything I say. Except for Gerard. No one can tell Gerard what to do. He doesn't take shit from anybody."

"Gerard is your friend."

"No. He envies me. You remember when he was saying I'm 'retired'? He's jealous because I earn four times as much when I do half the work he does. All he wants is to get rich and he's not going to."

"Isn't there anyone you talk to? You know, really talk to?"

"I don't have any friends. I'm going to build the castle; I told you about the castle. As soon as I get rid of Betty. I don't want her living in it. I'm going to build this huge mansion in the middle of Haiti, surrounded by tennis courts, swimming pools, and a golf course. Do you like to play tennis?"

"No."

"I'm going to have only older women there."

"What do you mean by 'older'?"

"They can't be younger than fifty. I like older women cause they act like nursemaids. They'll take care of me. They might all have to be dumb. I'll have a few huge dogs who'll stay outside and I'll have the best stereo system money can buy plus all the records I can get. I like listening to records. That's all I'll have."

"You can't cut yourself off like that from the world. It might work for a while, but then something bad'll happen to you and you'll have no way to deal with your suffering. Even if nothing bad happens to you your whole life, you're going to die and you're going to have to deal with your dying."

"I told you. I'm going to have lots of old women there who'll take care of me. I won't even fuck them."

"Jesus Christ. What about all the people here who are suffering and starving all the time? Haiti's the poorest country in the world. There are almost no roads. Most of the people can't read. The rivers are polluted. There're almost no hospitals. How can you totally forget about everyone?"

"Did you like it when Duval put his hand on your titty?"

"Jesus Christ, Roger."

"You know what I think? I think you like Duval. I think you're going to make love with him."

"Don't be ridiculous. I thought we got through all that. I love you."

While they're arguing, Roger stops the car at The Imperial. They get out of the car and walk into a disgusting room. No fan, and the heat's so thick it's solid.

"Why d'you want to come here, Roger? This room's repulsive." Clear plastic covers the bed mattress.

"Back at L'Ouverture, I saw Ally following us. He's trying to stop us from being together."

His huge cock rushes into her. He's too rough and he hurts

her. Maybe all the interest has gone out of our sex, she says to herself. Do I love him? Maybe I don't love him. It was just sexual it's amazing how strong sex is you forget about it when you're not having it good sex is everything. I guess I don't love Roger anymore. Do I love him? Do I love him? His fingers're stroking the slimy puffed cunt lips. "Oh Roger oh Roger. That delicately. That is so good." His fingers keep stroking the red lips in the same way. His fingers are stroking the red lips in the same way. Thoughts endless thoughts it's Roger's fingers who are stroking my cunt lips it's Roger's fingers who are stroking my cunt lips I am those fingers I am the tips of those fingers I've found a man who loves me and is taking care of me this black man really loves me and he's a man the main thing he's a man his chest is broad he looks like a macho pig he's a businessman he's going to watch out for me and give me everything I've ever wanted I don't care if he has nothing to do with my life except sex sex is so important. I'm coming oh thank God I'm coming, she thinks to herself, as his cock plunges back and forth inside her, I needed to come so badly I was so scared I wasn't going to come I need him so much, clinging to his huge brown chest rivulets of sweat running between their bodies his cock plunges back and forth inside her, I'll never be horny again I'll never be horny again. Desire takes over. Dreams ideas . . . everything awakens. Your body is the most beautiful thing I've ever known and your touch satisfies all the longings I've ever had. I need to feel and see your body to keep on living. I can't live without you because you're so incredibly beautiful and I know you love me. I'm beginning to believe that I'll give up everything for you, because, so far, in spite of my blossoming career and endless need to break all limits, my life has been nothing.

"Are you going to leave me? I know you're going to leave me for another man."

"Stop it. Think for a moment. Your mind's driving you crazy. I don't want anyone else. I don't even think of any other man. Am I acting like I want another boyfriend?"

"I'm realistic. I know you're going to meet another man and fall in love with him. You're going to forget about me."

"Oh shit I've started bleeding. At least I'm not pregnant."

"I don't like it when woman are on the rag. I make Betty use only tampax. She has to change them every hour and flush them down the toilet. I won't go near her until she's clean again. It disgusts me. You know what my sister once did to me when I was a young boy? I got into bed and there were all her used rags."

"Well. You can stay away from me if you want."

"I don't want you to leave me. That's all I think about. If it's not Duval, it's someone else. All the boys are after you."

"I'm going to tell you something about myself, I'm really a very private person I don't discuss this with anybody. How do I explain this? I spend most of my time doing this uh work, Zen. I'm trying to find out who I am, my mind is basically occupied with this. That's where my mind is. I go with one guy, OK I love to love and I love to fuck, but there's no spaces in my life for a lot of sex."

"What do you do when you do this Zen? Do you go to a temple and bow before the Buddha?"

"No. I sit in front of a wall and stare at the wall." Kathy stares at herself in the mirror to see if she's getting fat. She isn't.

"I can't continue seeing you if you're a Buddhist."

"Why not?"

"Buddhists don't like to fuck or get drunk or do any of the things I like to do."

"I'm not that kind of Buddhist. I just do this weird kind of thing so I won't be selfish all the time and so I can find out who I am. I'm not even sure I'm a Buddhist. At the Zen Center I go to back home Jerry and Robert and I, those are two people in the Zen Center, couldn't decide if we were Buddhists or not. What I do doesn't concern you."

"If you do it too much, it won't make you stop fucking me?"

She laughs and throws her arms around his neck. "Roger I couldn't stand to stop fucking you."

"I can't help it. I don't want you to go away from me."

Arm in arm they walk through the night. Into the Imperial restaurant-and-cocktail lounge. It's midnight when most of the poor Haitians are asleep. They order their dinner.

"It's very hard for me to live here because everyone here watches me and knows what I'm doing. I ignore all of them I do what I want. I always do exactly what I want. But I have to be careful. You know if someone insults me, if someone wants to kill me, I can't do anything."

The lights in the restaurant are red. The walls are brown and the waiters are black and white.

"Who would want to kill you?"

"I have my enemies. People resent me. People think I'm hurting them. Just because of who I am. I don't do anything bad. Last year this kid waited outside the Poisson. When I came out, he punched me in the face. I couldn't do anything because if I do, everyone'll blame me and say it's my fault. I had to get my friends to beat up the kid the next day. I tell you a story why it's dangerous for me to go around town alone. Last year a cop stopped me and wanted to see my identification. I didn't want to show him nothing. He didn't want to give in to me. He said he was going to take me in. I warned him."

"Didn't he know who you were?"

"He was with a lot of his buddies and he couldn't lose face. I still refused to show him ID. When he was about to put his handcuffs on me, I showed him some ID. The next day my henchmen beat him up. He died."

"You killed a cop? Just cause he was acting like a punk?"

"You don't understand what it's like for me. You see this scar?"

"Yes."

"One time, when I was in school in Arizona, this girl she's crazy for me. I don't want anything to do with her."

"You fucked her?"

"I fucked her a few times. It wasn't anything special. I tell her I'm not going to see her again. She doesn't say anything. The next day I walk out of the cafeteria there she is. She has a knife and goes for my throat. The next thing I know, I wake up in the hospital. I find out she's been calling and calling to see if I'm still alive. Then she comes to see me and tells me she loves me madly won't I please let her take care of me. Oh brother."

"Sounds like a classical situation."

"This one girl here, she tells me she's been to a voodoo doctor who's done a work so I have to fall in love with her. But I tell her I don't believe in that stuff. Women are always falling in love with me."

"Have you ever loved a woman?"

"I had this mistress once I paid her a lot of money. She cheated on me and I didn't know at the time oh brother. She took all the money I gave her. Then she got pregnant with my child and had an abortion without asking me if she could have one."

"Roger, I love you."

A black-and-white waiter brings them their food: a whole fried fish surrounded by fried plantains, salads, sauces, lobster, and some other food Roger tells him to take away.

"I have things hard. I want to be like everyone else, but no one will let me. When I was staying in New York City, every day I got mugged. That's where I got this bump on my head. This man beat the hell out of me cause he said I'm a black man. I couldn't fight back."

"Jesus Christ."

"I don't like New York City. The white people hate us there. I'd lose my life if I lived in New York City. Here, when white people visit my father, they treat my father and the rest of us with a lot of respect. People like, what's that really good brandy?"

"Courvoisier?"

"No."

"Martell?"

"Yes. Those people, and the people who own Grand Marnier, important people: they all visit my father and bring us fabulous presents. Sometimes I date their daughters."

"Have you killed anyone else?"

"I've never killed anyone. I have some friends who protect me when I need it. It's good. This way no one can find me doing anything wrong and no one bothers me because they all know I'm protected. I don't have any more trouble."

"But don't you care about the people who are less powerful than you?"

"I can't do anything out in the open, none of us can, cause the government's always trying to get us. That's why when I first met you I said it's not good to talk openly about dope. You remember? If anyone caught me with even a joint on me, the government would use that against my father. They already tried to arrest my father directly, but they couldn't do that cause my father's workers stood up for him. Now they're trying to get at my father through us."

She starts crying over her fried fish, fried plantains, salad, and beer.

"Why are you crying? Is something the matter with the food? I'll have them take it back." This makes her cry louder and louder. A strange forty-year-old man walks over to the table. "I'll do anything for you. I love you."

"Hello, Roger."

"Wait a second Lewis. Kathy, please tell me. What's the matter? I don't want to see you crying."

"We'll talk about it later," she says through her tears. "Uh hello. My name is Kathy." She sticks out her hand at the strange man.

"Kathy, this is my uncle Lewis."

He shakes her hand and smiles at Roger. "How are things going at the factory? I hear your family's going down to Port-au-Prince."

"Yes. We'll be going next week. My father has to take care of that lumber business and see about Carlos. I'm going to take Kathy with me."

"That's terrific." He slaps Roger's back. "I see they got my lobster in today."

"This was your shipment. It's not any good I'm not going to eat any more of it. Waiter, take this away. They use bad fish here and they don't know how to cook."

"That lobster came from Port-au-Prince by truck in this heat. There's no way it could still be good. You should know you can't eat lobster around here. You should get the fish they catch right here."

"I saw Carol yesterday. He was drinking champagne. I guess he's doing well."

"Easy come, easy go. I'm doing pretty well myself. How are the rum tanks coming along?"

"I'm worried about the pressure-gauger. I think that gauger we're setting up might blow on us, and then we'd be sunk. That new French engineer isn't any good. I'm going to have papa come up and check it out as soon as I can do it behind my father's back. Papa's a smart one; he knows every goddamn thing there is to know about machinery."

"Maybe I'll come up and take a look at it myself. Are you going to be around tomorrow?"

"I'm working every day now. I'm working my ass off."

"Well, I've got to get going now."

"It was nice having met you," Kathy says as she sticks her hand out at him.

"You're a beautiful young lady. Make Roger happy."

"I'll see you tomorrow," Roger says and his uncle slaps him on the back.

"What a nice man. Waah. Waah. Roger how could you kill someone?"

"Two more beers, please. What are you talking about? I've never killed anyone."

"Well you said you have these henchmen and they kill people for you. For no reason at all. That cop was just trying to save his face. He probably didn't want to be outpowered by a kid in front of his friends. And he lost his life. It's not that you kill people. That's not that important. It's much more. Waah. Waah.

All the poverty and misery and all the suffering. You suffer so much. You don't understand."

"I understand what you're saying. Let's go."

"Don't you have to pay?"

"No. They know who I am."

They walk outside and the stars are moving and the winds are moving in and out of the stars and the moon moves in an even arc the clouds moving in front of the stars in front of and behind the moon, moving faster than the moon, irregularly: the night sky is a grouping of second-to-second changing light and heat and moving substances. Everything moving and changing and pulsating and they call this "death" and they call this "alive."

The ocean is a black still mass, a black monster hiding under his own death, and the town is absolutely still. A dead mass of houses and shacks and slums piled together, jumbled, shackled, no reason at all, just there. The faraway mountains lead slowly down, flatter and flatter land, to the rich houses the rich houses look way down on the poor houses. To the left of the poor houses a secret police shark chute swings down to the sea. This is death. Stillness. The slight ocean rises hit a stone wall, leap up in the air five to thirty feet high. Suddenly white and movement you-never-know-where. Don't hear anything. Hear the water slap the stones. Winds hit the coconut tree leaves. Hear nothing. Sudden violent unsuspected movement everywhere.

Break all speed records. Keep going. You're the gray sportscar and you're moving. I'm the richest prick in town. Poor people don't need arms and legs. I'm the richest prick in town. I wanna go out farther. I wanna get more fucked up. I want to go out there right now. Me go way me me. Moving as fast as the car winds. Grab the cock and up the energy. Anything to up the energy. Get right out there. The faster I go the faster the stars go maybe we'll all stop moving.

"I love it when you touch my cock. Why don't you suck it?"

"Roger, I know it's none of my business but you can't treat the poor people like animals."

"How do I treat them like animals?"

"You don't even realize. Like when you ordered that whore to bring you cigarettes and she even bought them for you and asked you for the money, you wouldn't give her the money."

"I never carry money on me. Everyone knows that. If they want money, they can go to my father and he'll pay them."

"These are poor people. They can't afford to pay for your cigarettes."

"My brother goes out drinking with our workers just so he can order them around. He has lots of girlfriends." The gray sportscar races up and down the long black boulevard. There are no other cars. It reaches the end of the boulevard, circles around Pension L'Ouverture, and heads back down the boulevard. Each time the car goes back, its speed increases.

"The main thing is to have love in your heart. That's what I'm trying to do. If you can love, nothing else matters. If you loved everyone Roger, there'd be a revolution in this town."

"I've never been in love with a woman."

"You haven't? Wow. Last year I fell in love for the first time. I just went crazy. I'd do anything for the guy. He didn't care about me at all. I learned what it was like to really feel for someone."

"I don't like it."

"What?"

"This is no good. You're going to fall in love with another man."

"I should have never told you about that incident with Duval. I love you Roger. I don't love anyone else. I don't want to love anyone else."

"You're going to go back to New York and fall in love with another man."

"No I'm not. I know exactly what my life's like in New York. I can tell you exactly. I spend most of my time at the Zen Center. I don't have much time left over. I see this one guy, the one I told you about, who doesn't give a shit about me. He's just hooked on fucking me. He doesn't give a shit about me. But I can't stop seeing him and I can't see anyone else cause I'm so crazy about him. I'm not going to fall in love with anyone but you."

"Why doesn't this guy fall in love with you? I know he's gonna start to love you when you get back to New York."

"No way. The people I hang around with in New York don't love each other. Not this way."

"You're going to fuck someone else while you're here. You can't have just one boyfriend."

"Do you want me to fuck someone else?"

"I'd hate it." The car goes faster and faster. "I believe what you're telling me, that you don't want to sleep with anyone else. But the flesh is stronger than the spirit."

"Not in my case."

"Tomorrow I'm going to leave Le Roi at lunchtime so I can see you. Then I'll leave you and I'll return in the evening. We'll spend the whole evening together fucking."

"I'd love that."

"And we'll spend all Saturday together. Saturday night I'm going to take you to the voodoo dances. I remember what I've promised you."

The car keeps going around and around the boulevard. The fastest and the only car on the road. It's almost dawn.

THE CHILDREN

BOATS out on the sea. Dense dark clouds with openings in clouds. Look like lands. Lands are serrated areas of bright reds and bright pinks. The water's dark green-blue and calm.

The sea reflects all the light that's in the sky. Uncountable tiny yellow-white quasi-circles moving toward the shore are the color and luminosity of light. At the horizon in the center of the sea is this luminosity. Here the sea is lighter than the sky. The sky is a uniform blue so pale it's almost yellow. To the right some small fluffy clouds are almost disappearing into the paleness. The ocean grows greener. A few whitecaps. A small wooden fishing-boat moves across the sea from right to left. The boat is pale green and both the fisherman who stands in the back of the boat moving the boat with a long pole and the fisherman who crouches down in front of the boat are black. The boat's rim is red.

The roosters are crowing their lungs out and small goats are pissing on the sand and dry dust which covers everything and the pigs are rooting in the sand for whatever garbage the rising waves are leaving behind and white and red hens are scampering up the thin branches of the canap trees.

A group of eleven-year-old boys are sitting on a curb. Alex has two toothpicks, one long and one short, legs from rickets or polio and for the last two days has been running a fever. Kathy walks out of the pension.

"Did you bring me my food?"

"I couldn't get much out. They're watching me. I brought you the white bread. I'm sorry, Alex."

He turns away from her.

"Let's go for a walk," she says to Fritz who always has clean clothes. Fritz and Alex are her two closest friends.

Fritz, Alex, Kathy, and Tony the head of the gang and older walk along the stone wall. Tony puts his arm around Kathy. Alex refuses to talk to her and throws a stone at her. She turns around, pissed. "Why'd you throw a stone at me?" He throws another stone at her: "I want you to die." She's so upset, she starts to cry. All the boys refuse to talk to her. Finally Fritz explains to her that when someone wants to fight her, she has to fight back. Otherwise: everyone will lose his respect for her. If Alex tells her he wants to kill her, she has to tell Alex she's going to kill him. Then they can both forget anything happened. "I'm going to kill you if you give me any more trouble," she says to Alex. He smiles, and runs up to her, and holds her hands. There are tears in his eyes. They're walking back along the stone wall to the dusty white street curb. Fritz tells her she has to fight kung-fu. He demonstrates.

Kathy walks away from the pension. A little red-hair boy asks the white girl if she saw Mrs. Betty this morning. "Sure I saw Betty. She was at the breakfast table talking to papa when I came down for breakfast this morning. I didn't get to speak to her cause I had to run to the bank. I like Betty."

"You know why Mrs. Betty was there?"

"No. Why was she there?"

"We don't have to tell you. You know why she was there," says Fritz.

"She was there because she was talking to papa. Betty and papa are good friends."

"I think she was there for another reason."

"Are you talking about me and Roger? Betty knows all about that."

"I think Mrs. Betty's one very smart lady. She does something," the red-head boy says.

"What's Betty doing?"

"You'll find out what she does."

"I don't have any idea what you're talking about. Fritz, what's this boy talking about?"

"Don't you worry. I'll take care of you. Anyone who brings any trouble to you will have to fight me."

"I'm not worried about anything. I just want to know what's going on."

"Don't you worry. Mrs. Betty won't be able to do anything to you."

"What's Betty going to do to me? Betty and I are friends."

All the boys look at her with pity.

"Where were you last night?" Alex asks. "Did you have good eat?"

"I didn't go anywhere last night. You guys know that. You were watching my room all night. I was waiting for Roger, I had a date with him, but he never showed up."

"I think you ate well last night. I think Gerard came to visit you. You like Gerard?"

"Did any of you see Roger last night?"

"I saw him go into the Poisson," the red-head says. "He was alone."

"That's weird. Why would he go into the Poisson and not see me? I don't think Roger loves me anymore."

"Don't you listen to that little red-haired guy," Fritz says. "He makes you bad. Mr. Mystere didn't go into the Poisson last night."

"Why're you lying to me?" she asks the red-hair guy.

"I'm not lying. I saw the Mystere go into the Poisson."

"Did any of you see Roger today?"

"Nobody's seen Mr. Mystere for the past two days. Don't listen to that little guy. He just wants to cause trouble. All the time he tries to cause trouble."

"I'm gonna beat him up for you," says Alex.

"No. Don't do any fighting. I feel really upset."

"I think Mr. Mystere makes you bad."

"It's not Roger's fault. He just doesn't love me anymore."

"Don't you worry about nothing. If Mr. Mystere makes you bad, I fight him for you."

"I feel good now. You're making me feel happy."

"Mrs. Betty's my friend," the red-hair boy says. "She's very kind to me."

"I like Betty too. I think she's a great person."

"I saw Mrs. Betty talking to papa. She's going to make trouble for you."

"What kind of trouble can Betty make for me? I'm an American."

"Last year," Alex says, "Mrs. Betty was talking to a girlfriend of hers. As soon as Mrs. Betty turns her back, Mr. Mystere starts kissing the girl."

"That's tacky."

"Mrs. Betty sees what's happening. She's no dope. She goes up to the girl and says, 'That's my husband you're kissing. You have no right to kiss him.' She slaps the girl."

"What'd the girl do?"

"Mrs. Betty takes care of herself. She knows Mr. Mystere has to do what his parents say. She gets Mr. Mystere's father to keep him in line."

"That's true. Roger absolutely worships his father and does everything his father says."

"This morning," the red-head boy says, "I talked to Mrs. Betty."

Just then a completely and highly unusually clean blue-green jeep drives up in front of the curb. This car doesn't even have a spot on it. The white girl lackadaisically watches the jeep stop.

Three men get out of the jeep. They're as clean as the jeep. They're wearing blue pin-striped starched and pressed shirts, stiff white pants, thin brown leather belts, real brown leather polished shoes, and black sunglasses. Their bodies are thin and their hair is less than an inch long.

The white girl looks around and sees the boys running away. The three men stand over her. She looks up at them and doesn't say anything. She feels too dazed and lightheaded from the boiling hot sun to stand up.

After a while of staring, she asks them in her lousy French if they want anything. They don't reply. They just keep staring at her. She sighs and sinks down against the white stucco wall. The morning sun's getting hotter and hotter. After a while, they get back into the jeep.

As soon as the blue-green jeep drives away, the beggar boys return to the curb. Kathy's shaking. "Who were those men?"

"Oh, they were the police."

"The secret police?"

"Yes. The police," Fritz says. He's wearing a short-sleeve khaki shirt and has his hands in his pockets.

"What . . . what did they want with me?"

"I don't know. You must have been bad."

"Look, you've got to tell me about the secret police here. I've heard they kill people whenever they want to. Do they always do this to tourists? They stood over me and didn't say anything."

"No. They usually don't go near the tourists."

"Then why me? Have I been doing something wrong?"

"You must have been."

"What've I been doing?"

"I don't know."

"Why'd all of you run away when the police came? Why didn't you tell me who they are?"

"If the police catch us talking to you, they'll arrest us. They'll think we're bothering you. We had to run away. They won't arrest you because you're an American."

"Then why were they standing over me and staring at me like that? I don't like cops I'm really scared of them. You've got to tell me exactly what's happening. I don't understand what's happening."

"Don't you worry," Fritz sticks his hands in his pockets and spreads his legs, "about nothing. I'll fight those big men for you if they give you trouble."

"You're not going to fight those men. Don't be ridiculous."

"You shouldn't worry about nothing. In Haiti there are no problems." All the boys nod in agreement.

"I just want to know what's going on. I want to know if I've been doing something wrong."

Alex says, "You have a lot of evil thoughts."

"You mean I'm evil?"

"Yes. You're going to have to go to church to get rid of the evil."

"I don't want to go to church. I go to my own kind of church. Every day I sit by myself and pray. My kind of religion doesn't have a church and a priest."

"Alex is right," Fritz says. "You're a Haitian now and you have to behave like a Haitian. You run around with too many men."

"I do not. You know the only man I see is Roger. Am I supposed to go without a boyfriend?"

"You see Gerard and lots of other men. Last night you let some man into your room. All of us saw you."

"That's not true and you know it. I spent all last night sitting around and waiting for Roger. I love Roger. I don't love anybody else."

"Then why," the oldest and biggest boy asks, "when I asked you last night to take a little walk with me, you said you were too busy?"

"I was busy. I had a date with Roger, but he never showed up."

"You said you were busy and now you say you didn't eat last night. I think you're lying."

"I think you have a lot of bad in you," Fritz adds.

"You're all being ridiculous. I want to know about those cops. I hate cops. They ruin everything. What did they want with me?"

"You shouldn't see Mr. Mystere. He has a wife."

"I know he has a wife. I don't want to be in love with someone who's married. Do you think I can choose who I fall in love with?"

"Mrs. Betty's a nice lady," Fritz says, "she's always kind to us. She's not going to like the something you're doing with her husband."

"I'm only going to be here a few weeks I'm leaving. I don't want to break up Roger's and Betty's marriage. I think their marriage is terrific. Betty knows all about me and Roger and it's OK."

"Mrs. Betty's not going to like it when she hears Roger spends his nights in your room. Mrs. Betty's a very jealous woman."

"I don't want to hurt Betty and I don't want to break up her marriage. What'm I supposed to do: make myself stop being in love? I can't do that. Do you understand?"

"I understand," Fritz says. His bare foot kicks a pebble.

"Mrs. Betty's my friend," the red-headed boy says. "This morning I talked to her."

"Why don't you go with me the way you go with the Mystere?" asks Tony. "You have to give me comfort."

"Oh Tony."

"I want to know why not."

"You're too young. I'm twenty-nine years old and you're only twelve."

"In Haiti there is no age. I'm a man like the Mystere."

The white girl's silent for a moment. She feels ashamed. "You're right, Tony."

"The Mystere give you good suck? I give good suck. I have many girlfriends. Ask anyone. I have girlfriends who are older than you. There's one of my girlfriends. She's twenty-five years old. All the time she's after me. 'Tony Tony give me a kiss please just one kiss.' "

I don't believe you, she thinks to herself. She sees a tall, strangely thin woman high-high cheekbones and glittering eyes walk up to Tony and throw her arms around him while the woman kisses Tony, she stares at the white girl with her glittering eyes and Tony says, "You see . . ." The woman holds out a bunch of tiny purple-pink flowers toward the white girl Tony puts his arms around both of them, "I have two girlfriends." "No," the white girl says. The woman kisses Alex twice. "I'm number one," says Tony. The woman places two sprigs of the purple-pink flowers in the white girl's hair.

A nineteen-year-old boy is trying to teach the white girl how to read the Creole of a Jesus magazine. They're slowly translating into English a prayer to Jesus. "Tonight," Tony says to the white girl, "there's going to be a mist over the ocean."

OUR FATHER WHO ART IN HEAVEN

"This mist is called laughter."

HALLOWED BE THY NAME

"If you see this mist, you sleep all the time."

THY KINGDOM IS COMING

"Don't look. Don't look," the kids yell and turn her face away from the glittering eyes of the woman. The woman's standing an inch away from her. "Don't look at her." The woman reaches for her hand. "Don't let her touch you." The woman's hand's holding her hand. "Why?" she asks, "what's the matter?"

JESUS IS COMING JESUS YOU ARE
OUR SAVIOR ONLY YOU CAN UNITE
US ONLY YOU BRING US COMFORT

The women are standing an inch away from each other and staring at each other.

The nineteen-year-old boy explodes. "Don't touch her. Don't let her get near you. She has nothing to do with Jesus. She's trying to stop me."

"She wants a something from you," Fritz says. "She's a bad woman. She's going to do something to you. She's going to make the mist come and you're going to get very sick." She sees the woman's eyes glitter and glitter more.

The woman descends on the nineteen-year-old boy. "I don't care about you I do what I want. You can't stop me."

"I can't, but my father can. My father's a captain. You know who he is. He's a captain so you better watch your step. You know what I'm talking about." The woman with glittering eyes turns around and runs away.

All the little boys have their arms around the white girl. They're all touching her.

"Mrs. Betty's going to make trouble for you. Mrs. Betty's a smart lady. She's going to make plenty hot water for you with Mr. Mystere's father. You better watch your step," the red-head boy warns Kathy.

"How do you know Betty's going to make trouble for me?"

"She say so to me. She say she going to cause you a lot of trouble."

"She said she was going to cause me a lot of trouble? What's she going to do?"

"Don't you believe him," Fritz says. "He tells lies all the time."

"How can he say something like this if it isn't true? Doesn't he know what he's doing?"

"Don't you worry yourself. You get lots of thoughts in your head and you become bad."

"Listen Fritz. Sometimes it's necessary that people talk things out. Just to get them straight. All I want to know is what Betty said. I know what's going on and it's all OK. I just want to know what Betty said."

"Mrs. Betty said you're in a lot of hot water," the red-head says.

"How do you know this? Did Betty say it to you?"

"It's our job to know everything," Fritz says. All the boys agree.

"Then Betty didn't say this directly to you?"

"Don't you listen to him. Come with me." Fritz takes her to a corner of the curb. All the children follow him. The corner ends in burning white sun, burning white dust covers the sky and makes the concrete dirt sand and wood burn like heated car metal. This burning white dust leads straight ahead to the ocean. Thin women are sitting rocking babies and fanning coal fires and pounding something in straw baskets and talking to each other and the maids on the pension are handwashing laundry spreading it out in the sun to dry and preparing food for the night's dinner to the left of the white dust, facing the green ocean, a filthy sandy beach curves outward into the reefs and upward into low rocky hills. The women sit on the edge of this beach. The land is very flat and the women and houses are almost invisible. Small black pigs, goats, chickens, and some mangy dogs run around the women. Tall flashy men elegant shirts walk up and down the sidewalk to the right of the burning dust. A few bare-chested rolled-up pants men are trying to clear the small beach for the tourists by moving the heavier rocks from the sand to the more distant reefs. There are no old people because all the old people are dead. It's the middle of the day. "You know what somebody tells me about you?"

"No."

"This somebody says you do your something with Mr. Mystere because he gives you money."

"That's ridiculous."

"This somebody also says you do a something with lots of men for money."

"Do you mean I'm a prostitute?"

"You do your something with lots of men for money."

"Look: You know I go only with Roger, and no one else. How can I be a prostitute? I do something with Roger, but does that make me a prostitute? Do you think I shouldn't do anything with anyone?"

"We know about your something with Mr. Mystere. It's OK. You also go with other men for money."

"What the fuck are you talking about? That's a totally horrible disgusting thing to say. It's horrible to call a woman a prostitute. You know who I am. I'm your friend. How can you think such things about me? You must be crazy."

"I'm not crazy," says Fritz who's offended.

"I'm not crazy," says another boy.

"Then whoever told you this is lying."

"The somebody who said it to us doesn't tell lies," Fritz says.

"Who said I'm a prostitute?"

"You know who. That little boy, Tommy."

"I don't know who you're talking about."

"That little boy who's always running around the pension with a radio in his ear. He's the owner's nephew. He sees men going into your room every night. He says you're staying at the pension so you can get lots of money from the rich tourists."

"I don't even know this little boy. I mean I know him by sight, but I've never even said two words to him." She thinks for a moment. "He's got some weird thing in his head about me cause he always avoids me. I'm going to tell you something. If I really was a prostitute, I wouldn't be staying at L'Ouverture cause it's not possible for a prostitute to make any money at L'Ouverture. The tourists who come here aren't rich enough, you know they're the plane tourists rather than the boat tourists, and there isn't a quick enough overturn of tourists. And L'Ouverture isn't cheap. A prostitute would starve to death here."

"Then why does he say you take money from men?"

"I don't know. How the hell should I know?"

"There must be something in what he says." All the other boys agree with Fritz. "There's no smoke without fire."

"That's true," Alex adds, "there's no smoke without fire."

"You don't believe anything I'm saying."

"I believe you. I think you do a something with lots of men."

"The only person I do a something with is Roger. You know that. Have you ever seen another man go into my room?"

"No."

"You're watching my room all the time. I know all of you are. You know I never let anyone besides Roger in my room. So why do you believe whatever some little guy says about me rather than what I say about me? You don't even like him and I'm your friend."

"I don't believe Tommy and I don't believe you. I don't think nothing."

"How can you think nothing? You tell me this horrible vicious thing people are saying about me, you say you believe it, and then when I prove that it's false, you say the whole thing doesn't matter. It matters to me. I don't want people saying horrible false things about me. I'm in a foreign country. I don't know what's going on here if I get in trouble I don't know anyone I can run to."

"Nobody says horrible things about you. Lots of women are prostitutes."

"I'm not a prostitute."

"If you say you're not a prostitute, I believe you."

"I swear on anything you consider holy, the holiest thing you know, I'm not a prostitute."

"How much money do you make from men?" the red-head asks.

"Haven't you been listening to anything I've been saying?"

"How much do you charge each man?"

"I'm getting out of here."

Papa and Kathy are sitting on the dining-room terrace that overlooks the ocean. Papa is a seventy-six-year-old American perhaps ex-CIA ex-sailor. "Papa, the tontons macoute just stopped me. They got out of the jeep and stared at me then they drove away. What do you think they wanted?"

"You better watch out for those guys. People disappear around here."

"Do you really think I might be in trouble? They didn't say anything."

"As far as I know, I repeat, as far as I know, they don't bother Americans unless they think you're trying to overthrow their government. Then they don't even give you a trial. Now if you were a Haitian, you might be in hot water. Now I don't know anything for sure."

"Do you think there's going to be a revolution here? The people in this country are so poor. All those boys out there are going to starve this fall cause of the drought."

"There's not going to be a revolution here. There can't be.

These government blacks have the country sewn up. No one can get into this country to start a revolution. Cuba's on one side America's on the other side both of them are dying to grab the one resource that's left in this country: cheap labor, and Baby Doc's not letting either of them stick their noses in the door. Why just last year this boat, just a rowboat, comes over here from Cuba. This happens every so often here. Cuba's just around the next bend. The rowboat's heading toward this beach down here, right around that little hill." Papa points to the left, to a small piece of land that juts out into the ocean. "No one knows exactly what happened. We saw the whole damn army come out of the woodwork. The colonel and all his men in full uniforms, guns loaded, stood on this beach, ready to shoot. They covered the whole beach front. Got a few fisherman. The colonel and his men were waiting for that rowboat to touch the beach. How they knew that rowboat was coming, I'll never know. They know things around here. No one knows who was in that rowboat, how many men, what happened to them. Those men disappeared. You don't put men on trial for political crimes in a country like this. Why there used to be this real nice fellow, a big guy, came around here every now and then to sell some fish. A real nice guy. He didn't show up for a few days one time so I asked around. You know? If anyone knows what happened to him? No one knows anything. Finally I asked Raoul and Raoul tells me it's not good to ask questions. Just keep your mouth shut. You know that guy just disappeared."

"But what about back in the hills, papa? I heard there are guerrilla groups who work in the country."

"Who're you kidding? First of all, these people are," he whispers, "Voodooists. They'll tell you they're not, but they are, every last one of them. They're not going to fight Baby Doc, honey, cause they know he's Papa Loi."

"He is. He's got all the power."

"That's right. If he's got so much power, he must be Head Voodoo Man. These people aren't stupid. Plus the voodoo men, you know each village has a head voodoo man. The head voodoo man isn't the chief; he's equal to the chief. He's the doctor. Everyone comes to him with their problems. 'Doctor, my boyfriend's disappeared.' 'Doctor, someone's poisoned my dog.' So this voodoo man knows everything. There's nothing that can happen in the village that he doesn't know. And the voodoo man goes and tells the sheriff, or whoever's the big government guy in the district, what's happening in the village. And the government guy goes and tells the big government guys in Port-au-Prince."

"Do you think things will ever get better here?" She looks at the beggar boys who are sitting on the low ocean wall, the blue-green ocean, the men working on the beach, the goats, chickens, pigs, dogs, and sand.

"Well, sure, things are already better here. Used to be when a tourist ship'd come into the harbor, its captain would radio to the cops, 'Please put away your guns so the tourists won't see them.' They didn't want to scare the tourists cause it was bad for the tourist trade. Why there were shootings all over the place. The tontons macoute, you hardly see them anymore."

"I saw them. They scared the shit out of me. The boys knew what was going on and ran away. I sat in front of those cops and stared at them like a stupid dog."

"They used to be all over the place. And with guns. After all, they didn't pull any guns on you. I had a run-in with them once. About five years ago. We had to go from Cap Haitian to Port-au-Prince. In those days the only way you could make a trip like that was in a good jeep. And you had to stop at every police station to show your police pass and make a report. We stop at one station and goddamnit that army man can't read. He looks at our papers and he can't read a damn word. He's got his gun on us the whole time. You know you don't go to jail in Haiti for political crimes. You just disappear. Finally we persuade him to drive with us to the next village where there's a man who can read. That son-of-a-bitch cop gets in the truck with us, cocks his gun, and sticks his gun in our backs the whole way to the next village. And at that time I was in the employ of the Haitian government. These police don't work for money, you know. They're in love with their jobs. The regular cops in Port-au-Prince, the ones in yellow shirts, get paid like regular cops, but these guys don't get anything. Of course they take whatever they want from whoever they want."

"Papa, Roger told me he gives Betty a thousand a month above expenses. Do you think that's true?"

"Roger was lying. My God, he doesn't even have a thousand a month for himself. His father has money, but that doesn't mean he has money. You know what I'm talking about: your parents are the same way. That father keeps all the money for himself. That way he can control the boys. He doesn't let those boys have a penny. Why just last year all three boys, you know they're all married, go to him and ask for some money. 'We're all married, father, we've got wives and kids: we need some money now, etc.' So he buys them all cars."

"Why don't they tell him to go to hell? Jesus Christ, in the States no kid would put up with that kind of shit from his parents. Especially a kid who's over twenty-one."

"For heaven's sake those kids know the guy has money. They're just waiting around for the good stuff; hanging on to daddy until daddy decides to cough up. He's never going to cough up you know."

"So Roger's always going to be controlled by daddy?"

"Of course he is. Do you know how much that father has stored up? Why just that one rum tank: that's going to gross a half-million this year. Sure he has expenses, but what are those? Haitian labor's cheaper than slavery. The machines don't cost him that much, though they cost more than the labor. So figure it out, nice and slow. He has three rum tanks going for him. Plus the lumber plus the rubber plus the cocoa plus the coffee plantations."

"Oh."

"Ooh. Something penetrated into your little head. Ooh. Now you see what's going on. Half a million doesn't mean much, but when you add half a million and half a million and half a million and"

"Yeah papa, I understand. So that's why Betty's hanging in there. She's not such a dope."

"Sure. Betty has her nose out for the money too. You know she already tried to leave Roger. She went home once for good, about a year ago. But she came back."

"I know all about Betty's leaving Roger. I think she really loves Roger. You know they're not even really married. Roger never registered the marriage with the Haitian government. So Betty has no possessions of her own, no money, she has no claim on Roger."

"Well, Roger's a nice boy. He's still a boy, understand. He can't get his head out of that black stuff."

"Roger just likes pussy. Black white red old young. He's rough."

"This damn bum leg. It's hurting me worse than ever."

Roger doesn't love me anymore. I know. He likes women too much. Even if he does love me, he's under daddy's control and daddy's stopping him from being with me. I know he is. She doesn't say anything out loud. "Why don't you have a doctor look at it, papa?"

"I have. I've had five doctors look at it. They all say something different. Why that Spanish doctor who lives over the hill there was giving me Vitamin B-12 shots every other day. Those things are dangerous. He had to stop them cause they were getting too dangerous."

"How'd you get the leg?"

"I was shipping fruits and vegetables out to the Caics. You know, you can't ship anything into Haiti. No one buys anything here. The only way you can make money is to ship things out of Haiti. Mangoes cost a penny, two pennies each when they're in season and in the Caics you can get fifteen cents apiece for them. All the fruits and vegetables here are that way. At that time I was shipping fruits and vegetables out to the Caics. There's nothing on the Caics you know. Just a lot of dunes and sand. Some natives. We were sitting off the Caics and we ate a bad fish and the lot of us got sick. Puking sick. I puked for three days straight and I wasn't the worst one. There was no doctor around and there was nothing we could do. Finally we got hold of this nurse. I mean got hold of her. She was something. Jiggling all over the place. I just love those things. Mmmm-mm. Well, she shot me up in the leg with that stuff, what do you call it? the stuff they use to make people sleep on airplanes."

"Dramamine?"

"That's it. Dramamine. She must have hit a nerve or something."

"Dramamine's not a medicine, I mean,"

"She must have hit a nerve or something, I'm sure it was a nerve cause immediately the leg swells up like a balloon. It won't come down for three months and it hurts like the dickens. The goddamn thing's still swollen." It is. "My heart isn't so good either."

"Why don't you get over to Florida and see a good doctor?"

"I've lived a good life. I've done everything I've wanted to and I can't say I've hurt anyone too much. I always try to avoid hurting anybody: I see no sense in doing otherwise. I always pay my girls as soon as I use them. That way there are no hard feelings. I sleep well at nights and you can't say that about anyone who lives in the States."

"I always sleep well at nights." She takes a sip of thick rich coffee.

"When you get back to the States, get a book called *Papa Doc*. That'll tell you everything you need to know about this country. Of course you can't get the book here. Papa Doc was a live wire. He had all the money and all the power in the country. He started out with nothing, and he got it that way. He was a rapacious son-of-a-bitch. When he died, you see, the family got together. They had to decide who would inherit what. Just a little family

meeting like any family meeting after the funeral. They decided
to split it. The mother and the sister got the money and Jean-
Claude got the power."

"Jean-Claude's not poor."

"Of course he isn't, honey. But he's not bleeding the country
for all he can get the way that mother and sister are still doing.
Jesus Christ, women can never be satisfied. And his top ministers
get all the graft they can get. They don't even think twice about
it. Those blacks are still in power and, I say, they never completely
came out of the trees."

"Everyone in this country's black."

"No they're not. There're the blacks and there're the mulattoes.
Right now the blacks run the government, but the mulattoes have
all the money. The blacks and the mulattoes: they've never liked
each other. A mulatto man'll never go with a black woman. He
doesn't even like American women. He'll go with another mulatto, or even better, with a French or French-Canadian woman
cause that means he's overcome his African blood. Whereas a
black prefers an American woman every time. The mulattoes are
society: they do all the business and they have all the money. I'll
tell you something: that's where your revolution's going to come
from. Look at Henry. His father's English and his wife's father's
French. Gerard is almost white. Those are the ones who have
money in this town."

"But Roger's black?"

"Are you kidding? That father's almost as white as I am. And
look at Nicolas, the second brother. He's barely tan. I'll tell you
something. You look at Jean, Gerard's younger brother. His gums
are black as anything. Now and then you get a throwback, and
there's nothing you can do about it."

The boys and the white girl sit out on the stone wall. They
don't do anything. They sit there for about an hour. Then they
move back to the curb in the white dust. They sit down. They
don't do anything else. A few more hours pass.

"Have you brought it for me?" Tony asks.

"Brought what, Tony?"

"You know."

"Don't give me any problems. I'm not in a good mood."

He raises his fists at her. "He wants to kill you," the nineteen-year-old boy says. "You want to kill me, Tony?" "Yes."

"Why do you want to kill me?" "You know."

"It's no good to want to kill someone. The bad energy you put out comes right back at you."

"No. It goes out to you."

"Tony only likes white girls. He refuses to go with Haitian girls. Last year he fought Ally over a French girl Ally was with."

"Was Tony fucking her?"

"No. Tony wanted to fuck her."

"When are you going to give me the something I want?"

"I don't know what you want."

"Yes you do. Don't lie to me."

The sun is white-hot the air and the cement and the cars are hot.

"Tony, I can't."

"Why not? You give it to the Mystere. I know you do cause I've seen you."

"It's different with Roger, Tony. He's the only one I fuck."

"Why's it different with the Mystere? You think he has money and he can take you places and I don't have any money."

All the boys cluster around them. "I've told you again and again. I can't go with you cause you're much younger than me."

"You think this 'younger' means something. I can do anything the Mystere does. I see him take you to the Poisson and buy you beers. You think I can't do that? I have plenty of money. I buy you one beer, two beers. I take you dancing and buy you things. You go with him just cause he's going to buy you lots of things."

"I love Roger. I don't care about his money. I've got my own money."

"Then why won't you give me a little kiss? I need comfort just like the Mystere needs comfort. You know what comfort is?"

"Yes." She pauses. "OK. I'll give you one kiss, if you promise not to bother me again. You have to promise not to bother me again. Just one kiss."

"I promise." With a huge smile on his face, he closes his eyes, purses his lips. All the other boys gather round, nudge each other, giggle, try to touch her. She bends down and kisses his forehead. He opens his eyes. "That isn't fair. That wasn't anything."

"I kissed you."

"That was for a baby. You have to kiss me like you kiss the Mystere." Alex giggles.

"He's right," Fritz tells her.

"OK. But this is the only time. I'm not going to kiss you again."

He lifts his arm and puts it around her shoulder. He places his thick soft lips on her mouth and gently inserts his tongue in her mouth. His arms press her into him. He moves his tongue slowly in her mouth. After a few minutes he lets her go.

"OK?" she asks, dazed.

"When are you going to give me eat?"

"Tony. You promised that was all. You're not supposed to bother me again."

"You don't have to kiss me again. Now you have to eat with me." All the other boys are giggling.

"Tony, I'm really getting angry. You're going too far."

"What do you mean I'm going too far? You're always making these rules. I don't make them. You won't even give me a chance."

"I understand what you're saying. I just can't. It's me. It's my fault. In my mind you're too young for me."

"You're crazy."

"That's true," Fritz agrees. "You know what the women over there say to you when you walk by them to go swimming?"

"I know."

" 'La folle Americaine.' Do you understand what that means?"

"I know I'm crazy. Everybody's a little crazy."

"I'm not crazy. Tony isn't crazy. You're the one who's crazy."

"Wait a minute. Just cause I do what I want and what I want

sometimes doesn't coincide with what women normally do in this town doesn't mean I'm crazy. I'm not insane."

"You do things you shouldn't do. You go bathing where no other white people go bathing, where only the poor black people go, and you make love with too many men."

"I don't make love with too many men. The only man I go with is Roger. I talk to a lot of men, sure, like I talk to you, I talk to you all the time but I don't go with you. You mean I'm not supposed to talk to you?"

"It's OK for you to talk to us little guys. But you shouldn't talk to anyone else except Roger. Otherwise people'll think you're crazy."

"I can't do that. If the people here think I'm crazy, I can't do anything about that."

"Do you know how to fight kung-fu?"

"No."

"You don't. We fight kung-fu all the time. Look, we'll show you." The khaki-shirted boy and another boy stand five feet apart, bodies turned sideways, forward legs face front, arms extend and bend, hands straight and stiff, forward hands point at each other. The khaki-shirted boy says "Kung-fu." They move toward each other as if they're kangaroos on downers. They're about two feet apart they kick at each other. "Don't they do this in America?"

"Sure they do. Everyone sees the kung-fu movies. Especially Bruce Lee."

"He's dead now. I'm going to be Bruce Lee when I get older."

"I guess he is dead. How do you know about kung-fu here?"

"We know everything. The movie house down the street, you know where it is, shows one kung-fu movie and one romance movie every week. You want to go see it?"

"Not right now."

"I can't see the movie cause I don't have any money."

"I see why you wanted me to see the movie. How much do you want?"

"I want to see it too. I want to see it too. I want to see it too."
Three other boys crowd around the white girl.

"I'm going to fight kung-fu," Alex says. "Look at me." He and
Tony take kung-fu positions. Alex lurches and when he tries to
kick his good leg in the air, falls flat on his face on his crippled
toothpick leg. "Alex, are you OK?" the white girl asks. The other
boys giggle. Alex gets up and waves his hands.

"How much do you want?"

"Fifty cents."

"OK. If you really want to go, I'll give whoever wants to fifty
cents."

"I want a coke," the red-head says.

"OK. I'll give each of you fifty cents and you can do what you
want with the money."

"You owe me a coke," Fritz reminds her. "Yesterday you said
you were going to buy me a coke and you never did."

"I'll give you a dollar."

"That's not fair. Why should he get a coke and get to go to
the movies? We all want to do that."

"Shut up. I should never have said anything in the first place.
I'll give you all fifty cents and that's that." She doles out the
money.

"You owe me two dollars when I got that cab for you that day.
The one you took to visit Mr. Mystere," the smallest of the lot
says.

"Are you bringing that up again you scoundrel? You know
damn well I paid you. Listen you kids, I do not have endless
money. Compared to you I'm rich, but back home in the States
I am poor."

"When are you going back to your home?" Fritz asks. "I think
you're going back very soon. I think your mother and father are
waiting for you."

"I don't have a mother and father. I have a brother who's
waiting for me. He's terrific: you'd like him. I'm trying to get
him to come down here. If he does, I'll stay here a lot longer."

"If your brother comes down here, he's going to be very angry with you."

"Why?"

"He'll see you doing your something with Mr. Mystere and he'll make you stop seeing Mr. Mystere."

"No he won't. My brother doesn't care what I do."

"I don't believe you. If you were my sister, I'd keep my eye on you all the time."

"My brother's terrific."

"I think you're going to leave us soon. I don't think you're ever coming back," Alex cries.

"Oh Alex. That's not true. I'm not going to leave soon and if I do, it'll only be for a few months. I love it here. I'm happier than I've ever been anywhere else. All I want is to sit and do nothing. I have to leave cause I have to get some money so I can come back here. I'm not rich."

"I think you're going to leave and you're going to forget all about us."

"I'll never forget about you. I couldn't. I'll send you stuff from the States and I'll be back here soon as I can. I don't like it there; I like it here."

"I want the address of your mother and father so I can write them," Fritz says.

"I'll give you my brother's address. He's much nicer. My parents are creeps." She gives him her brother's address. The white ball grows small enough that some blue appears and long thin clouds moving rapidly past the blue and the burning white. There are no more fishing boats on the ocean. Girls in blouses and tight skirts walk together, giggling, on the boulevard. Tall young studs race by on motor scooters. A gray car whirs past and honks.

"That's Mr. Mystere."

"Where's Mr. Mystere, where's Roger?" she screams.

"His car just drove by."

"That wasn't his car," Fritz tells the girl.

"Was that Roger? Please, tell me. Please."

"That wasn't Roger," Fritz says. "They're just teasing you. Don't you worry about nothing."

"I don't think there should be any white people here," the smallest boy says. "This place is going to be like Jamaica. In Jamaica the black people tell all the white people they have to get out."

"I agree with what you're saying, but, it makes me feel funny, that you don't like me, well, cause I'm white."

"We have to be by ourselves. We have to do everything by ourselves," Tony says.

"I understand what you're saying."

"Can you do the Kingston walk?"

"The Kingston walk?"

Fritz sticks out his pelvis, lifts his legs high in the air, doesn't move his hips, shuffles.

"I've got to go to the hospital," Tony says.

"Tony, what's the matter with you?"

"You know why I've got to go to the hospital."

"I don't know why you have to go the hospital. Are you sick?"

"You know why he has to go the hospital," Fritz says.

"People stop me and I tell them 'Don't talk to me you can't talk to me anymore I'm dying.' I'm going to take myself to the hospital they'll say 'Tony, you're never going to recover. We can't do anything more for you.' I'll tell them this evil woman caused my death she's going I'm going to die now."

"Oh Tony, you're not going to die." They all do the Kingston walk. "Oo be doo oo be da na-na na-na, na-na na-na, oo be do oo be oo be be da."

"Les poissons, ils nagent dans la mer, Les poissons, ils sont tres cher," Fritz sings.

> "I wanna go home,
> Where-ere I belong,
> Cau-ause now I'm just a
> Lonely teenager, lonely tee-eenager.
> Seventeen, I ran away,"

"Chk a buka buka dchuk shlik ya hung, hung,"

"What's that, Alex?"

"That's Chinese."

"Oh. I didn't know you could speak Chinese."

"I'll teach you how. Hung guk, good good, hu hu long ha."

"Foe wah, li con good good lung chk hak."

"La spaghettina esta bono."

"Hey, that's a good one." The ocean leaps up into spray and covers them.

"Guk li pong ya, ma tay fong tu li pik so shlik punk li poe nah nah foe tay hong."

"Do you know Gene Kelly? When you go back to New York, you have to see him. He can give you comfort."

"Everyone in New York goes to see him. They bring him their problems and he takes their problems away. You know, a doctor? He's a doctor. When you go to see him, you have to bring him your problems."

"I don't have any problems."

"You have lots of problems in your head. I see them. Gene Kelly can make you better. He cures many, many people."

"How can I find him?"

"Everyone in New York knows where he lives. He's as famous as Bruce Lee."

"I think I've heard of him."

"Gene Kelly's a good man. You have to see him when you get back to New York, and then you be OK."

"I'm making big trouble for you," says the red-head. "I make big trouble for you and you don't get out of it so easily."

"What'd he do?" she asks Fritz.

"Nothing. Nothing." He waves his hands at the red-head boy to go away.

"I talk to Mrs. Betty today and tell her what's going on. She says she's going to make trouble for you and Roger."

"What'd you do? What'd you say about me and Roger?" Her eyes blaze.

"Go away. Get out of here." Fritz raises his fists at the red-head then turns around to the girl. "Don't you listen to that little fellow. He wants to make trouble. He's telling lies."

"Fritz, this is my affair. I have to find out what he said to Betty." Her blazing eyes turn to the red-head. "What did you say to Betty?"

"I didn't say anything. I don't cause any trouble. Mrs. Betty's my friend. I just tell her what's going on."

"What's going on?"

"You know what goes on. I see you and Mr. Mystere kissing on the roof. I see Mr. Mystere go into your room night after night."

"I see that too," Fritz says.

"Mrs. Betty doesn't like this. I think she's going to make a lot of trouble for you."

"Betty can't make a lot of trouble for me. There's nothing she can do. Look. The only person you're hurting by sticking your nose into this business which you know nothing about is Betty. You don't have any idea what's going on and you don't know what you're doing. You're just causing a lot of unnecessary trouble."

"I cause trouble to you," he mocks.

"No. You're stupid. Betty and Roger have a lot of problems which have nothing to do with me. Their marriage has been on the rocks for awhile and I'm not going to save it or break it. I don't matter. Betty knows all about me and telling her is only going to hurt her feelings more. It doesn't hurt me. So just keep out of this."

"Mrs. Betty doesn't like it when her husband makes eyes at other women. She's going to get Mr. Mystere's father to hurt you."

"What're you talking about?"

"I think the police are coming after you."

"The police? You don't know what you're talking about." She's trembling.

"Don't you listen to that little fellow. Come away from here." Fritz pulls her left arm.

"I'm going to cause a lot of trouble for you," the white girl says. "I'm an American so I can do it. You'd better watch your fuckin' step." The red-head throws a rock at her head. She ducks. "You try that one more time and you're going to be in more trouble than you've ever been in your life." He throws another rock at her head. She starts crying. "I think the cops are coming after you. Whore. Miss Whore."

"I'm going to kill him." She can't talk directly to the red-head. Her fists are clenched.

"Are you going to kill him?" Fritz asks. "Are you going to fight kung-fu?"

"How much money do you take from men? I tell you what everyone says." None of the other boys say anything.

She turns around and starts to run. Only she can't figure out where to go.

"Gerard. Can I talk to you for a minute?"

He shrugs through his blue-green jeep window.

"Are you sure you've got five minutes?"

"I've got five minutes and only five minutes. Open the door and climb in. It's more private in here."

Through the dirty jeep window the beggar boys sit in the dust and watch, Ally comes out of the pension, gooses a maid, drives away on his red Honda, the white dust covers everything, Fritz and Tony fight kung-fu. "It's about Roger. I don't want to bother you or anything, I just have to know I don't want to dump my private life on you."

"Spill it. We're all friends here."

"It's about Roger." She takes a deep breath.

"Want a Marlboro?"

"Sure."

"Here's a light."

"That night I met you and Roger at L'Ouverture, Roger and I spent the night together."

"That's great. Roger's a wonderful person."

"I think so too. Uh . . ."

"Roger wanted me to drive him back to Le Roi. At six o'clock he came pounding on my door . . ."

"I know. He was pissed off you didn't drive him back. He says you're not his friend."

"Roger's a nice guy, but he's full of crap. I have to work on that mountain five days a week. I only come down here for the weekends. The morning he knocked on my door was the only morning I had to sleep till eight o'clock instead of getting up at five o'clock. I wasn't about to get up for no one. Roger has plenty of friends who can drive him back to Le Roi."

"I want to know about his and Betty's relationship," she blurts out. "I'm all mixed up. Roger says he and Betty aren't at all close, he can do whatever he wants, but he never spends a whole night with me and Betty talks as if she and Roger are the same person."

"Roger doesn't care about her at all. He wants to get rid of her and live alone so he can do exactly what he wants to do all the time."

"I know that. But the day after I met you and Roger, I went to Le Roi to visit Betty and Roger, Roger told me to come. Betty kept saying "we," she never said "I," she talked about her and Roger as if they're inseparable. Then she told me Roger's family is crazy. I liked Betty. I thought we were friends. But today I get up and go out on the terrace for breakfast, the first thing I see is Betty and I feel these totally weird vibes. She's talking to papa and I just know she's talking about me. Something tells me not to say hello to her. She wants to make trouble. I just ran. I couldn't handle the situation. And two days ago I had a date with Roger. He didn't show up. He's never done that before. He didn't call or nothing. I haven't seen him in two days. I don't think I'm going to see him again."

"Calm down and take it easy. The main thing is to enjoy your vacation. Roger likes to have his fun. He's probably been at Le Roi, working very hard. He'll be back."

"Does Roger have a lot of girlfriends? I just want to know."

"Roger has never had women problems. Don't worry about

Roger. Take a little sun, make love when you want to make love, go out drinking, see Roger, the main thing is when you get back to New York you'll remember you had a nice vacation."

"Roger tells me he loves me. I don't know whether to believe him or not."

"He does?"

"That's what he said to me."

"Roger has lots of girlfriends."

"He does?"

"Why don't you forget it."

"You've told me what I wanted to know. Thank you," she starts to climb out of the jeep.

"Wait a minute. If you want to stay down here, I can offer you a job."

"A job! In Haiti! What kind of job?"

"What can you do?"

"I can't do anything. I can write, but that's nothing. I used to be a professional dancer."

"You can write for me."

"Write for you? No one in Haiti does any reading."

"I want to start a magazine here. I haven't thought this through clearly yet. But I have a conscience, I see what goes on, and I have to do something."

"You could give me the information and I could write it up under a fake name. No one could know you're the source."

"I don't know. It's very dangerous here. I want to do something, but I don't know what I can do. The main thing that's needed in this country are Creole schools. All the people except for the government elite speak Creole, but the government won't recognize the language, they say it isn't a real language. They make all the schools use French and all the newspapers use French, so most of the people never learn to read. My people speak Creole; they're African, not American or European."

"If you could get me a job, Gerard, I'd stay here. I'm only going back cause I need money."

"We'll talk about this some more."

Kathy and Fritz sit huddled, hidden by the shadows, at Pension L'Ouverture.

"There are lots of evil people in this world."

"No there aren't. There aren't evil people. People do what they have to cause they're stuck, and poor and miserable and they've been hurt so much. The main thing is you have to realize why people act the way they do."

"There are evil people. They made you cry this afternoon and I couldn't do anything about it." He starts to cry.

"I was crying. That little red-head wouldn't leave me alone. Why does he hate me so much? That wasn't so bad, what really hurt me was that all of you didn't stick up for me and you're my friends. Don't you know what friends are for? How the hell could you believe I'm a prostitute? That little boy kept saying things and you just agreed with him."

"I kept out of it cause I couldn't do nothin' against all those big boys. I walked away. You saw me." They sit in the shadows of the steps, the corners, huge white blossoms in the air hanging over the front porch their odor everywhere mosquitoes slight breezes, the white girl covering him cause if the pension owners and servants see the beggar boy, they'll kick him out. He starts to cry again.

"I don't know what to do. Knowing why people hurt me doesn't help."

"Those little boys wanted to hurt you. They wanted to hurt you. I'm going to beat them and kill them."

"No you don't. That wouldn't do anything. Fritz, Fritz, don't cry. There's nothing to cry about. I love you." She puts her arms around him.

"You don't understand what happened. You're in a lot of trouble."

"What do you mean?"

"I don't mean nothing. There's nothing I can do."

"Fritz. You've got to tell me what kind of trouble."

His fist digs into his eye and wipes away the tears. He lights a cigarette. Raoul the head-servant walks by and she tells him it's OK Fritz is here. "That little boy, Tommy, says you're a prostitute."

"I'll tell you what happened between me and Tommy. One night one of the first nights I was here I heard a knocking at my window. I was asleep I didn't know what was happening I thought it was Roger cause that's where Roger knocks so I said, 'Who's there?' 'It's Alfred.' It sounded like Alfred: I don't know I was asleep. I don't know any Alfred. I said, 'I don't know you. Go away.' The doorknob started turning. The doorknob to the back door that's always locked. It wouldn't stop turning. I get really scared. I freaked. I thought someone was going to rape me. In New York City women get raped all the time and they don't like being raped. I ran to the front door, threw the door open, and there was that little kid. Tommy."

"Tommy told me about that. He said he knocked on your door cause he wanted to be with you and you slammed the door in his face. You hurt his feelings badly."

"I didn't know who he was. It was the middle of the night."

"You know what that little red-head told Mrs. Betty?"

"What?"

"You can't tell this to anyone. I don't want to get into trouble."

"What'd he tell her?"

"Today he told Mrs. Betty that you and Mr. Mystere are doing your something."

"I know that."

"He told Mrs. Betty you're trying to break apart her and Mr. Mystere cause you want Mr. Mystere for yourself cause you want his money. Mrs. Betty said she's going to get Mr. Mystere's father to make Mr. Mystere stop seeing you."

"Roger'll do whatever his father tells him to do. Well, that's that. Jesus Christ, why don't you kids get your nose out of other people's business? This didn't concern you. It didn't matter to you in any way whatsoever. But you had to butt in on something you didn't understand and now you've hurt a lot of people, for no reason at all. Just for no reason at all."

"I tried to stop that little boy, but there was nothing I could do. I told you he was going to cause trouble."

"Well, now he's caused trouble. I hope you're satisfied."

"I didn't know what to do."

"Don't cry, Fritz. Please Fritz, don't cry anymore. Everything's OK. Nobody's been really hurt. Fritz, I love you, please don't cry."

"I didn't know what to do when you started to cry this afternoon. You made me cry."

"Well it's all over now. That little red-head boy is my problem, not yours."

"Those little boys are making you bad. I don't know what to do about it."

"I don't know what to do when people hurt me. The best thing is to forget about it."

"That's no good." Crickets made a lot of noise and an occasional wave splashed against the wall.

ROGER: "Hello."

    Kathy: "Uh."

    "How are you doing?"

"Uh."

"I've been wanting to see you a lot, but I haven't been able to."

"Why not?"

"We can't talk here. Let's go into that little garden in back of your room."

"I don't want to."

"I want to talk to you."

"OK. What do you want?"

"You know why I haven't been here? My parents forbid me to come here."

"Why'd they do that?"

"I told you there's been a lot of drugs here. The last day I saw you, the Chief of Police told my mother there's going to be a bust here."

"In the pension?"

"The police say there's an American who's staying at the pension who's distributing a lot of drugs."

"But I'm the only American who's been staying here for any length of time, except for those damn missionaries, and I'm not dealing drugs. I don't even use drugs. Not that that matters. Do they think I'm the dealer?"

"The Police Chief told my mother they have a complete list

133

of everyone who's been dealing and everyone in the town who takes drugs. They know everything. My name's on it."

"What do you think I should do, Roger? Is my name on the list?"

"I don't know."

"You know when those tontons macoute came after me, maybe that's why they were after me. There are drugs coming out of L'Ouverture, but they're not coming from me. Ally directs all the drug traffic. He's getting strung out these days on pills: a few days ago when I said I was going down to Port-au-Prince for a few days, he went down on his hands and knees begging me to bring him back some grass. Imagine being desperate for grass. Then when I mentioned my brother might come to Haiti, he asked me to ask my brother to bring him some reds. My brother should risk getting caught at the border just for Ally. Ally must be out of his mind."

"Ally's gone crazy from too many pills. I've seen it happening for a long time. He goes crazy when he can't get drugs and he wants to kill the women who won't sleep with him. The police know all about him. We shouldn't talk about this so loud."

"When did your mother tell you the bust is going to happen?"

"The policeman didn't tell her. But she made me promise I'd stay away from here cause I'm in a precarious position. If the police could find any member of my family with even a joint on us, they'd be able to arrest all of us and take away all our money. Have you noticed I've been dressing like a businessman instead of a worker lately and eating at the expensive hotels? My parents told me I have to start acting like who I am because of my position."

"Do you think they're after you?"

"The cops wouldn't dare touch any of us. But just in case my parents want me to go down to Port-au-Prince for a few days until the heat cools down."

"Do you think I ought to leave too?"

"Maybe you ought to get out of Cap Haitian for a while. You could go back to your country."

"Why'd you say that?"

"I'm worried about you. You have to be very careful in this country."

"Maybe I should get out of here for a while. I could use a change of air. Once things die down, I'll come back here."

"I'm going to get out of here myself. When this is all over, we can see each other again."

"How are you going to get down to Port-au-Prince? Are you going with your family?"

"I'm going in a car with my sister, my parents, and Betty."

"I thought you weren't going to take Betty with you to Port-au-Prince. At least that's what you said a week ago."

"Betty doesn't want to come with me, but I'm taking her. I don't want her staying alone in the house while I'm gone."

"Oh."

"Have you missed me a lot?"

"I don't know."

"You must be going with a lot of other men and have forgotten me."

"I haven't been fucking anyone else."

"I thought about you all the time. I came to see you the first moment I could."

"You did."

"I kept seeing you making love with Duval. I know he wants you. If you're not going with him, you're going with some other man. I think I must care about you a lot."

"You do? Oh Roger, I've missed you so much. I thought you didn't want to see me again. Two days ago I saw Gerard I asked him what was going on with you cause I didn't understand why you didn't show up for that date you didn't call me nothing. I think I really bugged Gerard."

"What'd Gerard say to you?"

"Oh. Well . . . I asked him about your and Betty's relationship cause I didn't understand what it was."

"I told you. Betty doesn't mean anything to me."

"That's what Gerard said."

"Did he say anything else about me?"

"He didn't really say anything . . . He said you were probably working hard at the factory and too tired to come to town. You'd see me in a day or two. That's all he really said."

"Well here I am."

"I know. I'm glad you're here."

"I'm going to take a walk now."

"What d'you mean: going to take a walk now? You're gonna leave?"

"I'm going to take a walk now. I'll see you later."

"Roger. Wait a second. Don't you . . .?"

They kiss.

"I'll see you later."

"You can't see me later. I won't be here. You go to hell."

"I hate your guts. You think you can do whatever you want to and just walk off . . ."

They kiss for a long time.

"Goodbye."

"Roger, wait a second. Just talk to me for a second."

"What do you want to talk about?"

"I don't want to talk about anything. Goodbye."

"I'll see you later when I finish my walk."

She pulls him to the ground. "Fuck me. Fuck me right now Roger." They make out for awhile.

"Let's go in your room."

"Stick your cock in me as hard as you can and fuck me here. I don't care who sees us. I want you."

"You've gotten me all wet."

"I'm wetter. Please fuck me. Here."

They stand up. "What d'you do that for? My new pants are torn. There's mud all over me. You're crazy."

"I was right in the mud. That was terrific. Why didn't you fuck me?"

"I'm not going to have anything to do with you anymore."

"Are you really angry? It's only mud and water. Roger, I love you."

"You tore my pants. Why'd you jump on me?"

"You were walking away from me and I didn't want you to. I haven't seen you for days and suddenly you show up and then you say you're going to take a walk."

"I told you why I haven't been able to come here. I have to talk to you further. Let's go to your room."

"Are you still angry with me?"

"Pull this chair to here and sit down on it."

"Like this? I don't like it. I like sitting here by your knees. I always liked sitting on floors when I was a kid I used to sit on the floor in front of my mother's bed all the time and watch TV."

"If you're sitting on the floor, I have to sit on the floor."

"Roger."

They make out.

"Do you like this?"

"I'm so hot for you. The minute you touch me, I start to come."

"Let's go to the bed." They go to the bed. "I've got to go now. I have to see another girl."

"You have to see another girl?"

"I made a date with another girl. I'll come back later."

"OK. Get out of here."

"You don't like that, do you?"

"I said: GET OUT OF HERE."

"I'll make love to you once and then I'll leave."

"You're not touching me."

"I thought you said you liked making love with me. I have to hurry cause I have to meet this girl."

"Jesus Christ. You're out of your mind. What're you trying to do? Do you think I'm some ragdoll or something you can throw around?"

"You don't like it when I go out with other women, do you?"

"I don't give a shit."

"I've never seen you this upset. You're very jealous."

"It's not that you go out with other women. Look. The men in New York treat me like I'm something special. They buy me presents, they take me out for meals, they treat me very gently. I'm a special kind of woman. I have to be treated well. No man's ever treated me like you're treating me."

"I'm not acting badly."

"You make a date with me and don't show up for days, when you show up five minutes later you say you have to take a walk. Now you tell me you've made a date with another girl while you're supposed to be seeing me. If you don't give a shit about me, why are you coming around and seeing me? I didn't call you up. I didn't tell you to come here."

"You have to act the way I want you to act. I'm much nicer to you than I am to most women."

"Most of the women you go with are dumb fluffy cunts who don't know what the hell they're doing. That's why you can treat them that way. I know a lot about how to treat men I'm good at sex and I want respect for my knowledge. I'm a woman."

"That's why I go for older women. I like them my mother's age."

"But I'm special. There's something special about me as far as sex goes. There's always been. You have to treat me that way or else get out."

"I've told you I love you more than any other woman."

"Then why do you treat me so badly? Have I hurt you in some way? If I have, I did it by accident I didn't mean to. I'm very egotistic."

"I already told you what it is."

"You did?"

"You're going back to New York and I won't see you again. That's why out in the garden I told you I was going to take a walk and that's why I made plans to meet another girl."

"But you're going to Port-au-Prince tomorrow. And you're taking Betty with you; you told me a week ago you weren't going to be taking her."

"Betty doesn't want to go with me, but I told her she has to cause of what my mother told me."

"Oh. Look Roger, it doesn't matter about Betty, I can't stick around here waiting for you to come back and never knowing when you'll come back. How long are you going to stay in Port-au-Prince?"

"Only a week."

"That's that. If I stay here more than a week, I'll have to give the airline another hundred dollars and it's ridiculous to blow a hundred dollars just so I can sit around waiting for your return and I'm not even sure you're going to return. You know you have to go back and forth just as your father wants you to. Do you think I should wait for you?"

"No. You're going to go away."

"Well, what the hell can I do? We're going to see each other again."

"I'm a realist. I know that most affairs, no matter how good they are, go away like the wind. Maybe ours will remain, and maybe it'll go away like it never happened."

"If we want to, it'll remain. If we work at it."

"This is our last night together. You know what I'm going to do? I'm going to stay here all night with you until my brother returns to pick me up. We're going to spend the whole night together making love."

"Roger . . . ?"

"What?"

"Roger? Would you do something for me? It's not really anything . . ."

"Tell me what you want."

"Would, would you give me something before you go away. I don't care what it is, just something I can wear. It doesn't have to be expensive or anything. It can be a beer ring. I just want something so I can hold you while I'm away from you."

"I don't have anything. You can have this necklace I'm wearing."

"Oh no. It's much too expensive. I just want something little."

"You know what I want. I want to suck your cunt again. Do you like that?"

"You know I love it. I like it the best. Oh touch me. Not that hard. Yes. Oh, just like that."

"That girl who used to be my mistress: once I sucked her cunt for hours and I came in my pants twice. I never took my pants off."

"I wish you'd suck me for that long. Oh don't move your finger. There. Just like that."

"Take me in your mouth while I suck your cunt."

"No. I'll get confused. I'll just suck you if you want, but I don't like doing both things at once."

Suck.

"That feels good."

Suck.

"Don't stop. Just give me another few minutes."

Suck.

"Please. Don't stop. I'm just about to . . ."

Suck.

"Don't stop. Not now. Oh no . . ."

"I'm going to leave now so I can see that girl."

"Roger, you bastard. You can't leave me like this."

"I told you. I have to meet someone else."

"I can't believe this is happening. You lousy stinkin' bastard. You stink like nobody's ever stinked in their whole life. You're a bunch of crap you don't have anything in your head your asshole's full of shit. You lousy little prick."

"I never made a date with no girl. I just wanted to see how you acted."

"You mean this has all been a lie? I hate you. Get the fuck out of here."

"You really want me to get out of here?"

"Get out of here."

"Are you sure you want me to leave?"

"Jesus Christ that feels good. Oh. Ooh oh. Oooh."

"Ah."

"Oh yes. Not like that. Faster. Please do it hard. Make me come. Ah. Ahh. Ahh."

"Ah."

"Ooh. Ooh. Ah. Ah. I can't do it."

"What's going on?"

"I'm too tight. I'm scared of you. I get this way when I've been hurt too much."

"You're trembling."

"Hold me."

They kiss lightly.

"Hold me like you care about me. I freak out sometimes and I have to be treated gently."

"Kathy, are you OK?"

"Just hold me a few more minutes. I'm OK now."

"Do you want me to leave you for a few minutes?"

"No. I'm OK now. We can start fucking again."

"I act the way I do cause you're going away and I don't want you to. I love you more than I've ever loved any other woman."

"Roger, please fuck me. Fuck me as hard as you can. Just fuck me. Ah. Ah. Ah."

"Ooh."

"Harder."

"Ah."

"Ah. Ah. Ah. Ah."

"Ah."

"Ah. Ah."

"I'm going to come now."

"You came, didn't you?"

"Didn't you?"

"Touch me a little with your fingers. Ow. That's too hard. I'm really upset. I can't come. I don't know what to do."

"Do my fingers feel good?"

"That feels good. That feels terrific. Don't go any harder . . . Oh . . . Oh . . . I love this. Roger Roger. Please Roger. Roger please please say Roger oh Roger. Ooh ooh ahaah ooh ooooh. Oooh. Oh. Thank you."

"Look at me."

"Mm. You're always hard."

"I love fucking you. When you go away, every day I'm going to remember how you smile when I fuck you."

"That's cause I love this so much. I'm going to come again. Oh."

"When you come, your eyes roll to the top of your head and you scream."

"I do?"

"Don't you hear yourself?"

"Another boyfriend used to tell me I screamed. Every time I was about to come, he'd put his hand over my mouth. Ooh. I'm going to come again. Come with me this time. I feel good now."

"You know why I couldn't see you these last few days?"

"I don't care."

"I was scared of getting busted."

"You told me."

"You don't understand. I'm bad."

"I like bad men. I'm not a nice person."

"I'll tell you something, but you have to promise you won't tell anyone." "I promise. What're you going to tell me?"

"I deal drugs."

"So that's why you were so worried when your mother told you L'Ouverture might be busted. You better get down to Port-au-Prince and stay there for a while. I hear in this country if you're busted for even a joint, it's a really bad scene."

"That's why I have to take Betty with me."

"Dealing a little grass isn't such a big thing. It's just that everyone in this country's crazy."

"I grow all the grass that gets sold in Cap Haitian out in the factory. No one can see me there. I also deal pills."

"I see. You'd better be really careful."

"You could be a government spy and I could be throwing my family's lives away by _telling you this_."

"Jesus Christ Roger do you really think I'm a government spy? You've been fucking me for weeks now."

"I don't know anything."

"Get the fuck out of here. I'm getting sick of all this suspicion and accusations. It isn't worth it. How the hell can I be a government spy when I sit around with the beggar boys and have the opinions I have? I told you to get out of here."

"Anyone can be a spy. There's no way to tell who the spies are."

"Well, I'm not a spy. If you think I am, that's your problem."

"If I thought you were a spy, I wouldn't be telling you all this."

"That's true. How come you've never been caught dealing?"

"I was caught twice in the United States. I told you about the time I went to school in Florida, with the blonde schoolteacher, I got thrown out of school for dealing."

"Oh yeah, I remember. You were in high school."

"I also got thrown out of another school in Arizona for carrying coke. I tell you, I'm a tough guy."

"I don't know if dealing drugs makes you tough. Aren't you scared of getting busted here?"

"My mother's good friends with one of the cops. He tells her when a bust's coming and then I go down to Port-au-Prince for a while. Also I'm very careful. Nobody here knows exactly what I do."

"You're telling me about it."

"You're the only person I tell and you're going back to America soon. You see I'm very very careful. Remember I told you the first time I met you it's dangerous to talk about drugs?"

"If you get caught, you're going to be in a lot of trouble."

"I'm never going to get caught."

"They all say that."

"No they don't. I'm the one who can do it."

"What else do you do besides deal drugs?"

"If I really tell you about me, you'll never speak to me again. You'd hate me."

"Don't you ever talk to people? That's a stupid question. Haven't you ever been friends with a woman so you could tell her what you're really like?"

"Nobody knows what I really do and who I am. You should stay away from me cause I'm bad."

"Well, I'm not going to stay away from you. I don't care how bad you are."

"Why not?"

"When people act bastardly toward me, it just doesn't bother me. The only two things that bother me are when people lie to me and when I get bored. I can't stand being bored. As soon as I get bored, I split."

"You won't leave me if you know all the things I do?"

"It'd probably make me love you more. I always go for the ones who burn me."

"You asked Gerard before if I go with other women and he told you yes?"

"I only asked him because I was confused about your relationship with Betty. I don't want to pry into your personal life."

"What Gerard told you is true. I go with many other women. I've always had lots of women. Does that bother you?"

"Why should it?"

"Before I married Betty, I used to go with five, six women at a time. Often Ally, Duval and I would trade off our women. I'd go with a woman, then when I was finished, Ally would take her, and he'd hand her over to Duval, or else all three of us would go out together and we'd share the girls we were with that night. Of course these girls weren't worth anything."

"Do you think I'm like those girls?"

"If I thought you were like those girls, I would have slept with you once and then let Ally have you. I only sleep with women once cause after once they start wanting things. Remember how upset I got when you told me that something happened between you and Duval?"

"Nothing happened between me and Duval. You misunderstood what"

"I got upset because you're going with me and Duval should have kept his hands off you. He knows that too because he won't speak to me anymore."

"Didn't all the girls you, Ally and Duval fucked mind you were doing that?"

"Most Haitian girls, all they want to do is make love. They're whores. They especially want to make love with Ally, Duval and me cause they know we have money and they think we'll give them things. When I was ten years old, we used to go down to the beach and lie in a circle. One girl would stand in the middle of the circle and take off her clothes. You know, she'd do a striptease. Then she'd go around the circle and give it to every guy who wanted her. We'd all lie in a circle and watch each other doing it while we did it. The other girls, the ones who come from wealthy families, no one sees. Their parents keep them under lock and key until they're fifteen or sixteen, and then they can only go out, under chaperone, with the boys their parents chose for them. They're being groomed for wealthy husbands because marriage can mean a lot of money to these people and their parents want to keep the money in the family."

"Historically that's how marriage has always been."

"I could never date one of those girls. You know the two girls who hang around here? They're Henry's nieces. You never see any men around them."

"They're really beautiful too. I wonder what'll happen to them?"

"One of them's studying to be a doctor. They'll get married to rich men."

"Have you ever loved a woman?"

"I don't give women presents. I had a mistress once before I married Betty. I gave her lots of money because she had to do everything I told her to."

"What sort of things did you make her do? Sexually."

"I gave her all sorts of money and then later, after we had broken up, I found out she had been seeing other men while she was seeing me."

"You didn't know at the time she was fucking other men?"

"She told me I was the only one she was with. Then she took all my money. The worst thing was: I found out after we broke up she was pregnant and going to have an abortion."

"So what?"

"It was my kid and she was going to have an abortion without asking me. She really hurt me."

"I hope you never get burned worse."

"I've been hurt by lots of women when I was younger. But now, no more. I don't let women get to me anymore; I'm very careful. All the women around here want to fuck me, oh brother, cause of who I am, so I fuck them once or twice and that's it. I make it clear each time I'm with a woman. I'm not going to do anything for her."

"There's nothing wrong with that. It's the lies that really hurt people."

"You're right. I don't act like Duval or Ally. This movie star came down here last year and Ally took her out."

"A movie star? Was she old or something?"

"No. She was young and pretty, if you like that sort of woman. I only like older women. She really went for Ally. Oh brother. He made her buy the drinks and pay for all the food. He brought me along whenever they went out. He told her I didn't have any money. One night he made her rent two cars so he could have one and I could have one."

"But Ally has a car."

"He wanted to ride around in a limousine. And he made her pay for all the champagne. I got really sick and puked."

"And she did all this?"

"He wanted her to buy him a car and she walked out on him. I think she was really upset."

"I guess she was."

"I told you not to get mixed up with Ally cause he's crazy. He just wants to hurt the women he's with. I don't do that. Since I've been with Betty, I go mainly with the women I find in the hotels and bars. All these women buy presents for me, oh brother you wouldn't believe the expensive things they give me bracelets and"

"I believe it."

"They want to do all these things for me and they want me to write them when they leave. I never send them letters. Once or twice I'll make a call. You know what I was really doing when I'd pick you up here, and we'd go from hotel to hotel?"

"I thought we were getting drunk and fucking."

"I was checking out the other hotels and bars to see if any new women had come into town. That's what Ally, Gerard, and I do here almost every night."

"I saw you looking around, but I never saw you pick up any women. You must be really clever."

"Remember when I met you that first night in L'Ouverture? I was checking out the hotel to see if there were any new women around."

"You didn't seem to be checking me out, I could tell Ally was cruising me cause he asked me if I wanted a present, but you were a cold fish. You wouldn't even say hello to me when Gerard introduced us. I thought you were a creep. That's why I was attracted to you: every other guy I had met was drooling after me and you wouldn't notice me."

"That's the way I am: I never go after the woman, I let her come to me. I didn't like you when I first met you. You know when I first started noticing you? When we were at The Imperial and Gerard was telling us that story"

"About your getting married. Gerard kept talking and talking and I kept looking at you. I wanted you before: when we were in the truck and you told me not to look at you. Remember?"

"I wanted you then too."

"The first thing I noticed was your Donald Duck T-shirt. I liked you cause I thought you were a hippy. I never would have gone with you if I had known you were a businessman."

"You don't act like you dislike me."

"Did you have a lot of girlfriends after you married Betty?"

"I don't have girlfriends. The women I sleep with don't mean anything to me. I'll tell you what I'm really like. I go with five, six girls at a time."

"How the hell do you do that? You are married and, since I've been here, you've been spending at least every other night with me."

"Every day I'm with four or five different women. I spend my lunch break with one woman: maybe I take her to the beach. Then I bring her home in the afternoon. I make a dinner date with another woman and I take her around to the hotels so I can check out what other women are around. Meanwhile I've made a date to meet another woman around ten o'clock in a bar. I go to the bar and spend an hour there. Like tonight I had made a date to meet a girlfriend of mine at Le Poisson."

"Then you were speaking the truth earlier: you really were going to meet some girl at a bar. I thought you were saying it just to make me upset."

"I have dates with women all the time. Sometimes I bring one girl with me to meet another."

"Don't your girlfriends get upset?"

"I've had girls walk out on me. One girl three nights ago slapped my face and said she wanted to murder me."

"Did anything happen?"

"There's nothing she can do to me. I like to see women upset. Sometimes I like to really fuck over women and see them cry a lot. I pull every trick I can think of."

"You don't like women, do you?"

"I love to make love to women. If I could, I would make love to women every minute of the day. When I can't fuck anymore, I suck pussy and that makes me hard again. I can suck pussy for hours and I still want more. I love to make love to women in bars and places I've never done it before. Where have you never done it?"

"Huh. I can't think where. I've never fucked in a sewer. Or a police station."

"Women love to be loved in public places. I can do it to any woman in a bar. Often I can do it to two or three women together: they don't mind."

"So how do you fuck women over?"

"I go into a bar with one woman and make her wait while I make love to another woman. Then while the first woman's sucking me off, I tell her what just happened. Remember that night we walked into the Poisson and that girl in the brown dress kissed me. She was waiting for me."

"But you didn't fuck her in the bar, you fucked me."

"I wanted her to wait for me, and then when I finally showed up, nothing would happen. I saw her the next night and she wouldn't talk to me. One of these days I'm never going to fuck women again. I'm going to be all alone."

"Why do you keep on fucking women? You obviously hate them."

"Women are whores. That's my opinion. I'm a male whore."

"Someone must have frightened you badly."

"I know how the world is. We're all animals. Anyone who thinks otherwise is fooling himself."

"Roger, fuck me again."

"You like it when I fuck you?"

"Fuck me as hard as you can. Make me forget everything that's ever happened."

"You like me when I fuck you?"

"How come you married Betty? You're a sex maniac and she's so innocent it's unbelievable."

"I tell you something. I married Betty cause she's a donkey. She has no friends and she has no one she can run to for help. I wanted someone who was nothing. Who was like an animal to me. I don't want her anymore anyways. I've told her to leave me, she could find men who are much richer, more handsome, and smarter than me, but she says she won't leave me. Yesterday she told me if she ever has to separate from me, she's going to enter a nunnery."

"That's what you get for marrying a donkey."

"I've hired lawyers who've offered to give her money to leave me, but she won't go."

"Papa says the only time a man hires inexperienced help is when he gets married."

"I'm going to get rid of Betty this year."

"How are you going to get rid of her? You've been trying to for the last year and you still haven't succeeded."

"I'm going to get rid of her this year and live alone."

"Why do you hate women so much? You know you hate women?"

"It's the women here: they all lie and do everything behind your back. They're real sweet, you know what I mean? Women act like they want to give you everything and then when you think you have them, they disappear."

"That's the only way they can act. They don't have any power."

"I see women lie to me all the time and I act the same way. I've never let a woman get too close to me."

"I'm the same way."

"I went with this one French woman last year a couple of times, but it didn't mean anything to me. She approached me and made me come back to her room with her. Then when she was sick of me, she went on to Ally."

"I've heard that most of the women tourists who come alone are looking to get laid as much as possible."

"The women always leave me. They say all these sweet things they tell me they love me like they've never loved any man, then they go back to their country and I never see them again."

"Well, you're a bastard too."

"You know why? When I was staying in the United States, not only in New York City but in Arizona, all the people who lived around me wanted to beat me up cause they said I'm a black person. They didn't care whether I had money or not. I was really innocent then. In Arizona this one guy who was a cop taught me how to defend myself. I hung out with cops cause they knew how things were. They taught me the things I needed to know. I like cops; I own two guns already. They know how to treat women. I saw this one cop give it to a woman, he almost took her scalp off. Oh brother."

"Why don't you try being friends with women?"

"I make love with lots of women."

"If you tried talking with women, you might find out they're as mean and vicious as men."

"I never talk to any women. If I let some woman find out what I'm like, she won't go with me again."

"I'm still with you. I'm talking to you right now. I'm as bastardly to men as you are to women only I'm more indirect about it. I've lived with three men and walked out on every one of them."

"That's cause you like sex as much as I do. The next time I marry, I'm going to marry an older woman like you and not a dumbbell like Betty."

"Someone like me wouldn't marry you. You can talk to me: that's the point; you can say whatever you want to me. I don't give a shit. I just don't like when people lie to me."

"I'm always honest to women. I tell them what I'm like and if they don't like it, they can go away."

"As long as you're honest, you can do anything you want with me. You can fuck around, fuck me over, I don't give a shit. I just have to know what's going on."

"As much as I've ever loved any woman, I love you."

"You know what I'm going to do? I'm gonna write you everything that happens to me: all the details. Who I fuck, how I manage to get money, all the weirdest things I do. That way you'll find out what a woman's really like and you'll know I'm being honest with you."

"Do you promise you'll write me? Maybe you won't so I'll wait until you write me and then I'll call you. You know what? You call me when you get back to New York and charge it to me. I'm going to write down my phone number and address on this paper."

"I'd be embarrassed to call you collect."

"You're going to call me as soon as you get back to New York. You're my girlfriend A-number-1."

The gray car honks. "Honk. Honk."

"That's my brother's car. I have to go."

"No. I don't want you to go."

"My brother's waiting for me."

"Just give me a minute. Just wait a few minutes."

"I want to fuck you again quickly. In your asshole."

"Oh please, in my asshole. I've got to have you again."

"Does that hurt?"

"It feels wonderful. You've got to come with me, fast."

"I've got to go now."

"Honk. Honk."

"Roger . . . I . . ."

"We say 'Goodbye' like this. We have to smile."

"Goodbye."

A TRIP TO THE VOODOO DOCTOR

AFTER a week and a half of anxiously waiting, Kathy decides to go to Port-au-Prince to look for Roger. As soon as she reaches Port-au-Prince, she forgets about Roger. Completely dazed, with a huge smile, she wanders around the hot docks that are the pits of Haiti's main city.

The congested streets, rotting pastel-colored wood walls piled on top of each other, legless and armless beggars on wheels, male and female one-basket merchants, rows of food and leather and plastic shoes and notebooks and hair curlers, one or two scared white tourists, starved children looking for the rich white tourists, nonexistent sidewalks and cars, lots and lots of cars, Chevrolets and Pontiacs and Plymouths and Fords and VW's and jeeps and a few American sportscars and the trap-traps, cars of every color and year, cars that don't run and hopped-up cars, all going at the same speed: slowly, and lots and lots of garbage, and rooms without doors in the rotting pastel-colored wood walls, and rooms without walls, everything and everyone piled up on and squashed next to each other, a big pounding scaly pregnant fish: all give way to wide empty streets. Wide empty sidewalks. Low block-big rectangular buildings. Everything here is white. It's hotter than where the people and all the buildings are crushed together. There seem to be very few people here because sidewalks and the streets are so huge. The air seems to be the same color as the buildings and the streets.

Moving from the congested market-slum-city, through this whiteness, to the ocean, each block gets longer and wider. The

third and final block is the longest and widest. It's huge. It's
surrounded by emptiness. The few people walking up and down
look like black marbles lost in the sand. A white person wouldn't
be seen at all. Moving from the congested market-slum-city,
through this whiteness, to the ocean, no one can breathe. The
ocean is a green plate. There's no sound because the streets and
buildings are big and empty and almost invisible. As if they're
shadows.

What are they shadows of? One narrow wood pier extends into
the water. The water makes no sound against the wood. A two-
sail boat lies a quarter of a mile off of this pier.

It's this hot and white because dust and pollution sweep down
from the mountains and the upper city into this pit. Then the
air and pollution move from this pit across the ocean and leave
a vacuum.

One wide black street lies parallel to the ocean front. Three
huge empty squares, amputated fingers, lie off of this street. The
cement squares don't contain anything.

A group of males are standing on the corner of the sidewalk
of the middle square. They're talking to each other. Two cops
in cop uniforms're yelling at a smaller group of men, a few whites
in this group, who're trying to get past the closed wire gates and
on to the far end of the pier. Kathy walks out of the middle of
the smaller groups of men and off of the pier. She's leaning
against a pole and watching what's going on. The world's hot.

"Hey, Kathy."

She looks around, but doesn't see anyone she knows. She
doesn't know anyone in Port-au-Prince.

"Hey, Kathy."

She looks over the street at the large group of men on the
sidewalk and sees an arm waving. She crosses the black street
and walks over to the waving arm. "Don't you remember me,
Kathy? I'm Sammy's brother. Don't you remember Sammy?"

"Jesus Christ. How are you? I've been away: I just got back to
Port-au-Prince yesterday. How's Sammy?" She feels embarrassed.

"Sammy wants to see you."

"I don't know. Uh, I'm kind of busy right now. Actually I'm looking for Rue DeForestre. I've got to make an airplane reservation so I can get back to the Cap as soon as possible. Can you tell me where the Rue DeForestre is?"

"When should I tell Sammy to meet you?"

"I don't know. Sometime later today. I have to get to the Rue DeForestre and I got totally lost . . ."

"It's just a few blocks from here."

"Where?"

"You can't walk there by yourself. I'll get someone to help you."

"I don't need any help. I just want to know where it is."

"Patrick, this is Kathy. Kathy, Patrick." A short-haired good-looking twenty year old.

"How can I get to the Rue DeForestre?" she asks Patrick.

"I'll show you. It's not far from here."

"Just tell me how to get there."

"You can't walk there by yourself. It's too far."

"I like to walk."

"White women don't walk around this city by themselves. The men won't leave you alone and you'll get lost."

"I can take care of myself. I just want to know how to get there."

"Do you not want to talk with me because you think I'll do something bad to you?"

"Don't be ridiculous. I just don't see any reason you should go out of your way so I can get to where I'm going. I like you."

"I have nothing to do. I'll walk with you."

"I can't pay you or anything."

"Why do you mention money? I want to be your friend. Do you think I want your money?"

"I'm sorry." She tries to explain. "I get so used to people asking me for money. I . . ."

"You don't want to be friends with me?"

"I don't even know you. I think I want to be friends with you."

"What hotel're you staying at?" the brother asks her.

"The Plaza."

"Sammy'll pick you up there at five o'clock this afternoon. Don't forget."

"OK." She turns again to her new friend. "I have to go to ABC Tours. It's on the Rue DeForestre."

"I know where it is."

They start walking upward, through the city. "Is it far?"

"Why do you ask so many questions?"

"I just want to know where I'm going."

"Why do you want to get to ABC Tours so badly?"

"I want to get back to Cap Haitian as soon as possible." She tells him how much she loves Cap Haitian, all about Roger and the beggar boys. "Are we almost there?"

"What're you in such a hurry for? Americans're always in a hurry. I lived in America for a while, that's why I speak English so well, I didn't like it except when I lived in Atlanta, Georgia. The life in Atlanta, Georgia is like the life here. Nobody hurries there, no one works, and there's lots of dope. Do you smoke dope?"

"Yeah."

"Do you want some now? I have some really good smoke. I can stop by my house and get it."

"Not right now. Maybe later."

"Don't you trust me?"

"I trust you. I mean, you're a strange guy and I don't know you very well."

"I don't want to hurt you. Do you think I want you to be my girlfriend?"

"Well . . ."

"Look. Put your hand in mine." She stares at his outstretched hand. "Go on. Take my hand." She's holding his hand. "See. I don't want anything more. Do you know why you can trust me?"

"Why?" Her big brown eyes look up at him.

"You look and act exactly like my older sister. How old are you?"

"Twenty-nine."

"No you're not. She's twenty-three."

"I AM twenty-nine."

"You can't be more than twenty. That's how old you are. Call me your brother."

"OK, brother."

"Take my hand again." He takes her into the green rickety wood room that's the travel bureau and out of it. "Why do you want to take the plane to the Cap?"

"How else could I get there?" They continue walking up and down the sometimes nonexistent sidewalks past the fake storefronts.

"Why don't you rent a motorcycle?"

"Gee, that's an idea. When I was a kid, I used to spend days hitchhiking on motorcycles. I've always had this thing about motorcycles and black leather. But if I drive a cycle up to the Cap, I won't have any way of getting it back. Maybe I can return it there? I could learn to ride a cycle in a day."

"I'll ride with you. Then I'll drive the bike back to Port-au-Prince."

"How much money would you want for that?"

"I don't want your money. I told you this already. I do it because you're my sister."

"No. I don't think I want to do it. How much would it cost me to rent a cycle?"

"Nine dollars a day."

"That's not much."

"Plus you give them a deposit. You get the deposit back."

"How can I get the deposit if I'm going to Cap Haitian and not coming back?"

"I can get it for you."

"No . . ."

"You still don't like me. You think I'm going to take all your money."

"I don't have enough money for you to take."

"If you rented a motorcycle, you could be in Cap Haitian tonight. You don't want to waste all your money on a plane. Why don't you take a look at the motorcycle store? It's just around the corner."

"Wait a second. If it costs me nine dollars a day I won't be able to get the cycle back till tomorrow, it'll cost me at least eighteen." She's adding everything up in her head. "Plus the deposit. That's more than a plane ticket."

"So you're not going to do it?"

"I have my plane ticket. I'm going to go back to the hotel now."

"Why don't you rent a bike just for the day? You can take the plane tomorrow or the next day. We'll go to the Barbancourt rum factory."

"I don't have nine dollars to blow on a cycle. I want to go home."

Patrick informs her there are other cheaper ways to go to Cap Haitian—the vomit bus and the government airplane, so she asks him about the government airplane. They decide he'll take her to the government airport so she can reserve a ticket.

They've been walking up and down the sidewalks for hours. Sometimes there's a huge bottomless hole in a sidewalk. Sometimes a sidewalk disappears. Sometimes the sidewalks and streets are clean the wood store walls are solid. As they descend through the city, the sidewalks getting narrower until they almost disappear, the streets disappearing, the stores are on top of each other. They're in the marketplace. The sidewalks lie under shoes, carved fake mahogany cause there's no real mahogany left in Haiti cause the woods that used to cover the island have been decimated, straw baskets full of plastic barrettes, Ivory soap, and underpants, mangoes, baskets full of all kinds of burnt sugar confections, dried fish. The long cigar-black street lies under brightly-colored private cars, private taxis, city-run taxis, tap-taps, bicycles, young boys with no legs, young boys with shriveled legs, and old big-belly women. One huge block contains one no-door building. Inside this building, space is immense. There are no walls except for the outer walls of the building and those walls are almost invisible due to the lack of light. Tables cover all of the sawdust floor, tables far as the eye can see, wood tables covered with baskets full of short and long rices, millet, wheat kernels, ground grains, dried corn and white and yellow corn flours, dried fishes, fish freshly caught from the ocean still unscaled and ungutted, different varieties of mangoes, canaps, figs, bananas, breadfruit, sour oranges, lemons, limes, onions and garlics, tomatoes, co-conuts, cashews, roasted cashews, sugar, brown sugar, almonds, peanuts, raisins, Camembert cheese, more. Scales hang over some of the tables. Narrow pathways in the darkness separate the tables. Women and men and children all dressed in brightly-colored cloth, almost hidden by the darkness, stand by the tables or shuffle by each other. Almost under the table, in the half-light, here and there, an old woman squats and separates kernels of corn in a huge straw basket and scales a fish with a big heavy steel knife in her hand. Outside the people are walking on top of each other, over each other; the sky's so bright its yellow is blue even though it isn't.

Kathy and Patrick stumble into a tap-tap. A tap-tap is a small public bus that's colored with green red pink yellow brown blue and black paint. The tap-tap's white. Virgin Mary's La Sirene's Jesus Christ's Duvalier's private girlfriends' names adorn every inch of the bus' walls. GRACE DE MARIE. PAIX POUR TOUJOURS. LE SAUVIER EST ICI. The tap-tap lets Patrick and Kathy off at the government airbase.

The government airbase is a huge almost empty field that's brown gray and, a little, olive green. A brown man stands in a gray metal booth in front of this field and controls who goes in and out of the field. There are a few other men inside the field. There are a few two-engine gray airplanes. There are a few huts on the ground. The airfield seems empty cause it's so big and cause it looks like death.

She walks out of the airfield and they climb back into a tap-tap. She thanks him and tells him she's going to go home now that she's done what she had to. He doesn't want her to go away from him. He tells her he wants to go to the beach. She doesn't want to go to the beach. He wants to rent a motorcycle and ride around Petionville. She doesn't want to rent a motorcycle. He wants to go dancing in Carrefour. She doesn't want to dance.

"I know this doctor I'd like you to meet."

"Do you mean a voodoo doctor?"

"He's a very important man. I want you to meet him because you mean a lot to me."

"I'd love to meet him."

"You have to realize this could be the most important thing that's ever happened to you. I want you to realize this. This man can change your life."

"I want to meet him."

"He's going to do a lot for you. I know he is. This man has helped a lot of people. He's a very good man."

"I don't want him to do anything for me. I just want to meet him."

"There's just one thing. You have to be willing to realize who he is."

"Do I have to pay him anything?"

"You'll have to buy him candles so he can do his work. That won't cost you much."

All the tap-taps in the city meet in the marketplace. They're back where they started from. Limbless beggars crouch under them. Skateboards attached to half-bodied people roll by.

They go off to see the voodoo doctor. The city cab soon leaves the straight black tar streets. It winds basically upward and to the left, sometimes round in circles, sometimes in huge snake-arcs, sometimes it goes opposite to where it wants to go, there's no time in Haiti. It goes everywhere. Through driveways and around falling-apart single building single-room stores. On gray broken cement roads that go under while the old mansions alongside the road go up so it seems to go under mansions. Ahead up a narrow street hedged in by two-story wood houses into a narrow gray wood garage then straight back down the street in reverse.

The neighborhood changes completely. The taxicab turns left on a corner, and stops.

A narrower pebbly unrideable road juts off of the dirt road the taxi's been riding on. The new road is covered with dust. Thick yellow dust. This dust hides women carrying huge parcels on their heads, walking in the ruts, and two-story stucco houses, painted all colors, yellow and black. They walk into the dust. The sun seems to get hotter and hotter. There's lots of noise and hot dust and heat. On one side the dust sharply descends through the air into a ditch crossed over by a modern trestle. They keep on trudging upward.

The pebbly road turns sharply to the right. About ten yards below this turn, there's a dark red stucco house. The red house has a porch.

The sun is very very hot. Kathy feels tired and excited. Kathy should wait on the porch while Patrick sees if the doctor's available.

Kathy's waiting. A huge man appears. Would Kathy like to go inside?

Kathy does what anyone tells her. She follows the man around the porch and the house past a tiny woman washing and hanging laundry to a tiny room in the back of the house which is only big enough for the narrow cot and cabinet-desk inside it. Photos and newspapers cover the walls and glass windows of the cabinet.

"Are you the doctor?" Kathy asks the man.

"The doctor?"

"Uh, I'm supposed to meet a doctor. A holy person. I thought that was you."

The huge man sits down on the bed next to Kathy and laughs. "Non. I am Kung-Fu."

Kathy looks at him in total fear.

"There are pictures of me at my kung-fu."

She sees pictures of him dressed up in his uniform. "Oh, you're a black belt."

"Do you know about kung-fu?"

"Not very much."

"I am very good, I like doing that: I don't like violence. I don't go with women because they're tricky. They don't do things honestly. I only go with men."

She relaxes and looks at the girly pictures. "Are those your relatives, that woman over there?"

"That's a picture of my aunt and her two children. They now live in Boston. Do you know Boston?"

"Very well. I used to live there."

"I'd like to go there." There's a huge market for the private yacht owners in smuggling Haitians to anywhere in the US. They talk about their relatives and kung-fu for a long long time. Kathy and the huge gentle man like each other very much.

When Patrick returns for Kathy, she doesn't want to leave.

"You said you wanted to see the doctor."

She tells the kung-fu man she'll return as soon as she's finished with the voodoo doctor.

Patrick and Kathy're walking upward in the thick dust. When they reach a black Pontiac parked by the corner, he tells her to wait there until someone comes for her.

How will she know who that someone is? She'll know.

Fifteen minutes pass by. She sees a girl in a bright bright green skirt walking toward her. She sees, in the distance, Patrick's hand waving at her. The girl smiles at her so she follows her.

The girl walks part ways up the same road, then turns to her left. There are no more roads. The girl walks into a mass of dust, on a mass of dust, down ten feet of only slightly horizontal rocks, into a section that's unlike anything Kathy's seen in Port-au-Prince.

There's a mass of dust-ground and approximately ten feet by

eight feet and six feet high thatched huts. People are everywhere. Small black goats and roosters and black-and-white hens and lots and lots of children. Everyone squawking and cackling crying gossiping. Hotter than ever. Women sitting in the dust and women sitting by round straw baskets full of one kind of food and one woman sitting under an improvised cloth canopy by a table holding a tray of some homemade confection and women walking around and women washing clothes in some bowls of water and women holding babies maybe suckling them. The girl walks past these people without stopping, she walks around a hut, down, turns a sharp corner around another hut, straight onward, past almost a row of huts. Kathy follows her.

The girl stops by the door of one of the brown ten feet by eight feet huts and enters. Actually there's no door, only a red curtain. The roof is corroded metal. A narrow cot lies against the back wall of the hut. A rough table lies against the left wall. Two wood chairs. To the right, a middle-aged man so wrinkled and thin he looks old sits in a chair facing a smaller wood table.

Patrick's sitting on a chair between the old man and the back wall. "You have to buy some candles."

"How much money?"

"Three dollars."

Kathy gives Patrick this money. He gives the money to a woman who's sitting in the hut. There are three women sitting in the hut: two on the bed and one (the girl who led Kathy to the hut) on the floor.

The père lights a white candle. Then he lights a cigarette with the candle flame and gives it to Patrick. He lights another cigarette and gives it to Kathy. He lights another cigarette for himself. Everyone smokes. The père sings a song something about Jesus. He speaks only Creole. Patrick translates for Kathy but Kathy suspects that Patrick isn't saying to her what the père says to him.

The père opens a small Bible and begins to recite a passage rapidly in a monotone.

Then his head sinks and he makes loud hiccups. "He's receiving the spirit." Patrick tells Kathy.

The père shakes Patrick's hand, then Kathy's hand. His grip is unusually strong and sharp.

The père rubs some liquid from a bottle covered with red cloth over his face and hands. He puts a match to the top of this bottle; the bottle lights up; immediately he puts his hand over the bottle top. The bottle sticks to his hand. He passes the hand-and-bottle round his head. When he pulls the bottle off of his hand, there's a loud pop and it looks like the skin of his hand is going to come away with the bottle.

The ceremony's begun.

It's very hot inside the unlighted hut, much hotter than it was outside the hut in the dust under the direct burning sun. Everyone inside the hut's sweating.

Kathy doesn't remember exactly what and when happens from now on because she's so hot and because she's getting dizzier and dizzier. Certain incidents stick out in her mind.

The père takes a drink from the red-cloth-covered bottle. He hands the bottle to Patrick to take a drink. Patrick drinks. He hands the bottle to Kathy to drink. Kathy drinks. It's cheap rum.

The père pours rum into an approximately foot diameter tin bowl. Many objects are in the bowl: a Virgin Mary, some rocks, some sticks, a small skull, some beads, the white candle. He puts a match to the rum, poof! Everything's alight.

The père asks Kathy to write in a small green notebook. She writes down her name. "Anything else?" Kathy asks Patrick. She writes down her age.

The père says he needs something so he can begin his work for Kathy. He writes about fifteen words down on a small piece of white paper. "Give him some money" Patrick tells Kathy. "How much?" "It'll only be about three dollars." "Is this going to cost me any more money?" "This is important. You have to realize that you're doing something that could be the most important thing for you. He wants to work for you and he needs certain things to work with." "I only have a twenty." Kathy gives one of the women the twenty. She goes out of the hut to purchase the somethings.

The père gives Kathy a small dusty bottle with some clear liquid in it. She swallows. He smiles and takes back the bottle. "That'll be better for you," says Patrick. "You'll see what'll happen."

It's incredibly hot in the hut. Sweat runs down everyone's face. Kathy doesn't think she feels anything.

Everything takes incredibly long.

The père's singing again. The women on the bed join in singing. Kathy sings along. How the hell am I able to sing in a language I don't know, Kathy says to herself. The père and the women're happy Kathy's singing with them.

The père lights a cigar with the white candle's flame. He gives it to Patrick. He lights another cigar with the white candle's flame. He gives it to Kathy. He lights another cigar with the white candle's flame for himself. Everyone smokes his cigars.

The père talks to Patrick. Patrick tells Kathy she'll have to give the père some money because he's working for her. She understands. He's a worker. "How much?" "Ten dollar." Kathy gives the père a ten-dollar bill. He carelessly throws the bill on the wood table next to a huge beaten-up skull. "I don't have any more money," Kathy says, "I can't give you any more money." She's worried.

"How much money do you make in the United States?" Patrick asks Kathy. "Seven dollars a day when I work." "Wooo. You know why all the people up there," Patrick points to the invisible hills where all the rich people in Port-au-Prince live, "are rich? The doctor works for them. The doctor is going to work for you. This is very very important. The doctor is going to work for you for six . . . seven hundred a week." Kathy looks into the witch doctor's eyes. "I don't want money," she says. "I want you to understand. More, I want to do good for others."

The père smiles and says, "You have a great force in you. You must go upwards." His hands motion strongly upwards. "I can help you to go upwards." Kathy smiles. She feels she and the père understand each other. She thinks Patrick's becoming a nuisance. "I would like that." The père shakes each of Kathy's hands quickly and firmly.

The père begins singing. Everyone starts singing.

The woman returns with about ten small envelopes, a bottle of cheap perfume, a bottle of rum. She gives fifteen dollars to Patrick. Patrick gives the fifteen dollars to Kathy.

The père takes the envelopes, perfume, and rum. He opens the rum, pours it into the dusty bottle, and drinks. He gives the bottle to Patrick. Patrick drinks. Patrick gives the bottle to Kathy. Kathy drinks. Everyone drinks a few more rounds. "I work with rum this first time," the père says.

The père lights up a cigarette with the white candle's flame. Gives it to Kathy. Lights another cigarette with the white candle's flame. Gives it to Patrick. Lights a cigarette with the white candle's flame for himself. Everyone smokes.

"Give me twenty cents for more cigarettes," Patrick tells Kathy. Kathy gives Patrick the money. "Also three dollars for another bottle of perfume. The father wants to do something special for you." Kathy thinks the père hasn't said anything to Patrick, but she gives the money anyways.

The père pours the perfume into an old thin bottle, about five inches high. Then he opens one of the small envelopes. He carefully shovels some of the lavender powder from this envelope into the bottle. Each of the envelopes contains a different color powder. The envelopes say things such as AMOUR, REINE DE GRACE. After he's opened and closed all the envelopes, he pours some of the rum from the dusty bottle, raw white rum, into the five inch high bottle. Everyone drinks some more rum. He shakes the five inch high bottle. He puts some brown dried leaves and branches into the five inch high bottle. He takes the rattle that's lying on the floor to the left of the wood table, shakes the rattle over everything. He puffs on his cigarette, blows smoke over everything, blows smoke into the five inch high bottle, and seals the bottle with an improvised paper cork.

The père rubs his face and hands with some liquid. He pours the same liquid on Kathy's hands and motions for her to rub her face. She does.

The père takes some salve and rubs it on her lips. He motions her to do she doesn't understand what. She kisses her arms and breasts. He smiles.

The woman returns with the cigarettes.

"He's given me a secret for you," Patrick tells Kathy. "What is it?" "I'll tell you later. I have something to tell you later." "Why can't you tell me now?" "He said I should tell you after we leave. He said you have to sit by the sea after we leave here. It's necessary you sit by the sea. I'll tell you then."

The père holds a pack of filthy cards in his hands. He puts three cards down on the table. Jack of Diamonds, dark queen, Ace of clubs. He reshuffles the cards and cuts. He puts some more cards down on the table. He reshuffles the cards and cuts. He asks Kathy to cut the cards. She cuts toward him. He smiles. He puts ten cards down on the table. He quickly puts them back in the deck.

The père speaks to Patrick in a quick monotone. "Recently someone's been speaking to you badly," Patrick translates for Kathy. Pause. "Is this true?" "Uh yeah . . . yeah maybe. I had a fight with a boyfriend in Cap Haitian right before I left. But it's OK now. We made up. That's not really speaking badly." The père speaks again in his rapid monotone. Patrick translates. "You've missed a very good chance in the US." "I dunno," Kathy says. The old man's not really hitting the mark, Kathy thinks to herself. "The father says he's going to work for you for six to seven hundred dollars a week. This is very important. He says you have bonne chance." Kathy talks directly to the père. "Je ne veux pas d'argent assez que je veux travailler pour des autres." The father smiles.

The father starts singing. Everyone sings along. One of the

middle-aged women who's sitting on the bed leads the singing.

Patrick talks to a woman next to him, who suckles a baby.

"He wants to give you something else," Patrick says to Kathy. The père's carefully spooning some powder from each of the small white envelopes on to a crumpled piece of paper. When he finishes with the last envelope, he seals the paper and says something in his quick monotone to Patrick. "When you're alone, you have to rub this all over your body. If you don't do this, nothing he's doing for you will work." The père nods. Kathy nods.

The père takes the red-cloth-covered bottle. He lights its top with the white candle's flame. Poof. Quickly he places the palm of his hand over the top. The bottle sticks to his palm. He passes this hand-and-bottle three times around his head.

The leading woman, a middle-aged woman, starts drawing a vever on the stone floor. Everyone else sings lackadaisically while she sprinkles the white corn flour from a china dish on to the floor. The sign's a long backbone line with curlicues coming out of its sides. One heart in the middle. At the bottom of this vever she draws a funny hideous head. Then she draws a second vever which Kathy's too out of it to see. When the woman's finished using the flour, he nods his approval.

The père places the human skull that's on the wood table on the funny hideous head. He places two rocks near the skull. He shakes the rattle all over the skull. He's not satisfied. He takes the light blue nailpolish bottle that's on the wood table and pours some small gray beads from the nailpolish bottle on to the center of the first vever. He holds the lighted white candle next to these beads. The beads light up, explode. He places the human skull on top of the exploded beads. He puts two rocks near the skull. He's very careful to put everything in exactly the right place. He sticks the lighted white candle into a depression in the center of the skull. He sprinkles rum around the lighted white candle without extinguishing the light. He takes a small red-plastic-frame mirror and passes the mirror three times around the center of

Kathy's body. He sticks the mirror in front of her face so she has to look at herself. Kathy's almost unconscious. He passes the mirror around her head three times. He places the mirror on the vever near the skull but not touching the skull. He places the five inch high corked bottle next to, leaning against the side of the skull. He picks a string of many-colored beads up from the junk of the floor to his left and throws the beads around the lighted white candle. He says something to Patrick. Patrick says, "She can't give you fifty dollars." The père and Patrick argue about how much money Kathy must give. Patrick says to Kathy, "Wait a second. Listen closely to me. You have to give something more. Otherwise all that he's doing won't work for you. What he's doing is very important. This is very important. You must realize that what he's doing could be the most important thing in your life." "How much?" Kathy asks Patrick. This is an art piece, Kathy thinks to herself. "Ten dollar. And when you get back to the United States, you buy him a watch. Not a good watch, you understand." Kathy gives a ten-dollar bill to the père. She has no more money left. He throws the ten-dollar bill on the skull. It falls in back of the skull. He pours rum around the lighted white candle without extinguishing its flame. He shakes the rattle over the skull and the vever.

The père draws a cross on Kathy's forehead.

The père motions Kathy to get up. He turns her around three times. He pushes her around the vevers three times clockwise. He pushes her around the vevers three times counterclockwise. He picks up the small plastic red-frame mirror and passes the mirror around her body. He shows Kathy to herself. He pushes her around the vevers three times clockwise. He pushes her around the vevers three times counterclockwise.

Kathy's facing the red curtain. The père tells Kathy she has to return here. She can bring a friend with her. He gives her the filled five inch high bottle and a green plastic soap case containing the powders. He tells her she can't look back.

Chickens and goats run around. The ground's so dry, it's almost sand. This sand flies everywhere. Children squall and yell. Women sit on the sand-covered almost nonexistent doorsteps of huts and low wood chairs outside the huts. Women talk to each other. Women with baskets on their heads walk in the fine dust. Women carry huge amounts of wet clothes in their arms. There are a few men.

"Goodbye," says the girl in the bright green skirt.

Kathy turns around and walks outside into the sun. She's more dazed than before.

THE ADULT LIFE OF TOULOUSE LAUTREC BY HENRI TOULOUSE LAUTREC

"Make sense," Fielding said. "Tell the real story of your life. You alone can tell the truth!"

"I don't want to make any sense," I replied.

I'm too ugly to go out into the world. I'm a hideous monster.

CHAPTER ONE

THE CASE OF THE MURDERED TWERP

TOULOUSE," says Vincent. "What are you going to do with your life? How're you ever going to make any money? You're a deformed crippled beast. Look at your hairy chest, your huge nodding head. Your legs are spindly. You thought just cause your parents're rich, you had the world on a silver platter. Money does control everything in this world.

"But just cause your parents have money, doesn't mean you have money."

"I don't give a damn," I mumble.

"How are you ever going to get famous and get fucked? You're such a lousy painter. You may be a great painter, Toulouse, but you're a real lousy one. And that's what matters: goodness.

"What you need is a man, Toulouse, and you're never going to get one. You're going to be lonely for the rest of your life."

"You're a raving maniac!!" I screech at the top of my lungs. "I believe artists can do everything! Artists can know all the joy and misery and terrifyingness and usefulness cause artists don't have to suffer! Even though I can barely walk; I'm always in pain; I'm always hungry.

"All I think about is sex. At night, nights, I lie alone in my bed: I see the right leg of every sexy man I've seen on the street, the folds of cloth over and around the ooo ooo . . . I ache and I ache and I ache. I feel a big huge hole inside my

body. I see a man I like about to stick his cock in my hot
pussy.

"I used to think being crippled meant being in constant
pain. I can stand pain. Now I know no man wants me. I can
hardly bear to live.

"Fuck art, Vincent."

Just then the owner of the Restaurant Norvins walks up to
us. She runs the hottest bar in Montmartre. In the back of
the bar's a whore-house. Her closest friend is Theo, a young
teacher.

"Honey," Theo's looking at Vincent longingly, "we're
trying to organize this party. It's gonna be in the back of here
in an hour. And we need help . . ."

Just then this young girl runs over to them. "Norvins," she
screams, "you've got to help me. I just saw this, this horrible
event. I saw a murder. MURDER! I myself . . ." "She's a
liar," Theo says to me in a loud whisper.

"I don't know what to do. I. I saw . . ."

"I've got work to do," Norvins says. She walks away from
us. "You're a little liar," Theo pinches the girl. "I never
believe what you tell me in class. What're you doing in this
whore-house anyway?"

"I tell you I saw murder . . ."

"I've got to help Norvins with the whore-house party . . ."

She turns around, dashes into the bar's backroom before
we can stop her.

"Art," I say. The room whirls around me: the black bar
shudders and turns.

"Art:" I continue, "I'm so unbearably desirous needy I
can't think about art. Who can think about art in this miserable city? I think about sex so much my art must be sex. I
think about sex all the time, and I try to stop myself. I tell
myself I have to be stronger. I'm alone. I should revel in my
loneliness. I'm in pain. I should revel in my pain. I shouldn't
want to be with another person so much. If I think about this

miserable situation too much, I'll realize I'm about to kill myself."

Suddenly a beautiful man rushes into the bar.

Veronique, Berthe, and Giannina run up to Vincent and me. "Where's Norvins?" they cackle. "I read in *Crime*," Berthe mumbles, "this guy fucks his girlfriend in her left nostril."

"Shut up Berthe." Veronique says quickly. "We've got to get these apples to Norvins. We're going to bob for apples at the party."

I'm looking at the beautiful man; I'm staring at the beautiful man; I'm sending out every vibration I can so he'll know I want him and only him. His hair's red. His cheekbones're high. He's older than me. His left hand's resting on my cheek. I can feel the hot cum pouring out of my cunt.

The bar swirls and swirls around us.

"Listen you goddamn shitface assbung," I announce, "you've got to fuck me. If you don't fuck me, I'm going to blow up every rat scum tenement in Montmartre. The cops'll shit in their pants. They'll have nothing left to do. If you don't fuck me Mr. Beautiful I'll kick your lousy dick inside out I mean it. You can't treat me like a piece of moldy shit."

"I think you're extremely beautiful."

"Fuck me. Fuck me. Fuck me. Take me to Brazil. Take me to Argentina. Take me to bed. You're the only person or thing who can make me happy. You can make me ecstatic right now." I throw my arms in the air, leap on the table. My crippled legs buckle under me.

"I'm too old for you . . ."

"I'm sick of younger men. They always screw me over."

"I can only screw you three times a day. I know that's not very much, not for a woman of your extreme . . ."

"I'm in love with you. When I'm in love, what do minor things such as screwing, old age, and lack of money matter? D'you have any money? Darling. Will you support me? Can

I be your child? I've never had any parents. I love you. I
love you. When're you going to fuck me? Now?"

"You must have had a difficult childhood. I can tell by the
difficulty you have expressing your desires. Listen, baby,
I'm going to fuck you so hard you won't even know what's
happening to you. I'm going to shove this hard throbbing
piston into your cunt your ass your asshole the holes between
your toes your nostrils every microinch of your ears your
hands your breasts the space between your flopping breasts
your mouth your eyes your sweating armpits your navel at
60 miles per hour 200 miles per hour 2,000,000 miles per
hour. So fast, my cock'll never leave you. My cock'll be 24
inches, 36 inches long. And you'll be feeling every inch of
it. Baby."

I can see his cock following me everywhere: through the
Champs-Elysees, Montmartre, the Seine. A huge golden
cock at least 70 inches long. Five feet; no six feet.

"And when you can stop writhing, my baby, cause I've
made you come so much and so hard, you're just coming and
coming and coming, all you're doing is coming, I'm going to
slowly, more lightly and slowly than's possible, lick every
part of your body, so slowly until my tongue comes to your
clit. Your clit sticking out, dripping, from your thick red
lips. Tongue will be a point; go dot dot dot hammer a tiny
metronome on your clit. Your whole body'll begin to shiver,
then . . ."

Wet steaming flesh.

Hot breath shuddering next to me.

His lips kiss me so gently I hardly know I'm being kissed.
I don't feel mad passion, I feel he loves me.

I'm not sure he wants to fuck me.

His tongue moves between my lips. Lightly grazes my
tongue. My mouth hardly feels his tongue. I figure he wants
to fuck me. I feel a lot of tenderness for him. Tenderness
that's opening me up physically.

Will I fall in love with him?

His red head's rubbing against my head. I rub my right shoulder against his left shoulder, like friends. I want him to feel love for me. I'll wait until he feels love for me. He's kissing me harder and harder. He's going to love me. He's going to take me into his secret warm cave. I'm slowly licking the inside of his right ear. He's shivering and moaning. I'm open. I want him to love me so badly. His hands're running up and down the tender insides of my legs.

"Baby," he's saying, "I'm going to fuck you and keep you. But not yet. You're going to have to suffer first. You're going to have to learn the meaning of suffering. One day you'll find me; and then, it'll be the end of the world. Fuck. Fuck. Fuck. Fuck. I love you so . . ."

He grabs his pants and rushes out of the bar.

I can't follow him cause I'm a cripple.

"These goddamn cunts." Norvins' towering body's making me ripple and swoon. "Have you seen Giannina around? Now that cunt's gone. She's the only one who knows how to put the apples correctly in the bobbing tub."

"I haven't seen Giannina."

"And what happened to that female twerp who said she had seen a murder?"

"She ran into the back room."

"All she wants is attention. Forget her. There's Theo." He runs out and leaves.

I'm a totally hideous monster. I'm too ugly to go out into the world. If I was living with a man, I would have someone who'd tell me if I'm hideous. Now I have no way of knowing if I'm hideous or not. I'm extremely paranoid. I don't want to see anyone. I'm another Paris art failure. I'm not even anonymous. All I want is to constantly fuck someone I love who loves me. Fuck. Fuck. Fuck. Fuck. Fuck.

No one will ever fuck me because I'm a hideous cripple.

I don't know how to present my image properly. When

I'm with people, I act either like a changing wishywashy
gook or like an aggressive leather bulldog. That's an image.
Obviously nobody wants to fall in love with me. I'm miserable, I'm completely miserable. I've got this hole inside me
my work won't fill. I have to work harder. I'm too freaky.
Why was I born a cripple?

Maybe some man will love me if I pay him for it.

Here all the women know everything. They know if they
don't spread their legs, no man'll notice them; when they
spread their legs, they get fucked not loved. They're worn.
They know they have to turn to the brothel.

They flock en masse to the brothel in the back of Norvins'
bar. All the pretty boys are there, earning their daily bread.
Pretty boys; studs; sexy ugly men. Whenever there's a party
in Norvins' brothel, it's the talk of the town.

I hate paying for love.

"Well, my dear," Norvins says to Paul, "it's about time
you're here. Your costume looks wonderful. You'll have to
set up your mirror behind the crystal ball so you can reflect
Giannina who's disguising herself as various men. Each time
you need to show some horny dame a future boyfriend,
Giannina'll appear in the crystal."

Paul Gauguin's the local cleaning woman.

"Is that that female twerp," Norvins whispers to Theo,
"who keeps lying? It's immoral for children to be in a brothel.
Get her out of here. Better yet: hide her in the library that's
opposite the dining room."

"Don't be ridiculous darling. You're just jealous cause
you're too old to wear children's drag."

"Carry this." Norvins hands a broomstick to Theo. "I've
got to present the prizes for bobbing apples."

All around me're couples. They laugh and kiss. It's

disgusting. I can't stand this loneliness. This party. I hobble up to one of the male whores, ask him if he's busy.

Fifty dollars an hour, honey.

I shudder. How disgusting. How painful. Love's the only revolution, the only way I can escape this society's economic controls. I can't pay someone to really truly love me.

Now this sleazy whore thinks I want him. Now he's rubbing the insides of my thighs. I love being touched there. I don't want to give in to this disgusting emotionless touch. I don't want to give in to anything. I'm burning. "Go away," I scream. "Get out of here. You're a creep. I don't want you. Even if I've paid you." Thank god he doesn't listen to me. I'm tough: I can take care of myself. He's putting his arms around me. For at least a moment I'll be able to relax. I'm deliriously happy. I'm thinking about how much and badly I'm going to get hurt. I'm going to get burned. I'm going to get burned all over. His arms hold me in this real warmth that makes the constant pain I feel go away. I'm no longer thinking. I'm in his arms forever and ever.

All I do is feel: His wet soft lips brush my earlobes, my short thick hairs which make my scalp tingle every time they're rubbed. My forehead. My eyebrows. My eyelids. My eyelashes. The skin between my eyebrows. My sideburns. I feel so warm and safe I want to give him everything that's me I want to forget myself: I turn my face trustingly toward his so that my full lips open, longing, feel his lips I can't tell what I feel I. I feel his mouth's wetness. I feel my body ache, and rub against his.

As he takes off his clothes, I curl around his big red cock. His cock's going to make the world change totally. I take his cock in my mouth, as far as it'll go, I'm testing; then out so I can lick its tip, so I can wet my right hand, corkscrew my right hand up and down the lower smooth slippery shaft. Am I pleasing him? His hands clutch my head. Push my head toward his curling red hair. More and more of his cock hits

the back of my throat. My fingers are drumming, not rhythmically, light and hard on his cock. My tongue moves not
rhythmically, light and hard, on his long hard cock.

"I'm fucking you for money," he tells me. "I'm fucking you
for money."

First he lies on top of me and fucks me. Then we both lie
on our sides and fuck. Then he lies on top of me and alternately fucks me in my cunt and in my ass. I come and I come
and I come and I come. He moves very slowly as he's coming.
He never looks at me. He falls asleep while he's holding me.

"Any man'll fuck me," Giannina tells Veronique in total
privacy, "once or twice. But it's like fucking the men in the
porno movies I'm in. And I get paid to fuck when I make
movies."

Veronique sighs.

"The fucking's always terrific. I come once twice lots I
come and I come and I come. The guy never gives a shit
about me. The only difference between the artists I fuck and
the studs in the movies is that I can talk to the studs in the
movies."

"I hardly ever come." Giannina gasps amazement. "I need
to fuck guys who fuck really slowly, for a long time, so it just
comes over me. I tremble and tremble and tremble."

"Veronique," Giannina says, "I think I'm falling in love
with Jim."

"What's the matter with that?"

"He doesn't want to see me again. He doesn't like me. I
don't understand why. We love fucking together."

"It's just your paranoia. I've had the worst week I've had
in a long time I'm so paranoid. We're both paranoid cause
we're Aries."

"I was lying on the couch with Jim. Watching T.V. I felt
I was with this warm person in a home. That hasn't happened

to me in months: being with a guy and not just fuck fuck fucking."

"Jim's settling down with Linda. He gets more prudish the more married he gets. He's been dropping all his girlfriends."

"Gee William's cute. He's got the continual hots."

"He kept looking like he was about to jump me. He was real drunk, that's why he was letting some emotion show. This life's keeping us lonely, Giannina. What these artists really want are pillows. Nice soft sweet female pillows. We can't be that way. We've got our own work. We're waitresses."

"Each time I get hurt, I close myself up."

"You act like you don't need anyone."

"The more I find I can live alone, the more I don't want to deal with the younger weaky formless men. The older men never have any emotions. Not toward me."

"The trouble is we keep having images of what we want. We don't let our emotions take over."

"At the end of the party," I'm telling Poirot, "she was dead."

"Where'd she die, Toulouse?"

"It was the end of the party. Veronique said, 'Where's that little twerp Norvins hates? The one who keeps saying she saw a murder. She didn't get lost or something?' We all looked for her. Suddenly Paul screeched. A body was hanging out of the bobbing apple tub."

"Do you always bob for apples? Whose idea was that?"

"I don't know. But she must have been killed during the party." We're sitting in Poirot's small flat on the Rue de Ganglia in Paris. Only one man servant, George, attends the flat. Poirot thinks for a moment.

"Tell me, this Norvins, who runs the bar, what's she like?"

"A good person. Efficient. Hard on her girls and her whores, but she has to be. Looks like a society dame. Veronique, Berthe, and Giannina're her waitresses."

"Did Norvins know the victim?"

"Slightly. She thought of her as 'the nuisance'. So did Theo and Paul. You can't let a young girl run in and out of a brothel as she pleases."

"Who exactly was at the party and what was the layout of the place?"

"The people I've told you. Plus Theo, a young teacher; Paul who was dressed as a witch she was telling everyone's fortune; Vincent my friend; and all the male whores Norvins uses they're all the same. It was basically their party. And two other teachers, Rousseau and Seurat. We call them teachers cause they're so good, they show the whores what to do."

"Were any of these people holding any sort of grudge against the young dead girl?"

"How could they? She was so, so full of shit. She did keep saying she had seen a murder, but no one believed her."

"Maybe she had seen a murder." Poirot's stroking his moustaches like a big fat cat. "Did she say when she had seen this murder?"

"I don't know."

"What's the layout of the brothel?"

Will I kill myself if I don't get a man?

What do I care who killed that twerp? What's her name? Marie.

Poirot'll figure everything out. He's my father.

I live alone. I've got enough money if my rich mother keeps forking it over. She's sorry for me cause I'm a cripple.

It's better to be a cripple in this world than just a plain ugly creep who writes books.

Every night I lie on my bed and am miserable. I look at the empty spot next to me. When I want to put my head on someone's shoulder, I . . . When I want to find out if I possibly don't look like an ugly cripple, I ask . . . When I want to feel someone's weight pounding into me, bruising me, naked flesh streaming against naked flesh naked flesh pouring wet against naked flesh, I . . . When I ache and ache and ache; I always ache; every day I ache; I . . . I need a man because I love men. I love their thick rough skins. I love the ways they totally know about everything so I don't need to know anything. They don't really know everything, but we'll forget about that. They take hold of me; they shove me around; and suddenly the weight of my own aggression's off me. I can go farther out. I can explore more. They're masculine which means they know about a certain society, this polite-death society which is their society, with which they know how to deal. So I don't have to deal with it. I don't want to. They provide a base for me in a society to which I feel alien. Otherwise I've got no reason to be in this world.

I can't get a man unless money's involved. I found this out in the brothel.

Maybe this is only cause I'm so ugly.

"Should I bother seeing people at all?" I ask Poirot.

Poirot's stumped.

"Whenever I see people, I can't stand them. They make my nerves snap. I can't stand seeing them cause I know they hate me."

"Did you murder the young girl?" Poirot asks.

"I don't like my friends anymore. I don't want to see anyone. I want to sit by myself, and play chess.

"I've got to paint. I've got to paint more and more, make something beautiful, make up for make away with this misery, this dragging . . ."

"You lack the analytical mind. You're too emotional to have planned this murder."

"The cops finally got Norvins' brother," Berthe exclaims. "They gave him the death sentence, and all he was doing was stealing."

"All I ever do is play with myself. I don't care about politics."

"When the cop arrested Clement, Clement hit him over the head with the end of a bottle. What d'you think of that? At his trial Clement said: 'The policeman arrested me in the name of the law; I hit him in the name of liberty'."

"Berthe, do you think it's better to fuck a man for money, or just to fuck for free?"

"Then Clement said: 'When society refuses you the right to existence, you must take it.'"

"I'll fuck any way I can get it. I love to fuck so much."

"The other day the cops arrested Charles Gallo."

"Huh," says Giannina.

"The anarchist who threw a bottle of vitriol into the middle of the Stock Exchange; fired three revolver shots into the crowd, and didn't kill anyone. When the cops got to him, he said, 'Long live revolution! Long live anarchism! Death to the bourgeois judiciary! Long live dynamite! Bunch of idiots!'"

"That stuff doesn't concern us. We're women. We know about ourselves, our cunts, not the crap you read in the newspapers. Who d'you think murdered the girl?"

" Maybe a person who lives in the same hell we live in. Sure we're waitresses. We're part of the meat market. We're the meat. That's how we get loved. We get cooked. We get our asses burned cause sex, like everything else, is always involved with money."

"I don't like to think and I don't trust people who think." Giannina kisses Berthe on her right ear.

"If we lived in a society without bosses," Berthe says seriously, "we'd be fucking all the time. We wouldn't have to be images. Cunt special. We could fuck every artist in the world."

"I'd like to fuck all the time."

"My heroine is Sophie Perovskaya." Giannina's slowly licking the inside of Berthe's ear. "Five years ago March first

The People's Will, a group she was part of, murdered Tsar Alexander II. As she died, she rejoiced, for she realized her death would deal a fatal blow to autocracy." Giannina blows into her ear. "I'd like to have the guts to follow that woman."

"I want to be a whore."

"Don't you understand the world in which we're living?" Berthe screams. "On Sunday May 21 the first detachment of Versailles troops entered the capital. This entrance caught the Commune unawares. Thiers' army made up of prisoners of war and provincial recruits shot everyone in sight. They killed 25,000 people. The Communards, retreating from Paris, burned as much as they could. Marshal MacMahon of the Versailles army declared order was restored. The death of the Paris Commune was the death of the workers' revolutionary power. Now we have to give up our lives to cause any destruction of this society."

Giannina kisses Berthe again and again. Her tongue slowly enters Berthe's full red mouth.

"We want men!" both women think. "Be a man to me! Fuck me. Fuck me. Lie on top of me. Drive it into me. We want women!"

Their warmth and need for warmth drive them into each other.

They feel confused. They're not sure they want each other, even though sweat's pouring out of their flesh and their cunt muscles're relaxing, opening with the agony of desire.

Naked flesh against naked flesh. Naked lips against naked lips. Naked cunt burning against naked cunt. Naked thighs against naked thighs. Bare shoulders twisting around bare shoulders. Naked tits against naked tits.

"Giannina" murmurs Berthe "sometimes I hate you. You're so beautiful every man's always creaming in his pants after you. I could never be so beautiful. When I'm with you, sometimes, I feel ugly." Her tongue flickers the aching nipples.

Her whole mouth goes to the nipple, and sucks.

The hair curling above the cunt, between the thighs, around the outer lips, in the red crack of the ass touches the thick pink outer lips touches the tiny red inner lips inside the outer lips touches the red berry at one end of the inner lips whose inside grows if it's grazed lightly enough touches the muscles and nerves spiralling as a canal away from the red inner lips. Berthe's thumb draws a slow pink spiral against the soft yielding breast flesh. Her right hand's fingertips grasp the heavy falling breast. The nipple rubs against the inside of her palm.

"Giannina, I don't want to. I think I'm falling in love with you. Help me not to, or don't let me get burned, I'm scared I'm going to be very very in love with you."

The wide open pink cunt lips. Giannina's fingers touch.

The thin slivers of red membrane.

As Giannina touches the membrane, lightly, very lightly, she sees the membrane move, the whole cunt quiver. Sigh. Lightly she draws her middle finger along the main fold . . .

She hears Berthe scream and scream. Berthe screams and screams. Berthe's in a world composed only of sensations. She doesn't know anything except what she feels. She rolls around on this wonderful mass of flesh and bones, yielding and non-yielding, her nerves rub into warm, wet, rough hairs. She writhes feels quivers shakes turns spins falls rises bounces squirms wiggles pants. Her sense of balance's rolling against Giannina.

Fucking. Fucking. Fucking. Feeling all the possible feelings which are needs in the world.

Giannina's the cat. She throws herself up, against Berthe because she wants Berthe. She wants to throw her body into Berthe's body because she wants to bask in Berthe's heat. Berthe's safety. Berthe's going to do it to her. Berthe looks so huge. Berthe's flaming hair. Berthe's blue eyes. Berthe's

huge hands. Berthe'll protect her: she can open herself totally
to Berthe . . .

Her cunt opens to Berthe's cunt. To all of Berthe's body
which's going to get inside her. Her mouth's open. Her
eyes're open. Her arms are open, groping wet heavy flesh.
Her legs're open. Wide. Her stomach's rending. Her whole
abdomen's opening. Her womb . . .

"I'm frightened. I want you. This's the sun. I want you,"
Berthe squeals.

"If you were a man, I could love you," says Giannina.

The Paris of 1886 is the Paris of the Conservatives, in spite
of the surprising, and painfully short presidency of the Radical
Rene Goblet; of General Boulanger; of the Opportunists
who're making Paris and France into an empire whose only
rival is Great Britain; of depression due to increasing imports
of American and Australian wheat, widespread phylloxera
destruction of grapevines, lack of natural sources such as coal
needed in this beginning industrial period. An act passed
July 1886 forbids the Orleans and Bourbon heirs access to
French soil. General Boulanger, the new Minister of War,
expels the Duc d'Aumale and the Duc de Chartres from the
Army. The general on the black horse's charming! Bismarck,
a bit too hastily, incarcerates a prominent unnamable French
person. Boulanger gets him released! But people're still
starving everywhere: strikes're increasing especially in the
mining, iron, and steel industries.

What can we know of such a period?

A particularly brutal strike and murder occurs in the
mining town of Decazeville.

The most important incident of the year, at least for us,
takes place not in France, but in Chicago, U.S.A. The most
industrialized city in the world. A city that's a giant factory.
In France the workers still support their bosses. The workers
want to be petit bourgeoisie. The new Marxist party, tiny

to begin with and composed of intellectuals, splits into the 'Possibilists' and the French Workers' Party. In Chicago the workers unite.

May Day, 1886.

The workers celebrate and demonstrate.

A strike's going on at the McCormick harvester works.

Two days later. Chicago cops shoot at strikers during a clash between strikers and blacklegs at the works.

Local anarchists hold a meeting at Haymarket, a large empty spot in Chicago, to protest the cop shootout.

The meeting goes peacefully enough. A heavy storm drives away most of the people. The police order the meeting to close. Samuel Fielden, one of the demonstration leaders, who's still speaking, objects. He tells the cop the meeting's orderly. The police lieutenant insists. Suddenly, a bomb explodes the crowd.

Who threw the bomb?

The day is wet, cold, and windy. One policeman, several other people wounded. The police start to shoot. Demonstrators policemen wounded killed.

The city panics! Bombers terrorists're going to take over! The police arrest nine prominent anarchists. One of the nine, Schnaubelt, disappears.

Another of the nine, Albert Parsons, who's been missing, turns himself in to the cops so he can share his friends' fate.

The defendant anarchists try to use their trial to put the conservative American government on the defensive:

Schwab (one of the anarchists): I demand the floor in the name of all the defendants.

Judge: You can't have the floor!

The anarchists: Speak, Schwab, speak!

Several jurymen: Your Honor, tell the defendants to shut up.

The D.A.: The defendants are to remain seated!

(All the anarchists stand up and scream.)

Judge: The court will not permit itself to be intimidated
by this uproar. I declare that, if the slightest disturbance
is injected into the trial, I shall bring in a verdict of guilt
against the defendants.

Several anarchists: Cut it short! Judge us now, without
letting us be heard! That won't take so long!

The anarchists (en masse): Condemn all of us!

All! All!

The court sentences four of the anarchists to death.

The court sentences four of the anarchists to long prison
terms.

During the appeal sessions, Albert Parsons speaks for eight
hours. Samuel Fielden speaks for three. Schwab calls for a
"state of society in which all human beings do right for the
simple reason that it's right and hate wrong because it's
wrong."

Lingg (a true terrorist who has manufactured bombs) expresses contempt for "your ORDER, your laws, your force-
propped authority."

The court changes none of the death or prison sentences.

My friends Vincent, Paul, Theo're starving. I'm dying for
lack of love. Suddenly I'm also starving because my mother
stops giving me money. I move into the brothel.

In the last bedroom of Norvins' brothel, a small dingy room
into which a beam of light occasionally filters, Rhys Chatham,
a prostitute, lives. Rhys is a tall red-hair, lanky, huge basket-
ball player's chest, broad shoulders, green eyes thin large
nose stiff spine. He's an ex-cop. In fact, he used to be Super-
intendent of the Paris police. He was a good, honest cop, as
cops go; he got his desire to work hard and be honest from
his religious parents. But he also wanted to find God, and
God isn't in the police force. This's the wildness and mean-
ness of Rhys' character.

"Masturbate in front of me," Rhys says to me.

CHAPTER TWO

LONGING FOR BETTER THINGS

"**Y**OU know that city called San Francisco," Giannina says to Vincent Van Gogh one day in the brothel. "Huh," says Vincent.

"You know. The place where all the criminals and perverts live. They've got lots of earthquakes there so the U.S.A. government encourages all its misfits to live there so maybe the earthquake'll kill them."

"Huh," says Vincent.

"I want to go there, Vincent. I love this American poet Ron Silliman who lives in San Francisco."

"Giannina you shouldn't be here, in the brothel. You're only a lowly waitress."

"I'm desperately in love. I'm going to kill myself if I don't get to San Francisco. Maybe I can become a prostitute; earn enough money to get to San Francisco."

"You're too much like a cat. You're not tough enough, and you don't like people enough. You're good in bed, G., when you love someone and only when you love someone. That's a problem."

"You're not so terrific yourself, big boy, and I've heard that you've turned a few tricks. I've seen you go crazy when you're in bed with me; you love what I do to you; what d'ya mean I'm not any good in bed? And I've never fallen in love with you! You're too young anyway!"

"Does this guy in San Francisco love you?"

"I'm not even sure he knows who I am."

Vincent sighs. These waitresses sure can be stupid. "Giannina," he moans, "don't go to San Francisco. In this city there's no such thing as love. We're all too much into doing our art: when we fuck, we fuck, but really, fucking's not very important . . .

"All there is is art . . .

"Giannina, we're all friends here . . .

"Giannina, you can't go running half-way across the world . . .

"You can't race to San Francisco after some guy who doesn't even know you or love you . . ."

Giannina the cat's not listening to this claptrap. She's too sensual to be smart. She's not sure what she wants. There's a faint idea in her mind, a kind of shitty goosh feeling. A glimmering knowledge of feeling for someone so strongly nothing else exists. A possibility of living in a world to which she's not always alien. San Francisco!

San Francisco!

"Listen," Poirot tells Rhys the prostitute, "we have to use our brains. If we don't find this murderer, more murders'll occur in this brothel.

"Who could have possibly murdered the girl?"

"I don't know," Rhys replies.

"O.K. According to the coroner's report, the girl was murdered during Norvins' party. Could anyone have gotten from the bar or from the outside street into the party?"

"No."

"Then it was someone at the party . . ."

"It was one of us . . ."

"Who exactly was at the party? Do any of these people dislike the little girl who was murdered?"

"Norvins was at the party. Vincent, you know, Toulouse, Paul, all those artists who hang out at the brothel. And their teacher friends: Theo, who's also Vincent's brother, and Pere Tanguy, headmaster of the school Vincent teaches at. Marie,

the girl who was murdered, went to that school. Marie's
family, her mother brother and sister, were there. They're
all prostitutes and older than Marie. Berthe, Giannina, and
Veronique. All of us: myself, Peter, Garrett. And Zidler, the
whore lawyer."

"Who are these people?"

"Veronique, Berthe, Giannina work as waitresses for
Norvins. They're too stupid to murder anyone. Peter Garrett
and I are Norvins' boys. Marie's mom, sis, and brother sometimes work for Norvins. Vincent Van Gogh Toulouse Lautrec
Paul Gauguin the artists hang around here cause they work
so hard, they need to calm down to play hard so they can
start working hard again. Theo and Tanguy hang out with
them. Zippy Zidler's the family lawyer for this whole
neighborhood."

"The murderer must be one of these people."

"Listen Poirot, you have to stop thinking like that. We all
love each other here."

"I hate every one and thing I know," that mad flighty girl
Giannini confesses. "All I think about is Ron.

"I think about his blond moustache.

"I think about his uncircumsized cock. I never saw one
before.

"I think about how he gets so scared in bed, when he
really loves someone, that his cock can't get hard.

"Now he's wearing a red flannel shirt. Thin off-white pants
that make his hips look wide. He's got a funny flat kind of
heavy body. A hat slung low over his eyes.

"He's so smart.

"He's very male: he goes after whoever he wants. He never
pushes.

"He's strong and quiet.

"He knows so much more than me he can teach me stuff
I don't know.

"He's so secure, he'll give me some stability. I'm too flighty.

"He doesn't love me which means he'll be mean to me so I can look up to him even more.

"He's less sensual than me."

"I thought you didn't know this guy, G. Maybe you just want to get out of this doom claustrophobic filth city like the rest of us. There must be someplace else besides here."

Giannina scratches her dark head. "I don't think that's the only reason I'm falling in love with Ron, though I certainly hate this city. I have to be totally dull in this city. If I open myself to feeling anything, I'll get totally destroyed."

"Yeah. Paris' a rotting stinking shithole. Every now and then, suddenly, I realize that no person should be able to live in such filth. I ask the person I'm with: 'why d'you stay here?' The invariable reply 'cause the pressure excitement keeps me working hard' proves my friend's becoming immersed in the filth.

"I don't know. I don't want to think about being here too hard.

"Sometimes I think I'm going crazy: I'm walking down the filthy street to work, and I think I'm going crazy. The skin on my head starts swelling. My fingers, hands, shoulders, legs, feet. My sinuses are pounding, I've got to run. The air's too thick. There's too many people. Thousands of people're sitting on rows of folding chairs in one tiny filthy room. Water's gushing out of their skins. I'm one of these people. Nobody says a word. Nobody complains. More and more people enter the room. They tell us to go to another room. We go to another room and sit on identical folding chairs. One person says they're about to close off the cities cause our government can't handle the city problems any more and doesn't need the cities.

"We'll never get out again.

"Ron is so wonderful, Vincent."

"Giannina, if you have to fall in love, fall in love with someone who's rich. We need money to get out of here."

"Ron was my closest friend when I lived in San Francisco.

"I never talked to anyone when I lived out there. I was very shy.

"One night I was sitting in a bar in North Beach with my friend Andrei. We were drinking Angels' Clits.

"A friend of Andrei's named Jim walked into the bar.

"After we had drunk a lot of Angels' Clits, we decided to bust up this poetry reading that was happening a few blocks away. Andrei and Jim walked me in a shopping cart into the reading. I jumped out of the cart just as it began to clatter down a series of steep steps . . .

"Andrei wanted to go into the reading cause in the reading people'd come to him and tell him he was famous. Jim and I lumbered into an empty theatre right above the reading.

"Jim began to eat me. His jaw dislocated. A guy named Stanley, another friend of Andrei's punched it back into place. We know Stanley was a Buddhist genius. People were coming out of the reading, so Andrei, Jim, Stanley and I stood by the door, greeted the people by kissing my nipples. I propositioned the women.

"Suddenly I noticed some man's eyes on me.

"He looked straight. I decided he was a creep.

"He said, 'Excuse me, are you Giannina? I'm Ron Silliman. Bruce Leary told me you're a waitress.'

" 'Yeah,' I said, and ignored him. I went back to kissing Jim.

"I don't remember the next time I saw him. I got to know Rae Armantrout, one of Ron's closest friends, who's bi like me. We hung out together. I guess I got to know Ron gradually. My closest friend at that time, Clay, decided he liked David Melnick and David's friends.

"I remember the first time I wanted to fuck Ron. We were on a bus on Market Street. I asked, 'Do you want to come home with me?' He replied, 'No.' I figured he didn't want to fuck me.

"About a month before I planned to leave San Francisco, I was planning to leave San Francisco temporarily." Giannina rubs her black-haired cat's head. "Ron moved to a house near my house. We started going drinking a lot. One night we were drinking in a bar called The Pub. We spent hours talking about writing and people. When we left, I put my hand on Ron's shirt, told him to button his shirt so he wouldn't catch cold. I figured if he wanted to fuck me, he'd touch my hand.

"He didn't."

Vincent's not even listening anymore to this inanity. He's got to figure out how to get out of Montmartre.

"We drank and talked together twice more. At that time I felt I had more in common with Ron than with anyone else I knew.

"The night before I was going to Paris, I went over to Ron's house to see him once more and say goodbye to him. We talked for hours, again about writing. Also, something about his ex-wife. He was becoming friendly again with his ex-wife. He was tired. About midnight I said, ' I'd better go.' He says, 'You can stay the night if you want.'

"I feel confused. I don't know what to do. I figure I should stay the night because I've been wanting to. I don't know how to approach Ron sexually. There's never been anything sexual between us. I walk into the tiny room in which's his bed, leaf through his new work. It looks terrific. I turn around to him. He's larger than me. Is he as frightened as I am?

"I'm not confused: I'm frightened.

"I don't understand why Ron's face's so close to mine. I'm not used to seeing Ron like this. His face looks strange: his yellow moustache his blue eyes. He looks too familiar and not familiar enough. We take our clothes off. He looks totally strange to me now he's naked. I can recognize his head, but

not his body. His head doesn't belong to his body. He's very
tender to me.

"I want hot violent passionate sex. That way the intensity
of my physical feelings will make me forget, not have to deal
with the person I'm with, the total confusion I'm feeling.

"Ron's so gentle with me. I can't handle it. He wants to
kiss my lips. I'm committed to going to Paris. I'm feeling
crazy. He tells me some woman he's been fucking's great in
bed. I should fuck her. I'm wondering if I'm good in bed. I
keep licking nibbling at, squeezing, sucking, rubbing his cock
so I don't have to look at his face.

"As soon as I can, I'm running out of the house, into the
San Francisco night, and home."

"Giannina, do you even know this guy?" Vincent asks.

"I love Ron mainly because I love his work. I always fall
in love that way. Ron's a great poet: His varied sensuous
language reflects and questions itself. What emerges, finally,
is a restless deeply perceiving consciousness. A consciousness, finally, I don't understand. I adore him."

"We'll get out by going to Tahiti," Vincent says. "We can
take a freighter past Morea to Papeete. Then we'll go into
the countryside. As far away as we can get from Paris. No
one ever works in this countryside. No one does art, for art
is a category separate from other activities. No one needs
such separations in Tahiti cause no one needs to escape. We
don't have to suffer all the time.

"From Tahiti, we'll sail to the Fiji Islands. We're gonna
get out of here."

"I want to live with Ron for a while," Giannina decides.
"I don't think he wants to live with me. I don't know how
he feels. I know he doesn't want to live with me. I know I'm
crazy saying this. If I don't say this, if I don't keep throwing
myself into the unknown, I'll die. Vincent, Vincent, do you
understand what I'm saying?"

CHAPTER THREE

THE DESPERATION OF THE POOR

IN Paris, the poor are desperate.

Vincent was born on March 30, 1853, at Zundert, a village of 3,000 inhabitants near the Belgian frontier in Brabant, Holland. His father, Theodore, the pastor of the village, was himself the son of a pastor who had 12 children. Three of Vincent's uncles're picture-dealers; one of them, also called Vincent, carries on his business at The Hague.

Theodore and his wife, Anna Carbentus, have six children: three sons, Vincent, and Theo who's four years the younger, Cornelis, and three daughters, Anna, Elisabeth, and Wilhelmina. The family's a most united one, like many others in a country where the domestic virtues and adherence to Christian doctrine are the foundations of society. Like so many others too, in Holland, the Van Goghs are middle-class citizens living narrow and monotonous lives, still further restricted by Calvinist austerity. Such families often dread the emergence in their midst of some rebellious member likely at any moment to shatter the rigid framework of the home and destroy its unity, an adventurer destined to carve an empire from the ends of the earth, a scientist who may later revolutionize the laws of physics, a thinker who breaks new ground, or an artist whose turbulent genius will scandalize his native land before it comes to idolize him.

The Calvinism of Holland produced a capitalistic spirit. It's doubtful whether anyone, the preacher Theodore . . . Anna . . . appreciated the child Vincent's virtues and needs.

Most poets and artists revenge themselves upon society for their early humiliations. But Vincent always blamed himself alone for his sufferings. A frustrated and misunderstood child, not given its due need of affection, ends as a man without roots, in rebellion or bewilderment, almost always embittered. Such are myself, Gauguin, and Van Gogh: sufferers who make others suffer. "One may have a blazing hearth in one's soul," I remember Vincent wrote, "and yet no one ever comes to sit by it. Passersby only see a wisp of smoke rising from the chimney and continue on their way."

At sixteen Vincent was given a post as salesman in the art gallery formerly managed by his Uncle Vincent at The Hague. He was then transferred by the latter to the Parisian firm of Goupil. The boy stayed in this gallery for four years and left it in May 1873 for the London branch. There he fell in love with his landlady's daughter, Ursula. She rejected him. He returned home. Four months later, he was back in the London Goupil Gallery on May 15, 1875, in a state of desperation.

"Toulouse," Poirot says to me one day, "we're going to have to visit Marie's family. They live in the poorest section of Montmartre. I hope you won't be disgusted by what you're going to see."

"An artist has to see everything," I loftily reply.

"Are you an artist, mon ami? I thought you were a whore. Grab your crutches if you don't want to trip over the drunken bums."

The streets of Montmartre are filthy. Garbage cans and dogshit lie strewn over the sidewalks. Bums lie under the garbage for warmth. Cats run through the collapsing railings; the buildings landlords have burned down to collect insurance, their tenants can no longer pay rent so why not burn down everything, this's the beginning of socialism; the churchyard graves.

There's only one law: don't stop walking as fast as possible.

Not for any reason. Thefts, pushing, kidnappings, tricks, murders: all these crimes take place in the open.

The street.

People die in front of other people on the street. There's very little room. Poirot and I have to rush down the Rue Cailancourt. We don't want to see any murders. If we see any murders, we might have to solve them.

We see a woman vomiting in the street.

"Mrs. Freilicher," Poirot bows, "we've been looking for you."

Her bleary eyes stare at us.

"We're investigating your daughter's murder. We thought you might be able to help us."

The woman vomits again. The vomit's red and green and blue and brown. It adds some color to the street.

"Lady, your daughter Marie died the other day.

"If we can find out who murdered her, we might be able to prevent future murders.

"Did your daughter have any enemies?"

The woman blinks at us. She understands nothing. Obviously poverty's destroyed her mind. "Mrrlrrp," her mouth gurgles.

"Marie said she had seen a murder. What'd she mean by this?"

"Marie's a liar." The old woman looks as dazed as ever.

"Mommy, mommy, mommy."

"Go away Missia. I'm talking to someone. Goddamn children."

A thin girl wearing black shirt and black pants runs in front of my eyes. She slaps her mother hard across the face. "Mommy. Pull yourself together. Something's happened to Melvyn!"

"Who gives a shit?"

The girl turns to Poirot. "Do ya understand? Melvyn my

brother's out there. A brick hit him; we were walking. He fell to the ground. He's dead."

"Where'd he die?" Poirot asks.

"Rue Cailancourt. A few blocks from here."

Right near the brothel.

"Missia, your sister died a few days ago in a house near where your brother just died. We're trying to find out who killed her. Your mother isn't able to help us. Right before your sister died, she said she had just seen a murder. Do you know if she had witnessed a murder?"

The thin girl looks at us as if she's testing us. What can she get out of us? What're we good for? She's got to survive. Her mother's a vomiting nuisance. She wiggles her hips. One of her eyes is lower than her other. "Marie was a liar."

"Then she didn't see a murder?"

"She was stupid." The girl's lower eye winks. Her straggly hair looks like it's wet.

"If Marie had seen a murder, would she have told your brother Melvyn?"

"She never saw any murder. Forget about it."

"Did she talk to Melvyn a lot?"

"Melvyn was like her. Greedy. That's why he died."

In December 1877, without waiting for an appointment— of which he was to be apprised a month later—Vincent went off to the Borinage district of Belgium, intent on revealing the light of the gospel to those who most needed it: miners living in extreme poverty and engaged in the hardest possible work. He flattered himself, with the touching presumption of a novice, that he was capable of bringing consolation and the Christian faith to these outcasts.

Then he began his apostolic career whose distressing episodes are so well known. He spent himself with selfless generosity: teaching the children, tending the sick, distributing his scanty possessions, money, clothing, and furniture. He overflowed with love, less for God if the truth must be told, than for humanity. In spite of his efforts to prove his compassion and devotion to the miners, he didn't succeed in convincing them. Moreover, since he's an indifferent speaker, his preaching had no effect on these unfortunate people whom he had thought the most likely of all to listen to him. Whatever advance and sacrifices he made, the Borain proletariat misunderstood him as had his own family. The repeated rebuffs which met his anxious longing to communicate with and be received by and among the workers threw him back, time after time, into his irremediable solitude. It was even questionable whether these hapless creatures would have agreed to an improvement of their lot. Bernardin St. Pierre used to say he never met any human being who didn't revel in his own misery. Vincent stripped himself of everything he had and made himself the poorest of the poor. He even blackened his face so as to look just like the rest of them. Whatever he did, he remained a stranger among the miners.

On April 12, 1881, Vincent took refuge with his parents at Etten. A cousin named Kee came to spend a holiday at Etten. Vincent fell deeply in love with her and proposed. It was a perfectly natural proceeding. He was 28 and wanted to found a family, to put an end to the loneliness that tormented him. Kee refused him. She said she had promised to remain faithful to the memory of her husband. And her parents were utterly opposed to the idea of a penniless son-in-law, with no settled work, and, of all things, an artist. Vincent persisted. She fled to her father in Amsterdam.

He wrote her again and again. She didn't reply. Desperate, he set off to see her. When he called at her house, she declined to appear. He insisted, with an obstinacy described by his uncle as "disgusting," on seeing her. He held his hand over a lighted lamp on the table and said he would keep it there till she arrived. Her horrified parents saw the flame begin to burn the motionless flesh. At last Vincent fainted.

He reached Antwerp on November 28, 1885, and at once rented a room at 194 Beeldekensstraat. In the daytime, he did his own work and attended courses at the Municipal Academy. From 8 till 10 evenings, he practiced drawing from life at a class in the Grand Marche. From 10 until midnight, he went to another life class. For all this art he needed expensive materials which he bought with the necessarily limited funds provided by Theo. When having to choose between working and satisfying his hunger, he was condemned to exhausting undernourishment. He lived exclusively on bread, a little cheese, and coffee. Consequently, he was in a state of perpetual weakness. He suffered from internal pains, lost about ten of his teeth, and coughed incessantly. One day, when he was feeling ill, he could no longer hide the truth from Theo: "I must tell you that I'm literally starving."

He left Antwerp suddenly, for Paris, where he arrived February 28, 1886. Poirot again interrupts my thoughts.

"Toulouse," growls. "You have to wake up. If you keep dreaming all the time, you're going to get killed. I want you to accompany me to T.T.'s house."

"Who's T.T.?"

"Rhys' brother. He knows everyone in Montmartre. He can tell us which of Norvins' guests at the party knew Marie. If any of them wanted Marie out of the way. Oh, also, if there've been any unsolved murders lately."

"You mean maybe Marie wasn't lying? Everyone says she was a lousy little liar."

"T.T. lives on the Rues des Martyrs. The other side of Montmartre. The only thing I know about T.T.'s that he's supposed to be a hermit . . ."

"I'm miserable. I'm totally miserable. I can't see anyone because everyone hates me. I don't want to see you here!"

"T.T.," Poirot says, "we're not going to hurt you. We have to talk to you about Norvins' brothel. There's been a murder."

"I feel so much, sometimes I think I'm going crazy. You won't hurt me? Where the fuck's my bottle? Come on in." I see a heavy-set man. Small face. Small eyes. Six feet three inches. Businessman's clothes.

"I'm an outsider. I can't talk to anyone. My emotions're so strong, they take me over. They drive me. They totally rule me."

"Listen T.T. Three days ago, someone murdered this twerp at one of Norvins' parties. Today a brick hit the twerp's brother's head and killed him."

"I know all about it," T.T. says. "I was at the party." He picks up a newspaper and starts shredding it. Hands me a bottle of rum.

I started drinking as much rum as possible.

"I've known Norvins for years. She was the last person I used to visit. Now I visit no one. She's a good woman: hard as nails. Every woman who succeeds in the business has to be that tough. It's the only way women survive. No wonder I'm refusing to leave this house, get involved in the violent hustling and desires of my friends."

I silently nod my head.

"I've got just enough money to remain in this prison, erect my own fantasies." He grabs for the bottle. Takes a few swigs. I'm sitting so the massive left side of his body leans against my right shoulder, arm, and thigh. "I sent Rhys to Norvins'. Rhys' young and needs guidance. No place for guidance like a brothel. The money he earns'll help me maintain this hermitage."

"Prostitution's supporting everyone these days," I murmur. I start drinking again.

"As I was saying, I was at Norvins' party. I hadn't seen Norvins for a while. The day after the party, I started being a hermit. I don't think anyone who was at the party really knew the murdered girl. She was just a nuisance. That's all Rousseau and Seurat really knew of her."

"She said she had witnessed a murder?"

"Yes. You know all these young girls'll do anything to get attention. That's all she wanted. She'd do anything. A desperate little girl. Anyway, no one noticed her once the party began. She must have been hiding somewhere. I remembered her when I saw her hanging over the side of the bobbing tub, dead."

"What I really want to know is whether there've been any unsolved murders in Montmartre lately."

"You think that brat was telling the truth . . . No one who's poor cares much about the truth . . ."

Suddenly I realize I want to fuck with this strange heavy man. I don't understand why. I shouldn't be attracted to him cause he obviously thinks I'm ugly. I must be getting desperate. I drink more rum.

"Every day thousands of murders occur in Montmartre. How else can a poor person eat? But what murders would Marie have possibly witnessed? There's the Ganneron shoot-out. In fact, it took place right outside Marie's building: 11 Rue Ganneron. The landlord of 11 Rue Ganneron tried to burn down the building. He realized he couldn't keep collecting rent from people who had no more money and were going through garbage cans, looking for food. He decided to burn down the building to collect city fire insurance. One of the neighborhood leather boys who lives in the building caught the landlord starting the fire. He rushed at the landlord, shiv in hand. This started the largest gang war that's occurred in years. The landlord's mongoloid son, who lives across the street, sees the leather kid making the death rush. He throws a knife into the kid's right arm. This son and the kid belong to separate, and very important, Montmartre gangs. So before ya' know it, it's an all-out gang war. BOOM BOOM BOOM. I saw one kid step out of 14 Rue Ganneron with a cardboard box containing fourteen Molotov cocktails. Stuffed with rags. Ready to go.

"The cops never interfere in Montmartre politics. They're too scared they'll get burned. They don't even clean up the dead bodies: the rats can do that."

"I think I'm looking for another type of murder," Poirot says thoughtfully.

I look at T.T.'s red face. As I see his eyes swerve towards mine, I quickly turn away my face. I'm scared he'll notice me. I'm scared that I feel so strongly. Does he want me?

"There was the Haitian voodoo killing: That happened three days before the twerp got bumped off. This guy and his wife weren't getting along too well. Well, they were getting along like most couples these days. He'd go to some whorehouse, not an uppity one like Norvins', for a quickie. She'd screw the garbageman or the delivery boy every now and then. All clean and sane. Like every one else, this couple gets poorer and poorer. The poorer they get, the more they take it out on each other. How're poor people supposed to live? The guy starts saving his shit: he smears it on the street outside his house. He probably thinks he's cleaning up the neighborhood. The wife starts screwing every man who'll go down on her. If she can't eat, she might as well screw. White-blonde hair. Luscious breasts. The kind of woman who gets every man hard who sees her and who won't give anything away. Her eyes're cold. She's too hungry. The husband wants to go to Haiti, Mexico City, Acapulco. He disappears. When he returns, he's very quiet. He complains he's got a radio in his head and the radio's getting the wrong channel. The U.S.A. government stuck the radio in his head in Mexico City. He's programmed not to say any more. One day he's going to kill some important political figure. Everyone in Montmartre thinks he's crazy. There's no politics in this slum. He's known as 'Baron Murder'. One day, on the Champs de Mars, the wife, who's called Connie, is found dead. Her white hair flows on to the sidewalk. A white satin sheath cloaks her huge tits. The huge slit in her throat contains no

more blood. She was out walking with some boyfriend: one
of the neighborhood brats saw her. But he couldn't tell who
was with her. And the husband's gone.

"Connie's friend, Arthur, also got bumped off. Connie and
Arthur, when they desperately needed money, would work
for this solicitor. Name's Zidler, or something like that.
Actually . . . as I remember . . . Arthur was the one working
for Zidler. There was a dope war going on at the time. It
may still be going on. Zidler's located on the Avenue St.
Charles right off the Place de Clichy. Near Rue de Ganneron,
ya' know? The Avenue St. Charles people, all Africans, want
to clean up their street. The street doesn't want to get cleaned
up. The pushers bump off a few residents. So the residents
form a vigilante committee: any pusher who comes near the
block's gonna get it. Then the cops rush in, full blast! Bang,
bang, bang! They've got to help their friends the pushers.
Arthur's somehow in the middle of all this. He's using Zidler's
office as a pusher-station. On the side, he's doing some
forging. That's the theory. He's also screwing this hot
number, Clay Fear, who's got a jealous boyfriend. Who
knows? One night, Arthur's found stabbed in the back. Right
in Zidler's office. What a thing to happen in a respectable
solicitor's office! Three days before Connie's slaughter. No
one knows why he's been murdered.

"Then there's Mrs. Alexander's death. She's an old rich
woman who lives off the Rue de Clignancourt. Anyone could
have bumped her off, she's so mean. She lives in Montmartre
and she thinks poor people don't exist. One night she dies.
Death happens to everyone. Who cares if she died naturally
or not? Her will says she leaves everything to some whore
who was living in her house and making it with every bit of
trash off the street. This whore used to do all Mrs. Alexander's
correspondence. Zidler, Mrs. Alexander's lawyer, says the
whore forged the will. No money for you, honey. So the
whore leaves. She was only trying to survive."

"I've got to get back to the brothel so I can requestion Norvins about these murders. T.T., could you get Toulouse home? She's quite drunk."

"I'm madly in love with you, T.T.," I whisper. "My cunt and womb are flaming so much I think I'm becoming a nymphomaniac. If I want you this much, you must want me."

"I think I want you very much Tooloose. I've never had a cripple before." I feel my face muscles twitch. I can't move. I see his face muscles twitch.

Suddenly we're kissing. We're kissing like both of us have never kissed before.

It seems to be Vincent's longing for the wholesome and his loathing of shams which makes it hard for him to endure Paris. In this late fall of 1886, he begins to despair. In his fur cap and goatish cloak he tramps the snow-covered streets in deep depression. He has no idea where to go, where to find a trace of warm human feeling. He has no friends to call upon. Anyhow, their paltry rivalries disgust him.

As I fuck T.T., all I think about is my brother Vincent.

CHAPTER FOUR

THE CREATION OF THE WORLD

A T night, after all our customers have gone home, Peters, Rhys, Garrett, and I lie in the brothel living room. We try to forget our weary bodies by telling each other bedtime stories. Stories that'll make us dream and sleep.

Peter's rubbing his sore red cock. "I'm going to tell," he says, "the first story tonight:

THE CREATION OF THE WORLD

A cat who has one green whisker and one white whisker keeps getting drunk. She's in love with a big hairy baboon who won't notice her.

When she gets drunk, she lies next to anyone: an elephant, a rat, a stick, even a human. She rubs and rolls and pounces and roars and shuffles and whimpers and prowls. She then smells all the smells in the world.

"Mr. Baboon," she say, "what can I do to make you love me? I'll do anything for you I want you to know that."

The baboon, barely noticing her, says, "You can't make me love you. But it's a depression this year: the rain won't come down because it's in a bad mood; there're almost no plants; I can't get enough to eat. You can bring me some food to show me how much you love me."

The little cat licks her white whisker then she licks her green whisker she runs rushes pounces leaps saunters everywhere, and she brings the baboon all the food that exists in the world.

The baboon looks at all the food that exists in the world. He smiles. He opens his red mouth so wide he blots out the sun. Into this vast wasteland he throws all the bananas all the plums all the mangoes all the kiwis all the apricots all the eggplants all the sugar cane all the honey all the basil all the edible plants and liquids that exist. He swallows. Now there's no more food left in the world.

The little cat looks up at the big hairy baboon. "Do you love me, baboon, now that you're fat and happy?"

"You can't make me love you," growls the baboon. "But the snakes are giving me trouble this year. They want me to pay taxes on the trees I use as my home. I want to have power over the snakes."

The little cat sighs. She'll do anything so the big hairy baboon'll love her. She catches all the mice and rats in the world, plays with them until they're dead. Then she ties them to her tail, one after the other. A long string of mice and rats. All the snakes that exist start following this one little cat.

The cat gives her mice-and-rat tail to the baboon. Now the baboon controls all the snakes in the world.

"Do you love me, darling?" murmurs the shy little cat.

"You can't make me love you stupid!" the baboon growls. "All I care about is power. I want to control everyone in the world."

The little cat shivers. She doesn't want to help the big hairy gross baboon control everyone. She runs into an old falling-apart house, and hides.

There're no more plants and liquids in the world, so all the animals are forced to eat each other. This is known as scarcity and depression. The lizards alligators crocodiles eat the fish. The hippos snap up the crocodiles. The red ants nibble at the hippos. The anteaters yump up the ants. The wild black hairy boars swallow the anteaters. The hungry black leopards attack the boars. The wild antelopes' horns pierce through the hungry black leopards. The elephants gobble up the wild antelopes. Huge hungry bones-sticking-out tigers drive their jaws into the elephants. The big fish who are left, cause all the little fish are in their bellies, the big sharks snap up the huge hungry bones-sticking-out tigers.

And what about the humans? They were all eaten up long ago. They never did know how to survive.

The big hairy baboon whose stomach is as big as his head, eats every animal he can get his hands on.

All the fish go into his stomach. All the insects go into his stomach. All the birds, the pretty little parakeets who fall in love with whatever animal they're around and who think they are that animal, the doves who're constantly committing suicide because they're so stupid, go into his stomach. All the plant-eating grass-eating animals, the giraffes, and the horses, and the zebras, the water buffalo who loves to fuck go into his stomach. Now the gross baboon's stomach is bigger than his head.

The baboon's so big, the huge hungry bones-sticking-out tigers and the lean sleek black leopards, the crocodiles alligators and piranhas of the big-teeth jaws can't figure out how to sink their teeth into him. The baboon's stomach is too full. So the baboon eats all the animals with huge teeth. Now the gross baboon's stomach's as big as a tent.

The huge elephant tries to kick the baboon. He starts running at this monstrosity of a baboon. There are no plants no rivers to cut down the elephants speed. Thump, thump, thump! The huge elephant feet. Tramp, Tramp, Tramp. Huge holes left in the surface of the world. Closer . . . Closer . . . The elephant's almost next to the hairy baboon. The elephant's almost on top of the hairy baboon. The baboon can no longer see the elephant: the elephant's running so fast. He sees a grey mist cover the flat barren surface of the earth.

WHOOMP! The baboon's stomach is so huge and hard, it's harder than the hardest rock in the world because there're so many animals plants and liquids in this stomach, this stomach is so dense and immense; the elephant falls right over it. PLUMP! The elephant falls flat on his long sensitive nose. Before he can tell what's happened to him, the horrible evil gross baboon has eaten him up.

Now the horrible baboon's stomach is so huge, it rubs against the white moon. This stomach is so dense, it weighs as much as the earth. So there exist three balls: earth, baboon, and moon.

The little cat's been watching everything.

She's been watching everything from her hide-out in the old dilapidated house.

She's starving. She has to find food so badly she comes crawling out of her hiding-place.

The only being who exists besides her is the gross hairy baboon.

The baboon sees this skinny, crawling, purring creature. He wants her so badly that, finally, after all this time, he's in love with her. He wants her more than anything else in the world!

He sings the following song to make her come purring to him:

Finally I've found you love
I realize I have to open up

The shy little cat doesn't move. She's much too weak.
The baboon sings another song:

I'm scared you'll hurt me
I've never let myself love anyone

I don't want you to hurt me and I
don't want to stop being this open

The cat doesn't move. She's too hungry to love anyone.
The baboon sings another heart-rending song:
I don't understand love
it's not rational

The little cat doesn't move. She just doesn't care.
All existence's silent.

The little cat's dreaming: She's dreaming of a forest where white leopards lie down among the free-floating giraffes black rivers run silently by tiny bears graze in the low bushes the wind smells of shit and grass and crushed leaves and cinnamon bark huge hippos yawn and catch flies in their mouths a human staring at his long red prick he doesn't know what to do with it a wasp lands on it and stings while the black rain liquid drips on the shiny plants down in the black soil and up through the thick green shining plant black liquids coursing through the forest grounds coming out of the animals the crocodiles who wait to snap at the stupid deer the wolves who talk to each other the little cat plays with everyone by rubbing against the hot skin then running just slightly faster than the other animal, teasing coming small white bears rise up bat their paws against each other's face. The little cat's not dreaming anymore.
This is how the world came to be.

And now that the world exists . . .

" 'STOP IT, TED,' I SCREAMED WHEN HE FINALLY RELEASED ME. BUT HE DIDN'T HEAR. HE WAS LIKE A MADMAN: OVERCOME WITH LUST. I WAS TOTALLY IN HIS POWER, COMPLETELY HELPLESS."

Fear, like an electric shock, ran through my body as Bill turned the car onto the deserted country road. I knew what was coming, the grand finish toward which the events of the evening had been leading. I hadn't tried to stop it. Deep down inside I knew that it was what I really wanted, and as the car bumped down the old dirt road I prayed inwardly that this time everything would work out, that I would be able to go through with it. Bravely I tried to fight down the familiar feeling of terror, but the attempt was useless. Slowly, surely, it began to take control of me, increasing as we rocked closer and closer to the end of the road.

I watched Bill as he drove, wondering if he had any idea of the way I felt. No. Of course not. He thought I was just another girl, maybe prettier than most, but basically like everybody else. He had no idea of the struggle going on inside my head or the dark secret that lay in my past. But I knew that all too soon he would find out what I was really like. Then he would be gone also, just like all the others.

We were near the end of the road and Bill slowed the car to a stop along the side. He switched off the lights. Then, stretching his arms above his head, he gave a long, contented sigh.

"Wow," he said, "it's a terrific night! Listen to the birds."

"I am," I said, trying to sound calm even though my heart was beating so violently I could hardly even speak.

Bill turned his face to me and smiled. It was dark and I could barely make out his features. His light brown hair looked black. The moonlight glittering in his eyes hid their blue and turned his freckled face ash-white. Although I knew he was good-looking, the darkness made him seem more a monster than a man. Without wanting to, I started to shake. Bill reached out and put his hand lightly on my leg.

"What's the matter? Are you cold?"

"Yes, a little," I answered quietly, even though my inner voice was screaming, "No, I'm not cold, you fool: I'm scared half to death."

"Come here, baby. I'll warm you up."

I wanted to go to him and I didn't want to go to him. I wanted him to love me like I wanted to eat. I didn't want him to turn me away. Then I'd be out in the cold again. Like I always was.

I was scared. I was more scared than I'd been before. I had done this. I had gotten myself in this situation. I could have been stronger. "Baby," his hot breath was rasping my flesh. I could feel his hand play with the tips of my breasts under my bra. I jumped back.

"What's the matter, baby. Scared of daddy? Come to daddy, baby, o baby . . ." He started moaning again and put his arms around me to draw me into him. His huge lips descended on my lips and I felt his tongue, his tongue in the middle of my mouth.

Something in me clicked. I wrenched myself out of his arms.

"What's the matter with you?" Bill looked at me queerly. "You sick or something."

"I, I can't, Bill. I wanted to, I wanted to do everything with you, but I can't."

"You've been coming on hot and heavy all night. You couldn't keep your hands off me until we got out here. What d'you think I am? I'm not going to let you tease me and control me." His eyes looked mean and heavy. I had never seen him like this before. Now he made me really frightened. He put one hand on the opening of my shirt. "You're going to give, girl, you're going to give me what you've been promising. I don't take teasing from no one."

"Bill," I gasped, "I just can't. Please don't be angry with me. I can't stand it when people are angry with me. I can't explain. Just drive me home . . ."

He almost hit me, and then he stopped. I could feel him make the decision. He put his foot on the gas pedal and the car started up. All the way home I felt miserable. I couldn't say anything to him. I couldn't give him what he wanted. When he said good-night in a cold mechanical voice, all I could do was murmur good-night and get out of the car.

I stood looking at the moon for a few moments before unlocking the front door and going inside. The evening had started out so beautifully, so romantically. But I had managed to ruin it. Like so many times before, I had become terrified at the thought of physical intimacy with a man. It seemed like I would never be able to keep a fellow of my own. The once lovely night had become a melancholy symbol of everything my life had ever been . . .

As I lay down on my bed, my future lay bleakly before me, that of a lonely old maid, yearly growing more sour and miserable. I had hoped Bill would save me from such a life.

Somehow I made it through work the next day. I was nervous and irritable. I'm always like that when I get upset because I'm angry at myself and don't know how to handle my anger.

Finally, when I got home, I fell into a soft arm-chair. I collapsed. Since the living room lights were out, I knew my parents weren't home. Finally, I could let myself go and I sobbed and sobbed.

I don't know how long I lay sobbing in the dark. The doorbell rang, but it was in the distance, and I didn't want to answer it. "Go away," I said as loudly as I could.

"Claire, it's me, Bill. Please let me in."

I didn't want to. I dried my eyes and let him in. He looked sheepish, and a bit scared. I could tell that even though I was trembling so hard I could barely stand up.

"What do you want, Bill?"

"I want to apologize for my actions last night. I didn't mean, to treat you like that. I wanted to be good to you and I loused everything up."

I understood that he wanted to save his sexual pride and still adjust to what I wanted. How could I tell him that I didn't want anything? That I would never let a man touch me because of my hideous past?

"Bill," I said, "I thought that with you it'd be different. I really liked," I couldn't say "love", "you and I wanted you. All night I was trying to get you to make love to me and when you did, I just couldn't . . . uh . . . You're in the right, Bill, not me."

"It doesn't matter who's right and who's wrong, Claire," he said gently. "We're not playing power games. I love you. I want to know why you wouldn't let me make love to you."

He was so gentle to me and so loving. I couldn't keep myself closed, and dark and hideous, even though I knew my dreadful secret would drive him away from me forever. "Bill. Bill.

"It was a Sunday morning, Bill. Mother and Dad had gone to church but I stayed home so I could cook a huge Sunday brunch for the whole family.

"As I was mixing the eggs and milk in a bowl my brother Ted came into the kitchen. Ted had just gotten back from Nam and he hadn't quite adjusted yet to our peaceful home. He seemed unable to talk and he seemed real scared, like everything was just about to attack him. I knew he didn't sleep well at nights cause I heard him screaming at night through the wall that separated our two bedrooms.

" 'Hi Ted,' I said. I wanted to show him that home was okay. Friendly. I wasn't going to attack him.

"He didn't answer me. After a while he said, 'Come upstairs. I've got something to show you.' He had a strange glassy look in his eyes.

"I wanted to talk with him so I went upstairs eagerly.

" 'Look, Claire,' he said, pulling a pair of red silk pajamas out of his suitcase. 'This is what the Vietnamese girls wear.'

" 'Gee, Ted, they're beautiful.'

" 'Why don't you try them on? You can pretend you're a little Vietnamese girl.'

" 'I grabbed them and ran into my room. When I returned, Ted was sitting on his bed. 'What d'you think, Ted? Am I O.K.?'

" 'Come here,' he said.

"At first I didn't know what he was saying.

" 'Come here you little bitch yellow girl. Come here pussy. Come here gook twat. Come here, come to Teddy-boy.'

"I couldn't come. I was shocked and frightened. As I started to run out of the room, his hand caught my arm and yanked me back to him and under him so that his heavy body was crushing mine.

" 'That's right, baby. I'm no enemy. I'm going to give you what you want, what all of you yellow bitches want, I've got the thing that's going to conquer your country.' His huge lips bore down on my lips and his hands began to crush my shoulders.

"I shoved his face away. 'Ted, I'm your sister. I'm your sister! Let me go!'

"He grabbed my head with his hands and his right hand covered my mouth. As he shoved my head back against the bed, his other hand tore off the red silk pajamas. His eyes were glazed and drool was coming out of his mouth. He looked cruel and he was hurting me badly.

"I kept struggling as much as I could, hoping, hoping for anything.

" 'Baby, that's the way I like you. The more you move, the hotter you make me. You're so little and delicate, I just want to feel you. I want to feel you all over me.' Then he started to pant. His breath was hot and fetid. I was about to faint. His demanding mouth bit down on my tongue and then on my unformed breasts. He was hurting me.

"His right hand unzipped his pants and he lowered himself into me. Lowered his hardened manhood into me so that I thought he was tearing my skin, thrusting an iron-hot cleaver into the most secret part of my body. He kept forcing himself into me until he began to shudder, and shudder harder. Finally he bore into me so hard, some part of me, burning, gave way. I felt no relief.

"He rolled off me. Suddenly he began to see me. A look of horror replaced the dazed grin on his face.

" 'O my god,' he gasped. 'What have I done?'

"I grabbed my clothes and ran. I locked myself in my bathroom and turned on the bathtub. Frantically I kept trying to clean myself.

"Later that night I learned that Ted had rushed out, taken the car, and driven off a cliff."

When I finished talking, I realized that Bill was still in the room. He was shivering.

"What have I done to you, Claire? I should have known. Look," his hand gently took my hand, "do you think you'll ever be able to trust me?"

"Yes," I said. "But I'll have to go slowly. I'm still very scared of men."

"It'll take a long time," Bill said. "But one day you'll want me to touch you and hold you and do all those other things. As for now, I love you, I love the real you because I know everything about you.

"Everything else will happen."

Now I think I must be one of the luckiest girls alive. Every night I thank God for sending me my Bill. If it hadn't been for him, I would have gone through life a lonely and bitter old maid. Instead, with the help of the man I love, I have become at last a real woman. The past few months have been a dream, and I know that there are even greater things in store. Next week, Bill and I are getting married, and with all that we have going for us we can't help but be happy."

"If you're nice to me and send me presents, especially money so I can get this trash printed," I exclaim, rolling drunkenly over my matchstick legs, "I'll tell you another story:

the true story of a rich woman:
I WANT TO BE RAPED EVERY NIGHT!

I was walking along the street. I wasn't doing anything. I was looking for some action.

It was night, late at night, Times Square. The blue yellow green red white and violet neon lights were still blinking. They wouldn't stop blinking for another two hours. And it would still be dark. It's always dark on Times Square: only rats live there, rats and some of those creepy insects that only come out at night.

My name is Jacqueline Onassis.

I kept walking down the slightly wet shining street. The neon lights were blinking at me, winking, inviting hot desires I had never known existed. In one dark alleyway, seven naked woman are waiting to slowly peel off my clothes. One has her tongue under my left arm. One has her hand buried in the soft flesh of my thigh. Hot. There's a woman waiting for me who's madly in love with me. In fact she can't live without me. Every waking minute of the day she sees my face, my face twice its normal size hovering in front of her eyes, my hands tangled in, pressing, messing her wet cunt hairs. She dreams that I'm wet: my thighs are pillars. Joined at the top. Water streaks down their insides. I'm so wet and anxious that sweat's pouring out of me. "Come get me," I whisper to her. "Come get me and handle me."

The street was still wet and shiny. I felt a hand lightly touch my shoulder.

I quickly turned around.

"Look," a young dark-haired man said to me, releasing his erect cock from his pants. "See what you do to me? Every moment I see you. Three nights I've been following you. Three times I had to relieve myself."

I laughed. "Didn't anyone tell you that was bad for you? You could stunt your growth doing it so much."

He didn't laugh. "When are you going to spend a whole night with me? Just one time that we could make love . . ."

I laughed again. "You're too greedy. I'm a married woman with responsibilities. I must be home every night so that I see my children when I wake up in the morning."

"What would be so terrible if you did not?" He pouted.

"Then I'd be remiss in the one duty that my husband demands of me," I said. "And that I would not do."

"Your husband does not care. Otherwise he would have come to see you and the children at least once these past three months," he said.

My voice went cold. "How do you know that? What my husband does or does not do is none of your business."

He sensed instantly he had said too much. "But I love you. I am going crazy for wanting you."

I nodded slowly. Relaxing. "Then keep things in their proper perspective," I said. "And if you're going to keep playing with your cock, you'd better get to the nearest bar before a cop arrests you."

"If I do, will you suck me?"

I was high. The private section of the Metropole was packed. The strobe lights were like a stop-motion camera on my eyes. The heavy pounding of the rock group tortured my ears. I took another sip of wine and looked down at the crowd.

I was annoyed with the black-haired man. He seemed to take too much for granted. In some ways he was like a woman, only in his case he seemed to think that the world revolved around his cock. I was beginning to be bored with him but I didn't see any other possibilities. It was the boredom that led me to smoke a joint. Usually I never smoke in public. But when the Englishwoman offered me a toke in the ladies' room, I stayed.

After that I didn't mind the evening at all. It seemed that I had never laughed so much in my life. Everyone was excruciatingly bright and witty. Now I wanted to dance, but everyone was too busy talking.

I got out of my chair and went to the dance floor alone. Pushing my way into the crowd, I began to dance. I gave myself to the music, happy that I was in the middle of New York City where no one thought it strange that a woman or man wanted to dance alone. I closed my eyes.

When I opened them, the tall good-looking black man was dancing in front of me. He caught my eye but we didn't speak. He moved fantastically well, his body fluid under the shirt, which was open to his waist and tied in a tight knot just over the seemingly glued-on black jeans.

I began to move with him.

After a moment, I spoke. "You're from the South, aren't you?"

"How did you know"

"You don't dance like the men up here. They jerk up and down."

He laughed. "I never thought of that."

"Where are you from?"

"Cracker country," he said. "Georgia."

"I've never been there."

"You're not missing anything." He looked at me. "I like it better here. We could never do this down there."

"Still?" I asked.

"Still," he said. "They never change."

"My folks sent me up here to a private school when I was eight. I went back when my father was killed—I was sixteen then but I couldn't take it. I head right back to New York the minute I got enough bread together."

I knew what New York City private schools cost and they weren't cheap. His family had to have money. "What did your father do?"

His voice was even. "He was a pimp. He had a finger in every pie. But he was black and the honkies didn't like that, so they cut him up in an alley an' blamed it on a passing nigger. Then they hung the nigger an' everything was cool."

"I'm sorry."

He shrugged. "My father said that was the way they would do it someday."

The music crashed to a stop and the group came. The record player began a slow number. "Nice talking with you," I said, starting back to the table.

His hand on my arm stopped me. "You don't have to go back there."

I didn't speak.

"You look like a fast-track lady and there's nothin' but mudders back there," he said.

"What've you got in mind?" I asked.

"Action. That's something I got from my father. I'm a fast-track man. Why don't you meet me outside?"

Again I didn't speak.

"I saw the way you looked," he said. "You gotta be turned off that black-haired man over there." He smiled suddenly. "You ever make it with a black man before?"

"No," I answered. I never had.

"I'm better than they say we are," he said.

"Okay." I said. "But we'll have only about an hour. I have to leave then."

"An hour's enough," he laughed. "In one hour I'll have you to the moon and back."

When I came out he was on the street opposite the discotheque, watching the last of the stores close up for the night. He turned when he heard the sound of my high-stacked shoes on the sidewalk. "Any trouble gettin out?" he asked.

"No," I answered, "I told him I was going to the ladies'."

He grinned. "Mind walking? My place is just up the street past the Paradise."

"It's the only way to get to the moon," I said, falling in step beside him.

Despite the hour there were still hookers walking back and forth. They were engaged in their principal form of amusement, looking at each other and trying to dodge the cops who cruised by. For many it was the only thing they had to do for they were fourteen years old or older and too old for the streetwalker trade. When most of the people in a city have no money and no source of money, they live without mercy.

We turned up the street past the Paradise with its smell of dried cunt juice and piss stains and began to see the cold, now deserted, sidewalk. Half way up the block he stopped in front of the dirtiest apartment building. He opened the door with a huge key. "We're six flights up."

I nodded and followed him up the old wooden staircase. His apartment was at the head of the seventh flight. There were no lights in the hall.

I stepped inside the apartment. The room was dark. I heard a click. The room was filled with a soft red light which came from two lamps, one on either side of the bed against the far wall. I looked at the room curiously.

There was no other furniture besides an armless metal chair. A bathtub covered by a wooden board served as a table. I didn't see a toilet, only a sink.

He went over to the bed and reached under a pillow. He took out a joint. Lit it. The sweet acrid smell reached my nostrils as he held it toward me. "I don't have anything to drink."

"That's O.K.," I said, taking a toke from the reefer. "This is good grass."

He smiled. "A friend of mine just in from Istanbul dropped it off. He also laid some righteous coke on me. Ever use it?"

"Sometimes," I said, passing the joint back to him. I put down my bag and moved towards him. I felt the buzzing in my head and the wetness between my legs. It was really good grass if one toke could do that. I pulled at the knot of his shirt. "I have an hour."

Deliberately, he placed the joint in an ashtray and then pushed the see-through blouse down from my shoulders, exposing my naked breasts. He cupped one in each hand, squeezing the nipples between a thumb and forefinger until the pain suddenly flashed through me. "White bitch," he said smiling.

My smile was as taunting as his own. "Nigger!"

His hands pressed me to my knees in front of him. "You better learn to beg a little if you want some black cock in your hot little pussy."

I had the shirt untied. I pulled at the zipper on his jeans. He wore nothing underneath and his phallus leapt free as I pulled the pants down around his knees. I put a hand on his shaft and pulled it toward my mouth.

His hand held my face away from him. "Beg!" he said sharply.

I looked up at him. "Please," I whispered.

He smiled and relaxed his hands, letting me take him in my mouth while he reached to the bed and lifted up a small vial filled with coke. The tiny gold spoon was attached to the cap with a small bead chain. Expertly he took a spoonful and snorted it up each nostril. Then he looked down at me. "Your turn," he said.

"I'm happy." I was kissing him and licking at his testicles. "I don't need any."

"White bitch!" He pulled at my hair, snapping my head back. He lifted me to my feet, filled a spoon, and held it under a nostril. "You do as I say. Snort!"

I sniffed and the powder lifted from the spoon into my nose. Almost at the same second he had filled the spoon under the other nostril. This time I snorted without his saying a word. I felt the faint numbness in my nose almost immediately. Then the powder exploded in my brain and I felt the strength pouring right into my genitals. "God!" I exclaimed. "That's wild. I came just sniffing it."

He laughed. "You ain't seen nothing yet, baby. I'm goin' to show you some tricks my pappy taught me with that stuff."

A moment later we were naked on the bed and I was laughing. I had never felt so good. He took another spoonful and rubbed it on his gums, making me do the same. Then he licked my nipples until they were wet from his tongue and sprinkled a little of the white powder on them and began to work them over with his mouth and fingers.

I had never felt them grow so long and hard. After a few moments I thought they were going to burst with agonizing pleasure. I began to moan and writhe. "Fuck me," I said. "Fuck me!"

"Not yet," he laughed. "We only beginning."

The next moment the lights were extinguished, and this wild cannibal sprang into bed with me. I sang out, I could not help it now; and giving a grunt of astonishment he began feeling me.

After a moment I was screaming as I had never screamed before. Each orgasm seemed to take me higher than I had ever been. I reached down for his phallus and finding it, pulled myself around so that I was able to take him in to my mouth. Greedily I sucked him. I wanted to swallow him alive, to choke myself to death on that giant beautiful tool."

"O, cut the shit," Norvins says, dragging her huge body into the room. "The boys are snoring away, Toulouse, and you're still talking."

"Norvins," I've got tears in my eyes. "Do you think Peter committed the murders?"

"Peter? Peter the whore?"

I nod yes.

"Don't be ridiculous. Peter's a lamb."

"Peter had this really weird childhood: His father did propaganda work for the American government. His mother was a member of the Young Socialist Party and a headshrinker. His younger brother raised rats. He grew up in the U.S.A. and in Germany. No stability. Plus he was fat. Unattractive. He was always unsure of himself. Since he was a musical genius, he trusted himself implicitly. That sort of thing often leads to murder."

"Why would he have murdered the twerp?"

Suddenly I realize I don't know what I'm saying. I'm too tired to think. All these stories are whirling around in my head, my head's whirling like a moon gone crazy, I'm going to stop thinking. Marcia . . .

A ten-year-old kid who's beautiful, innocent, and unworldly.

Suddenly a door closes behind me.

I'm left alone. The men I know have been mistreating me. They all think, because I like to fuck, they can do what they want with me. Step on me. Beat me. Never give me presents. They only fuck me when they have no one else to fuck cause they know I'm always ready to fuck. If I fall in love with a ten-year-old brat, maybe I'll find the road to happiness.

Marcia . . .

What would it be like if Marcia one day doesn't resist—if,

as my fingers caress the creamy inner surface of one thigh, slightly above the knee, she relaxes, allowing her thighs to open like a book with smooth pages. What then? There comes a softness at the tips of my fingers, a wet, breaking softness under a mat of fragile hair. What does she have deep there, at her pit, between her legs, like a furry animal? Does it have a life of its own? Is it a strange beast lying in wait, with its heaped softness simply bait for the unwary? I'd give anything to know.

I fall asleep, a curtain of softness descending over my senses. My last image is of Marcia, her head tilted back, her chest erect, and, like a vast portal at which I'm longing to prostrate myself, the soft yet muscled forward thrust of her dusky white thighs.

In another part of Montmartre, in an old crumbling deserted house on the corner of the Rue de Clignancourt and Rue Picard, a section of Paris that's still country due to the slight patches of grass, lives a couple a man and a wife who've been together, god willing, for the past thirty years.

These two old people are the only survivors of the once powerful Alexander family. They are not even Alexanders, to tell the truth, for the last Alexander, the rich old beautiful bitch Mrs. Alexander, has died, but they have been servants to the Alexanders for so long that they have inherited, or kept alive, the mysterious Alexander attributes. These two people influence peoples' dreams. Rhys, Peter, Norvins, Poirot, haughtily as they bear themselves in the noonday streets of Montmartre, are no better than slaves to these servant Alexanders, on entering the topsy-turvy commonwealth of sleep.

Two other people live in this rusty wooden house. A young architect who built the house and surrounding garden and who now cares for this living tangle of trees bush and water, and Marcia, the young daughter of Vincent Van Gogh and a clap-ridden sleaze-hag prostitute Vincent fell in love with in The Hague around 1881. Marcia's one of the most innocent of all creatures. She's very pretty; as graceful as a bird, and graceful much in the same way: floppy; as pleasant about the house as a gleam of sunshine falling on the floor through a shadow of twinkling leaves, or as a ray of firelight that dances on the wall while evening is drawing nigh. She gilds all with an atmosphere of love and joy.

The architect is quite another sort of person. He considers himself a thinker, and is certainly of a thoughtful turn, but, with his own path to discover, has perhaps hardly yet reached the point where an educated man begins to think. The true value of his character lies in that deep consciousness of inward strength, which makes all his past vicissitudes seem merely like a change of garments; in that enthusiasm, so quiet that he scarcely knows of its existence, but which gives a warmth to everything that he lays his hand on; in that personal ambition, hidden—from his own as well as others' eyes— among his more generous impulses, but in which lurks a certain efficacy, that might solidify him from a theorist into a champion of some practicable cause. Altogether, in his culture and want of culture—in his crude, wild, and misty philosophy, and the practical experience that counteracts some of its tendencies; in his magnanimous zeal for man's welfare, and his recklessness of whatever the ages had established in man's behalf; in his faith, and in his infidelity; in what he has, and in what he lacks—the artist might fitly enough stand forth as the representative of many compeers in his native land.

The sun's beating down on the tangled branches, the long-waving grass, the weeds, the rock piles, the strange mazes of the garden. Marcia's standing in front of a stream, her back to the house, clad in a halter and pair of underpants. The sun beats down on her. She reaches behind her and unfastens the halter, then, half turning, steps out of the underpants. She steps into the stream, bathes herself, then she puts on her underpants. Slowly she pulls the halter around her chest and ties the neck strap.

The young artist feels faint beads of perspiration across his forehead. This is the first time he's ever seen a ten-year-old girl completely naked. He never thought they could be so beautiful and exciting.

Walking quietly, he passes into a thicker part of the woods where he can no longer see her. He closes his eyes, and sinks, still trembling, to the soil. For a long moment he sits there, the pain of the heat surging inside him bending him almost double.

Slowly he reasons with himself. No. He mustn't. Not again. If he gives into it now, he'll always give into it. At last, he begins to feel better. He puts the French pictures Norvins gave him on the ground, so he can bury them.

All you need is a little self-control and determination. He places the pictures face-down on a tree stump. He begins to feel proud of himself. He's not going to look at those pictures ever again.

He lies down, on his back, on the earth. The sun beating down on him makes his mind wander. He forgets the pictures.

As he's about to fall asleep, he hears footsteps. He doesn't want to wake up. He remembers. He freezes. Dazed from the sun, he lurches toward the tree stump.

She's standing by the tree stump, the pictures in her hand. She looks up at him in surprise. "Scott, where'd you get these pictures?" she asks, a curious excitement in her voice.

"Give them to me!" he demands, walking toward her.

"I will not!" she retorts, turning her back to him. Her left leg kicks up into the air. "I haven't finished looking at them yet."

Lithely she spins away from his outstretched hand, across

the grass, to the far side of the stump. "Let me finish," she says calmly. "Then you can have them back."

She turns to avoid his heavy grasp but his hand catches her shoulder. The pictures fly from her hand as she falls against him. She reaches for the pictures. His hand catches at her halter strap to keep her from getting them, and the strap breaks in his hand. He freezes and stares at her white chest.

"You broke my strap," she says quietly. She makes no move to cover herself. Her eyes watch his face.

He doesn't answer her.

She smiles slowly and raises her hand to her breast, rubbing her palm gently across the nipple. "I'm just as pretty as any of the girls in those pictures, aren't I?"

He's fascinated, unable to speak. His eyes follow the movement of her hand. "Aren't I?" she asks again. "You can tell me. I won't tell anyone. Why do you think I let you watch while I was bathing?"

"You knew I was watching?" he asks in surprise.

She laughs. "Of course, stupid. I could see you in the water. I almost burst out laughing. I thought your eyes would pop out of your head."

He can feel the tension begin to build up inside him. "I don't think that's funny."

"Look at me," she says. "I like you to look at me. I wish everyone could." She swivels around so that her knees stick away from her thighs.

"That's not right," he says.

"Why not?" she demands. "What's wrong with it? I like to look at you; why shouldn't you look at me?"

"But you never did," he quickly replies.

A smile comes to her lips. "Oh, yes I did."

"You did? When?"

"The other afternoon when you came back from Norvins'. I know what you do there. There was no one home and I

watched you through the bathroom keyhole. I saw everything
you did."

"Everything?" The word escapes his mouth like a caress.

"Everything," she says smugly. "You were exercising your
muscle." Her eyes look into his. "I never knew it could get
so long. I always thought it was little and kind of droopy like
it was in the beginning."

There's a tightness in his throat. He can hardly speak. He
begins to get up from the tree stump. "I think you'd better
get away from here," he says hoarsely.

She looks up at him. Smiling. "Would you like to see all
of me?"

He doesn't answer.

Her hand reaches up and unties the neck strap of the
halter. Half turning, she steps out of the underpants. He
stares at her naked body, feeling his legs begin to tremble.
He sees her eyes move down on him. His shirt hangs open.
He looks at her again.

"Now take off your clothes and let me see all of you," she
says.

As if in a daze he lets his shirt, then his pants slip to the
earth. He groans and sinks to his knees in the earth, holding
himself.

Quickly she moves to him and looks down at him. A faint
sound of triumph comes into her voice. "Now," she says,
"you can do it for me."

His hand reaches up to touch her chest. She lets it rest
there a moment, then suddenly moves away from him. "No!"
she says sharply. "Don't touch me!"

He stares at her dumbly, the agony pouring through him
in waves.

Her heavy-lidded eyes watch him.

"Do it for me," she says in a husky voice. "And I'll do it
for you. But don't touch me!"

CHAPTER FIVE

HOW LOVE CAN LEAD YOUNGSTERS TO MURDER

S COTT'S, the young artist's, real name is James Dean.

Marcia's real name is Janis Joplin.

James and Janis fell madly in love when James, or Jimmy, was still working on *Rebel Without a Cause*. They were children and not yet hardened, frightened into feelinglessness by the Hollywood scene: still able to fall in love. Fall in love frantically, desperately, without any reservation. With all the insane hopes, fantasies, myths, and desires children have. Jimmy was twenty-four years old. Janis was only nine. They were unhappy, scared. They didn't understand the world they had been thrown into. Not only could they escape into each other; they also were able to reinforce each other's fantasy that the constant loneliness and paranoia of the world no longer existed for them.

Theirs was the perfect American love affair.

Rebel Without a Cause tells a story as old as *Tom Brown's School Days*: a boy's adventures, travails and triumph on his first day at a new school. Jim Dean plays the part of the fledgling Jim Stark, a new boy at Dawson High. What makes *Rebel* different from traditional schoolboy adventures is that school is no longer the only relevant field of action. Most of *Rebel* takes place away from Dawson High, late at night, in a teenage underworld of violence, romance and death. There are also new, more powerful authority figures: parents and the police.

In *Rebel Without a Cause* Jimmy Dean plays himself. He's

victim and hero: the kid who learns to be bad cause he can't be good in a society whose goodness stinks. The kid who keeps his innocence and vulnerability while he learns. The corrupted society. Jimmy not only played in this film, he also helped director Nicholas Ray create the film. Jimmy did this while he was lonely, overwhelmingly lonely, confused by his homosexuality and the sudden success he was having. The Hollywood world in which he made the film was, as is reality, far more complexly corrupt than the society in *Rebel Without a Cause*. Everyone in Hollywood carries hell in his or her heart.

If Jimmy was lonely, Janis was even more lonely. She had fled the boredom and the hostility of her hometown Port Arthur, Texas to find a place that was like her: bubbling and wild. Venice, Hollywood, all that part of southern California at that time was full of freaks, but Janis was too insecure, too unsure of herself to talk to anyone.

One day, when Jimmy was sitting in the Warner Brothers' cafeteria, he met Janis. He noticed a young girl sitting at the table across from him. She was so young she should have been with her parents, but she wasn't. She seemed so innocent Jimmy was intrigued. "Hey," he said to the long-haired kid, "what are you doing around here?"

"What d'you mean, 'what am I doing around here'?" she pugnaciously replied. "I have as much right to be here as you do." Janis noticed how good-looking Jimmy was, but she wasn't going to show she noticed.

"You're just a kid."

"I am not." She pushed up her filthy shirt sleeve and showed him the tracks covering the lower part of her arm.

Jimmy sneered. "So what. Only brats who want to act grown-up do that. Real actors have to take care of themselves."

Janis felt put-down. "Fuck it up your ass. Star." She tossed her long brown hair. "Anyway I'm not an actress. I'm a singer. I sing the blues."

"Hey, Jimmy, you're on," Natalie Wood's voice rang out. Natalie was playing Judy, the main girl in *Rebel Without a Cause*.

Jimmy decided he wanted to see this brat again. She wasn't like any other girl he had ever met. "Listen." His finger pointed at her face. "Wait here, I'll be back in three hours."

When Jimmy drove his MG right up to the door of the Warner Brothers' cafeteria, Janis' heart began to flutter in her chest. What a wild thing to do, Janis thought to herself. Here's a man whom I want to be able to tell what to do. He's tough and he's wild and he's mean. I need a mean man cause I'm mean and wild myself. I'm too intelligent for a woman. I need a man who can help me a little cause this death society doesn't like intelligent women. A man who can teach me something. I need a man who can step on me a little. A woman's gotta be stepped on, otherwise she stops being hard and mean and she can't deal with society anymore. I mean, I've got to make it and I've got to keep on making it. Dum, dum, dum.

This man isn't like those Port Arthur creeps. Those jocks and rednecks who made fun of me and told their children to stop associating with me, cause I wasn't feminine enough and pretty enough and I didn't DO THINGS RIGHT.

This guy probably doesn't like me. Hard men never go for powerful chicks, the ones like me, who got visions. They got their own visions and they just want some pretty chickie who'll say yes to them and make life easier for them. That's all they want.

But I gotta get loved and I gotta get love from a guy who's real to me. I need a tough leather guy. So I'll just take whatever this boy offers, Janis decided, I'll do whatever he wants, as much as I can, so that he'll love me a little. If he kicks me in the groin, and throws me away, so what, at least

I'll have of gotten a little bit of good loving. When it's over, it's over.

As soon as Janis got in the car, Jimmy stopped noticing her. He wanted her to reject him. As if alone, he began to race his red 53 MG down Santa Monica Boulevard, Venice Boulevard, right on to a deserted portion of the Venice beach. He pulled the car up to an old, old for California, ramshackle beach house.

He got out of the car and, hands in his pockets, started slouching toward the ocean.

Janis wasn't going to be put off like this. Goddammit, he was going to notice her. Notice me! Notice me! her body cried. She ran into Jimmy and started punching him.

"Just cause you're some fuckin' MOVIE STAR," her eyes, skin, and hair seemed to light up and explode, "you think you can ignore me. You're just like all the other creepy men I've ever known." She was trying hard not to cry.

Jimmy smiled. He looked shy and childlike. "O.K. Let's see if we can become friends." They grabbed hands and fell down in the sand. Jimmy's body was thin and muscular. Janis was already in love with him.

"I'll tell you everything," Janis said. "I want to sing, man. That's all there is to me. I got this vision and it's driving me crazy. Like Zelda Fitzgerald.

"You're not going to understand cause you're a man."

"I understand what it is to be driven. My mother died when I was nine years old. She just left me like that. Then my father sent me away. I knew I was bad and I knew I had to create my own world. Really. Not just fantasize. Create my own world."

"You still don't understand." Suddenly Janis didn't care anymore if she was impressing him. She was caught up in her own pain. "Men can do what they want. Those who got visions can try to follow them. Women in show business, man, they sing their fuckin' insides out cause they give up more than you'd ever known. If they got kids, they give them up; any woman gives up a home life, an old man, probably, a home a friends; you give up an old man and friends; you give up every constant in the world except music. That's the only thing you got man."

"It's the same for a man," Jimmy said thoughtfully. "An actor doesn't ever have a constant like music. Everything in the world is simply a tool for him, nothing more."

"But you can get laid, man! Every movie star gets laid! But I'm a woman: I don't want an ass-kisser, I want a guy who's bigger and stronger and ballsier than me. When I'm on the road, where am I going to find a man like that? Men like that want ass-lickers. They don't women they're constantly going to have to fight. I'm always going to be alone, man."

Jimmy looked at Janis seriously. She was being honest and, like him, she sensed her own badness. "I'm lonely too, Janis. I'm trying to make myself be someone else, be JAMES DEAN, but I'm killing myself, I don't know who and where I am. As for sex," he looked at her closely, "I haven't been to bed with anybody. I've told all the girls I've met to kiss my ass because they're sterile, spineless, stupid prostitutes. What d'you think of that?"

"I think we're going to be friends, man." They looked at each other for a long time.

Both of them felt they had found something they had lost a long time ago, before they could remember. Now they could relax. They started playing with each other and giggling, just like kids.

Often they talked about themselves and their problems, about movies and acting, about life and life after death. Then they'd walk side-by-side, not actually speaking, but communicating their love silently to each other.

They were beginning to have a complete understanding of each other.

They were like Romeo and Juliet, together and inseparable. Sometimes on the beach they loved each other so much they just wanted to walk together into the sea, holding hands, because they knew then that they would always be together.

It wasn't that they wanted to commit suicide.

They loved their lives, and it was just that they wanted to be that close to each other always.

They didn't want to be seen together at film premieres and nightclubs.

They didn't want to be in the gossip columns or be seen at the big Hollywood parties.

They were kids together and that's the way they both liked it.

They began to see a great deal of each other when they weren't making films or singing. They were young and wanted to enjoy life together and they did.

More than any other person Henry Kissinger is determining our lives in the 1970s.

On January 20, 1969, the government of the United States fell into the hands of a group of men who were undistinguished in intellect, personality, or vision. Swept into power at the end of a tormented decade, they were chosen not so much out of admiration or enthusiasm as out of fear, hatred, and desperation. No one would deign to bestow upon them the superficial accolades that had frequently adorned their predecessors, even in the worst hours of poverty and cruelty and war; in these administrations there are no Thousand Days, no New Frontier or Great Society. It was as if everyone had instantly grasped their obvious inferiority, and hoped only that the country could somehow muddle on until a time in the future when, refreshed and reinvigorated, it would catch hold of itself and produce leadership where a simple void had existed before.

In this bleak and unpromising setting, for those who think they know or presume to judge, one figure stands out. Unlike

the rest, he is sharp, determined, relentlessly intellectual—
one of the brightest men, some say, this country has ever
produced. Open-minded and pragmatic, he is not tied to the
mistakes of the past, even to those he himself had once
spoken for. Brash and impenetrable, yes, but there is still
a humility about him that his steelier and more arrogant
predecessors clearly lacked: he possesses a stark recognition
of America's and his own limitations, and he has promised
again and again that neither will be tested at its extreme.
The days when America would pay any price, would bear
any burden, would meet any hardship, would fight any foe
to achieve the defense of liberty had made for a certain public
spirit and elan; but, in retrospect, they led to overcommit-
ment, to useless loss and destruction around the world. And
in those hours of crisis, the President of the United States
was surrounded by men largely lacking in open-mindedness
and critical perspective, men who blindly insisted that the
country continue on the same futile course of action that they
themselves had launched. But now, it would be different;
there would be a sense of proportion. One often wonders, in
fact, how he emerged in this crowd of banal and mediocre
men, and more important yet, how influential he will be and
how long he will last.

The main question of our age is: how can all-out war and
total nuclear destruction be avoided? Kissinger's answer is:
by limited war. Kissinger was led to believe in limited war
through his faith in the universal applicability of Metternich-
style diplomacy, a diplomacy that presupposed an area of
common interest and understanding, as well as one of
conflict, between the contending parties. "In seeking to avoid
the horrors of all-out war by outlining an alternative, in
developing a concept of limitation that combines firmness
with moderation, diplomacy can once more establish a
relationship with force even in the nuclear age."

What are the requisites of such a diplomacy?

A diplomat, to be effective, must possess a certain degree of credibility. Under the circumstances of America's world-wide commitment—a commitment that, by its very scope, would seem to defy belief—and of the general unstable world condition due among other causes, to be advanced nuclear technology many nations now possess, Washington's and Washington's international representatives' credibilty must be total and constant. Washington's diplomats must have the freedom and the power to handle incredibly subtle and diffi-cult tactical maneuvres. That means that diplomats must not be harassed by public opinion or the necessities of domestic policy.

According to Kissinger, ". . . it is the President who decides and he, therefore, has to feel comfortable with the way his choices are presented to him or indeed whether he wants any choices." The Presidency is necessary only for decisions on America's role in international affairs. As the chief diplomat, the President is his own Secretary, his own adviser, his own deskman. One of the consequences of Kissin-ger's "diplomacy"

The story of *Rebel Without a Cause* played a large part in Jimmy's and Janis' romance and so must be told:

Rebel Without a Cause is the story of Romeo and Juliet. Jimmy is the first person we see in *Rebel Without a Cause*, lying dead drunk on the sidewalk, curled up next to a toy monkey he is whimsically trying to cover with a piece of paper, while credits and title flash by in flaming letters.

Without being introduced or identified, Jimmy acts out his own prologue to the movie. He plays an isolated, defenseless child, deliriously enclosed in his own protective fantasy, stranded like some inhabitant of another world on a grimy concrete ledge. Jimmy modeled his pose on one of his favorite paintings, Manet's *Dead Bullfighter*, and in his slow, deliber-ate-actions, the hero is introduced to us almost in embryo, a child with his mechanical toy who wishes nothing more than to be left alone with his dreams.

In the course of this night journey Jimmy (Jimmy Dean) is hauled into Juvenile Hall—a cold, sterile maze with glass partitions and jangling phones, gloomy and bizarre, with endless forms and mechanical procedures. These wards are the result of parental indifference and inability to understand their children. Despondently, the "juvenile delinquents" wait for the real culprits to collect them.

Jim's been hauled in because he's suspected of having beaten up some man. Society sends all its youngest casualties to Juvenile. Plato's (Sal Mineo's) also in this decompression chamber because he's shot a puppy. Judy (Natalie Wood), in searing red coat and lipstick, has been picked up for wandering around late at night.

Ray (the Juvenile Detective): Why were you out walking the streets at one o'clock in the morning, Judy? You weren't looking for company, were you? (She starts to cry.)

Judy: He hates me.

Ray: What?

Judy: He doesn't like anything about me. He calls me . . . He calls me . . .

Ray: He makes you feel pretty unhappy?

Judy: He calls me a dirty tramp—my own father!

When Ray calls Jim in, he immediately recognizes Jim's act: "You'll don't kid me, pal. How come you're not wearing your boots?" When Jim tries to take a swing at Ray, Ray invites Jim to "blow your wheels . . . take it out on the desk." Jim blurts out, "If I could have just one day when I wasn't all confused . . . I wasn't ashamed of everything. If I felt I belonged some place." Ray releases Jimmy for lack of evidence.

The next day, the students of Dawson High sit in a dark-

ened auditorium, confronted with a giant replica of the
heavens, listening to the dry, droning voice of a lecturer as
insectlike as his projector, and they watch this artificial show,
a Hollywood projection of the universe! As the lecturer says,

> For many days before the end of our earth, people will
> look at the night sky and notice a star, increasingly bright
> and increasingly near,

Jim enters and says in a stage whisper to the teacher checking
names at the door, "STARk, Jim STARk." Jim's the new boy
in school. The class turns; the lecturer hesitates; Jim slithers
to a seat.

> Jim tries to make himself part of Buzz' (Corey Allen's) gang:
> Lecturer's Voice: . . . and Taurus, the bull . . .
> Jim (in good imitation): Moo! (He waits for approval.)

But Jim's attempt to horn in on the gang has the opposite of
the desired effect: it provokes them and they taunt Jim with
the idea that he may be a coward:

> Scene: Angle shot of Judy, Buzz and group (seen from Jim's
> angle). He is in the foreground. They are staring at him.
> Nobody laughs.
> Crunch (flat): Yeah, moo.
> Buzz: Moos, That's real cute. Moo.
> Goon: Hey, he's real rough.
> Crunch: I bet he fights with cows.
> Buzz: Moo.

Plato, who's trying to make friends with Jimmy, whispers
some advice:

> Plato: You shouldn't MONKEY with him.
> Jim: What?
> Plato: He's a wheel. So's she. It's hard to make friends
> with them.
> Jim: I don't want to make friends. (He turns back, unhappy
> at having revealed himself.)
> Lecturer's Voice: Destroyed as we began in a burst of gas
> and fire.

The lifeless professor who manipulates the cosmos with his dumbbell project ends the world:

Lecturer: The heavens are still and cold once more. In all the complexity of our universe and the galaxies beyond, the earth will not be missed . . .

Through the infinite reaches of space, the problems of man seem trivial and naive. Indeed. And man, existing alone, seems to be an episode of little consequence . . . That's all. Thank you very much.

Plato: What does HE know about man alone?

Outside the school, Buzz jabs his knife into Jim's whitewall while Judy's nylon-stockinged leg dangles suggestively in front of the tire. Jimmy, sitting on the parapet with his back to the gang, lets out a slow, painful breath of air. There's no way he can avoid the trouble behind him. He climbs down and moves toward the group. Goon, then the rest of the gang, and finally Buzz start clucking at Jim.

Jim asks if they're calling him chicken. He'd had to leave another school for "messin' up a guy" who called him chicken. He tries to refuse the knife Buzz forces on him, but the gang knows he really has no choice and eggs him on.

The two boys circle each other, like wolves vying for territory. Buzz seems to snarl, thoroughly enjoying the encounter, while Jim hestitates, then lunges and gets jabbed in the stomach. Buzz grins. Jimmy makes another quick leap and is cut again.

Jimmy wins the knife fight, but he still can't get into the gang. Now Jimmy has to win Buzz in a chickie run.

Jimmy takes his dilemma home. Can his father help him? Jimmy's father is wearing an apron,

Jim: Can you answer me NOW?

Father: Listen, nobody should make a snap decision—this isn't something you just—we ought to consider the pros and cons—

Jim: We don't have TIME.

Father: We'll make time. Where's some paper? We'll make
  a list . . .

Jim (shouting): WHAT CAN YOU DO WHEN YOU
  HAVE TO BE A MAN?

Father: What?

Jim: You going to stop me, Dad?

Father: You know I never stop you from anything
      (Jim suddenly makes his decision and sheds his jacket
    for the red one.)
      Believe me—you're at a wonderful age. In ten years
    you'll look back on this and wish you were a kid again.
    When you're older, you'll laugh at yourself for thinking
    this is so important.

Jimmy runs out of the house to meet his next battle, incredu-
lously repeating, "Ten years . . . ten years . . ."

Wind shrieks over the exposed plateau which is several
hundred yards long. It cuts into the darkness like the prow
of a ship and ends in empty air. Several cars are scattered
about defining a sort of runway in the center. There are
several kids present but very little talk . . . They stand in
small clots, murmuring and smoking.

Buzz (quietly): This is the edge, boy. This is the end.

Jim: Yeah.

Buzz: I like you, you know?

Jim: Buzz? What are we doing this for?

Buzz: (still quiet): We got to do SOMETHING. Don't we?

It's the last time they speak, for during the run Buzz
catches his sleeve on the door handle and can't get out.
Trapped in his car, he careens over the side, and his life ends
in a "burst of gas and flames." Jim, looking over the cliff,
realizes he's lost his first friend.

Buzz's girlfriend, Judy, rides home with Jim.

Jimmy slips into his parents' home. To cool his overheated
brain and heal his frayed nerve ends, he rolls the cool glass
of a milk bottle across his forehead.

Jimmy sees his father watching T.V. His father (Jim Backus) doesn't want to notice him. Jimmy can't leave: he can't let go of his father.

Jimmy's mother enters the room. Jimmy tells them he got in trouble out at the bluff. His parents tell him they've seen a "bad accident" on the T.V. Jimmy tells them this accident was real and involves him. His parents don't understand. Jim puts his hands around his father's throat, drags him down the stairs, pushes him over his easy chair and onto the floor. His mother runs after them, shrieking, "STOP IT! YOU'LL KILL HIM. JIM! DO YOU WANT TO KILL YOUR FATHER?"

Jim runs away from his parents. He looks for the only other adult he believes can help him—Ray, the juvenile officer. Ray isn't at the precinct, but the gang is. They think Jim's going to tell all so Crunch decides they'd better take care of him.

Jim doesn't want to go home. He has nowhere else to go. He finds Judy waiting in his parents' driveway. She's run away too:

Jim: I swear sometimes, you just want to hold on to some- body! Judy, what am I going to do? I can't go home again.

Judy: Neither can I.

Jim: No? Why not? (no answer) You know something? I never figured I'd live to see eighteen. Isn't that dumb.

Judy: No.

Jim: Each day I'd look in the mirror and I'd say, "What? You still here?" Man! (They laugh a little)

Like even today. I woke up this morning, you know? Then the first thing that happens is I see you, and I thought this is going to be one terrific day so you better life it up, boy, 'cause tomorrow maybe you'll be nothing.

As Jimmy gets to kiss Judy—their first kiss

There's a place where Jimmy and Judy can hide: an old mansion Plato knows about. An abandoned villa, with its sunken gardens, waterless foundations, stone balustrades and rococo candelabra.

This is the new world:

Plato (he holds up the candelabra): What do you think?

Jim: Wow! Well, now, then, there . . . Let's take it for the summer.

Judy (laughing): Oh, Jim.

Jim: Should we rent or are we in a buying mood, dear?

Plato: . . . Only three million dollars a month!

Jim: Why don't we just rent it for the season?

Judy: You see, we've just . . . oh, you tell him, darling. I'm so embarrassed I could die!

Jim: Well, we're newlyweds.

Judy hums a little lullaby to Plato and he falls off to sleep, but his dreams of the future become nightmares. As the gang members arrive, Plato, as frightened as a child and he is a child, shoots one, screams "You're NOT my father!" at Jim, and rushes off into the bush as the police arrive. Judy and Jim run down the hill after Plato, who has broken into the planetarium and hidden himself in its dark, empty space. The cops arrive at the planetarium door. There are light, bullhorns, Officer Ray, Jim's parents, Plato's maid, and cops.

Cops with guns surround the planetarium. Officer Ray tells the boy in the planetarium to come out with his hands up.

Plato (shivering like a puppy): Do you think the end of the world will come at night, Jim?

Jim tells Plato he'll trade Plato's gun for his jacket. Then he'll unload the gun and give it back to Plato.

Jim (handing Plato the empty revolver): Friends keeps promises, don't they?

Jim walks with Plato to the planetarium door. Plato hesitates when he sees the menacing searchlights and the faceless crowd outside. Plato runs away from Jim and Judy and sobs "They're not my friends!" The police open fire and the child falls dead.

"But I've got the bullets!" Jim shouts to everyone and no one. Jim goes over to Plato, the second friend he's lost today, and zips up Plato's jacket.

"He was always cold."

The dumbbell professor who gave the astrology lecture walks up to the planetarium and doesn't understand anything, is that the Presidency has gained more power in decision-making, and Congress and the Pentagon, among others, have lost power.

The second requisite of Kissinger's "diplomacy" is that diplomatic decisions are made according to historical necessities. A diplomat has to follow a course of action which is manifestly correct, rather than give in to the transitory whims of public opinion. A diplomat thinks conceptually because he thinks in terms of wide-range even visionary historic goals.

What are the pragmatic consequences of this conceptual thinking?

Above all, Kissinger fears any power who, for the sake of an idea, as did Hitler, will deny and try to destroy the area of common interest and understanding the other powers have set up. Kissinger most fears ideology. He sees America as the defender of the free world simply because America is still the main non-ideological power. Since the Soviet Union is the main ideological power, the fundamental priority of Kissinger's policy is to convince Moscow that it is fruitless to conduct international business on ideological grounds. And the clearest expression so far of Kissinger's opposition to the idea of an ideologically oriented foreign policy is Washington's rapprochment with the People's Republic of China.

Another consequence of Kissinger's conceptual thinking besides his hatred of ideology and revolution, for Kissinger is the arch-conservative, is the concept of "linkage". The rationale of linkage is that all the world's trouble spots exist on a single continuum which connects the Soviet Union and the United States. In this context, the resolution of an individual issue depends not so much on the merits of the specific case as on the overall balance of power in the world. Kissinger's tendency has been to link Europe, the Mideast, and Vietnam without much regard to political or conceptual subtleties. Seeing no viability in modified linkage, he has chosen total linkage over no linkage at all.

Given this situation, America needs a sturdy and dependable group of allies. Kissinger's main disagreement with President Kennedy was Kissinger's assertion that America could not limit the Soviet Union's power by itself. For this reason America has had to militarily and psychologically overcommit itself.

At the same time Kissinger is trying to reduce America's military presence and the power of the Pentagon. So more and more, the United States, to maintain its credibility, must use threats. Threats tough enough to work. Kissinger and Ford would like to avoid nuclear war, but the excessive political commitments of their regime are edging them closer in that direction.

Kissinger is the intellectual. It is interesting, in reference to Marxist-Leninist theory, that Kissinger's policies are not only economic and are powerful, Kissinger himself, philosophically influenced by Hegel, believes that individual men can make real decisions that affect the world: ". . . on cooperating the intellectual has two loyalties: to the organization that employs him and to values which transcend the bureaucratic framework and provide his basic motivation. It is important for him to remember that one of his contributions to the·administrative process is his independence, and that one of his tasks is to prevent routine from becoming an end in itself . . . It is essential for him to retain the freedom to deal with the policymaker from a position of independence, and to reserve the right to assess the policymaker's demands in terms of his own standards."

Kissinger moved from Harvard, via Rockefeller and Henry

Cabot Lodge, to Washington. Yet Harvard University had been, and will continue to be, the focus of Kissinger's life: he had been launched on his fortune there, and his most enduring friendships and personal associations are still there. Harvard has trained many men including Schlesinger, Bundy, and Galbraith for the White House; there has always been a beeline from Harvard to the White House.

Kissinger is an individual who has always been obsessed, even before his arrival in government, with making his mark on history. It would not be at all surprising if, besides seeing Nixon and Ford administration foreign policy as a historical turning point, and besides conceiving of himself as a notable historical figure—which, no doubt, he does—Kissinger imagines, in his moments of greatest personal self-esteem, that he is one of Hegel's great men, one of those rare individuals, those carriers of mankind's historical spirit, about whom Kissinger's favorite philosopher once speculated so long ago.

Both Kissinger and Kissinger's policies, according to Kissinger, above all must reflect the historical conditions we see today and the historic possibilities we see for tomorrow. They are moving with history and moving history themselves. But a policy and a man who speak not to concrete realities or to contemporary concerns, but merely to what the man sees as the vindication of history, are a policy and a man who harshly exclude those human beings who are not living with the historians of the future in mind, and who completely disregard whatever torment and anguish happen to be generated at this time.

There's a new woman in the life of James Dean, "Kandid Kendris" wrote in her column:

—a wild youngster who's putting a new sparkle in his eyes.

For the first time since he came to Hollywood, Jimmy's dating in public—and the woman he loves being seen with is Janis Joplin, one of America's newest blues singers.

His dates with this excitable 9-year-old make Jimmy glow. The couple has been seen gazing into each other's eyes at cozy, exclusive Topanga Canyon restaurants and laughing and whispering cheek-to-cheek on Jimmy's motorcycle. On one date—in an unprecedented public display of affection—Jimmy kissed her.

"I was only a few feet away when it happened," said a photographer who's been observing Jimmy's new dating since it began in August. The photographer, who asked not to be named, said he's never seen Jimmy looking more relaxed and radiant. "He doesn't even avoid the camera when he's gone out with her."

The new woman in Jimmy's life is a former keypunch operator with the Los Angeles Telephone Company and the most exciting new singer on the scene. She lives on the Venice beach.

Janis, who's made no effort to hide her friendship with Jimmy, had her first known date with him on August 20. She met him at the Warner Brother's studio. They went to a drive-in to see *The Sun Also Rises*.

After the movie, they spent a lingering evening on the Sunset Boulevard, in the pool halls, and left around 3 A.M.

Jimmy and Janis dated several times after that in August and September.

A pool hustler who saw them together told *The Enquirer*: "They would talk together in hushed tones in the back, and once I overheard them having a conversation about leaving Hollywood. They really seemed to have a good time together."

Everywhere the couple went, they left an impression of warmth, even heat. At Schwab's Drugstore, a soda jerk told *The Enquirer*: "Jimmy and the girl had dinner here recently. They chatted and laughed a lot, and seemed to know each other very well. Jimmy Dean looked very happy."

At another drugstore, Googie's, a manager identified photos of Janis and admitted: "the girl was with Jimmy Dean. She didn't give her name, but she was very loving and pleasant to him, and obviously a pal."

Janis is well-known in rock-and-roll circles. It's difficult to determine whether her family is wealthy or not, for Janis looks like a beatnik.

Hollywood, all its evil, was beginning to destroy Jimmy's and Janis' love. Every word these two youngsters whispered to each other in public, every word of trust and affection, every gesture of trust and desire, was immediately reported in the gossip columns, the scandal sheets, the teenage heartthrob mags. Reported and distorted. Were Jimmy and Janis beginning to believe these distortions of their feelings and of themselves?

JANIS AND DRUGS. Janis Joplin, the gutsy, raunchy and very vulnerable singer that everyone's talking about, a psychiatric social worker from Venice told *Photoplay*, is taking drugs. A lot of drugs.

"According to Janis," said the social worker, "she's having a nervous breakdown. Her parents are psychotics, and she's been trying to break away from them. 'I don't want parents,' she told me. 'I was born from nothing.' Even though she's told her parents to stop calling her, they now call her and hang up the phone when she answers."

"At the same time the enormous amount of publicity Janis has been receiving on account of her affair with JAMES DEAN has made Janis feel more unstable. Janis has to flee to something, and she's fleeing to what's easiest for her: drugs."

Janis refused to talk seriously about her use of drugs. The only thing she said to us was: "I never wanted to sing publicly, man. Much less be a STAR! I just came to Hollywood and sang cause that way, I thought, I could get LAID a lot and get a lot of drugs."

One of Janis' friends, who wants to remain nameless, told *Photoplay* that she had the impression that Janis is now receiving insulin shock.

Janis was too young and too vulnerable to battle Hollywood's glamorizing dehumanizing death machine. And drugs were destroying whatever chance she had to toughen up and keep her love for Jimmy, her ability to love anyone, in a private fortress. Drugs were making her duller and, finally, even more vulnerable.

The evil of Hollywood. The coldness of Hollywood. The other side of Hollywood: if someone wants to become a really good actor or actress, that person has to become someone else, in fact become every he or she plays. Actors have to destroy themselves. They don't have time for love.

Jimmy began to realize that his affair with Janis was forcing him to remain human. Remain stuck on the ground when he wanted to soar into the air, a myth. As he put it, "Up here, I hate all earthlings."

But love is strong. Stronger than the desire for immortalization. Stronger than the desire for death. Jimmy and Janis had to flee Hollywood. They went to Montmartre, Paris, France and changed their names.

CHAPTER SIX

THE FUTURE

BEING wet and dark with someone.

Being touched and being able to know the person will touch you again. Being in a cave you don't want to leave and don't have to leave. Being in a place in which you're able to be open and stupid and boring.

You're open and wet and your edges are rough and hurt. You remember that you've always been this: totally vulnerable. You don't want to forget who you are. Being with someone has made you remember that you're totally vulnerable.

Marcia and Scott now always felt these ways. Being out of control and not knowing it. Being in total danger and believing that you're safer than you've ever been in your life, you're inside and so you can open yourself and make yourself raw to the other person.

Suddenly seeing something you've never seen before. You're willing to compromise yourself for this person. Forget what you've just thought. You don't have any more thoughts of yourself. You want to know everthing about the other person:

What was your childhood like?

What do you like to do the most?

Have you ever fucked any weirdos?

When did you start being an adult?

You think you are the other person. You begin to forget what you feel.

Scott and Marcia now were living on the street cause they didn't have any money. Caught between the devil and the deep blue sea: The other person's frightened of you. He's scared if he lets you into his wetness and heat, you'll disrupt everything. You want him wet and hot so badly, you act so heavy, he gets more scared, you put him out of your head. You want nothing to do with him. Finally you can think one thought which isn't about him. The second you see him again and his hand barely grazes your hand, your heart flops over, you almost faint, you feel like you're turning inside out. When he holds you, you forget the room exists. You can't act like he's the most casual fuck in the world. You can't tell him you're madly in love with him cause then he'll never see you again. You're screwed.

Marcia and Scott didn't even notice they didn't have any money. You're a man. You're not going to take anything from anyone cause you're a man. When you see her your mouth dries up and your eyes can't leave her face. You want her so much you can't handle it. You flee. You tell her you don't want her warmth. You tell her to go fuck herself. You can't let her go because you and she are, at one point, one. The more she wants you, the crazier you get. You have to let her go and you want to sink into her body.

You tell her you're in love with other women. When you wake up in the morning, holding her warm sleeping body in the curve of your body, you tell her you want to fall in love with someone.

Marcia and Scott hardly had enough money to eat and they were sleeping on the street. They'd lie on top of one blue blanket and place newspapers over their huddling bodies. Being at ease and in paradise. Every person you see looks proud and interesting. Every person you meet gives you information you want to hear. Every object in the store windows looks beautiful and yet doesn't drive you crazy with desire. Doesn't torment you with the knowledge of how poor you are. Every new street, every alleyway you see is a new stage of the voodoo ritual you're part of: A series of rooms. In each room a new magic event which changes you takes place. You're fascinated and scared. One room contains swamps and alligators and floating moss and voodoo doctors. In another room your sex is cut open and you become a third weird sex. You feel freaked. In another room, a little table, covered with a white cloth, serves as an altar upon which offerings are placed, and a candle burns on the dirt floor as its base, where the vevers are drawn. For the greater part of the time, Ogoun, and then Ghede mount the houngenikon. You place your hand on the heads of lions and wolves whom you're now equal to and who stand next to you. You find yourself outside: in a green grassy world, outside the wooden building.

Marcia and Scott knew that if the cops ever noticed they were people and not pieces of garbage strewn on the street, the cops would beat them up and put them in jail. The cops would forcibly separate them. Being so happy that you forget everything. You don't know whether you love or don't love. Forget you ever felt anything. Forget you can feel anything. You sleep cause you have to sleep and you piss in the streets. You're learning to know everything a new way.

Marcia and Scott now lived off Marcia's scant earnings as a street chanteuse. Feeling so strongly you're at the edge of a cyclone or huge hurricane. You're about to go over, if you don't constantly fight, into some new territory where the winds are whirling madly and there's no stability and your head bursts open. You still can't contain yourself, the feeling's so strong, your heart's pumping too fast and your flesh is burning: your only sense of yourself is that the world's sky has turned over inside you and that churning air is rushing out in every direction into the rest of the world and you can't fight it and the churning air becomes a force, a demonic force that exists outside of you as do all the forces of the world.

All you can do is learn. Maybe, gradually, you can learn to control this force: to keep it open so that you don't destroy the other person and/or the other person doesn't destroy you which is how most love affairs end. But all you do is stupidly and obviously unsuccessfully fight the force that is tearing all of you apart.

Capitalism as a world system had its origins in the late fifteenth and early sixteenth centuries when Europeans, mastering the art of long-distance navigation, broke out of their little corner of the globe and roamed the seven seas, conquering, plundering, and trading. Ever since then capitalism has consisted of two sharply contrasting parts: on the one hand a handful of dominant exploiting countries and on the other hand a much larger number of dominated and exploited countries.

In the beginning the relations between the developed and underdeveloped parts of the world capitalist system were based on force. The stronger conquered the weaker, plundered their resources, subjected them to unequal trading relations, and reorganized their economic structures (e.g., by introducing slavery) to serve the needs of the Europeans. In the course of these predatory operations vast colonial empires were built up and fought over by the Spanish, Portuguese, Dutch, French, and British; and the wealth transferred from the colonies to the metropolises was an important factor in the economic development of the latter.

Gradually the element of force receded into the background to be replaced by "normal" economic relations of trade and investment—without, however, in any way weakening the basic development/underdevelopment pattern, or stopping the transfer of wealth from the periphery to the center. Adam Smith was one of the first economists who tried to describe, order, and further this new society of trade, this society in which, for the first time in the world, all men could attempt to determine their own economies without regulations of kings or traditions.

After its victory in the Napoleonic Wars and the related dissolution of the Spanish and Portuguese empires in the Americas, Britain—which was already industrially far ahead of the other developed countries—moved into a position of virtual monopoly of world trade in manufactured goods. The simple laissez-faire capitalism had developed, seemingly from necessity for competition causes expansion, into imperialism.

Around 1885, A. F. Mummery, a successful British businessman, was speculating as to the cause of those periodic slumps in trade which had worried the business community as far back as the early eighteenth century. He decided that the cause of depression lay in the fact of excessive saving, in the chronic inability of the business system to distribute enough purchasing power to buy its own products back.

A shy and retiring economist named John A. Hobson agreed with Mummery. Together the two men wrote *The Physiology of Industry*, setting forth their heretical notion that savings might undermine prosperity.

Hobson continued to worry about the problems of capitalism, and in 1902, he wrote *Imperialism* which is a critique of the profit system. In *Imperialism* Hobson claimed that capitalism faced an internal and insoluble difficulty and that it was forced to turn to imperialism, not out of pure lust for conquest, but as a means of ensuring its own economic survival.

The inequality of incomes, the rich and the poor, the developed and the underdeveloped countries, said Hobson, led to the strangest of dilemmas: a paradoxical situation in which neither rich nor poor could consume enough goods. The poor don't have any money. The rich lack the physical capacity for that much consumption.

So, as a consequence of an inequitable division of wealth,

the rich—both individuals and corporations—are forced to save.

This saving leads to trouble. The automatic savings of the rich strata of society had to be put to use, unless the economy was to suffer from the disastrous effects of a steady withdrawal of purchasing power. The question was how to put the savings to work. The classical answer was to invest them in even more factories and more production and thus to ascend to an even higher level of output and productivity.

But, said Hobson, if the mass of people were already having trouble buying all the goods thrown on the market because their incomes were too small, how could the capitalists sell their new products?

Overseas. Imperialism is "the endeavor of the great controllers of industry to broaden the channel for the flow of their surplus wealth by seeking foreign markets and foreign investments to take off the goods and capital they cannot use at home."

All the developed nations are in the same boat. They all need new markets. Imperialism necessarily becomes the road to war.

Out of this situation arose the First World War (1914–1918) which had as major consequences for the global capitalist system: (a) extensive reshuffling of colonies and dependencies in favor of the victorious countries; (b) emergence of the United States as economically the strongest capitalist country; (c) socialist revolution in Tsarist Russia, the weakest of the imperialist powers; (d) birth and/or vigorous growth of national liberation movements in many underdeveloped countries, for the most part strongly influenced by the Russian Revolution. Thenceforth the dominant capitalist powers had to cope not only with their own internecine struggles but also with challenges from the rival socialist system and from increasingly militant liberation movements in their dependencies.

The Second World War and its outcome faithfully reflected these realities. Started as a war by the "have-not" imperialist powers (Germany, Japan, Italy) to redivide the world, it soon acquired, with the Nazi invasion of the U.S.S.R., a capitalism-versus-socialism character as well. For reasons of survival the threatened capitalist powers and the invaded Soviet Union made common cause, defeating the Axis challenge. But there was not and could not be a return to the status quo ante bellum. America, enriched by the war while all the other imperialist powers were severely damaged, became the undisputed leader of the world capitalism.

At this point many of the largest American corporations are located, at least in part, outside the U.S.A. By 1970, more than 25% of all these corporations' workers lived outside the U.S.A. By 1970, according to Commerce Department statistics, foreign sales accounted for almost 13% of the total sales of all U.S. manufacturing corporations. By 1971, the American global giants, determined to avoid the high American taxes and make higher profits, were diverting a quarter out of every dollar of new investment to foreign expansion.

More specifically, what does it mean for Americans and for the American federal regulatory process when the economic environment created by America's largest companies is increasingly beyond the control of the American government?

The more the corporate giants locate their production centers outside the U.S.A., the more unemployment in the U.S.A. increases. Money becomes tighter. When money is tight and there's an intense competition for funds to lend, big banks obtain such funds when small banks cannot. Thus in 1973, according to the Federal Reserve, nine New York City banks, six of which belonged to the Rockefeller-Morgan group, accounted for more than 26% of all commercial and industrial lending by banks in the U.S. About half of all the money lent by these New York superbanks goes to global corporations—with the result, as George Budzeika of the

New York Federal Reserve Bank has noted, that about 90% of the entire indebtedness in the United States petroleum and natural gas industry, two-thirds in the machinery and metal-products industry, and three-fourths in the chemical and rubber industries are held by these same nine New York banks.

It is the big banks, the very ones whose lending policies must be controlled if the government is to manage the economy successfully, that have the resources to escape control. Because large banks can evade mild credit restrictions, serious efforts to cool the economy by means of monetary policy must be so Draconian as to create even higher unemployment and idle factories. Heavy unemployment is not politically desirable.

For Americans, this situation means inflation because the corporations' current borrowings are permanently accelerating much faster than the corporations' increase in current holdings. Given the international status of the multinational corporations, the American government has no way to control the increasing inflation.

We're being crunched between rising unemployment and increasing inflation.

If employment possibilities increase, so will wages—not only because there are more jobs for more people to fill but also because employers in a time of labor scarcity must pay more. So we're experiencing increasing inflation, increasing unemployment, and decreasing wages.

Meanwhile there's less and less chance for the American worker or the American bum to get a share of the wealth that exists. Because the industrial giants such as I.T.T. have absorbed thousands of smaller companies in the last generation, a share of stock in these corporations represented a much larger portion of America's productive wealth in 1970 than it did in 1950—and a significant part of the stock of the largest corporations is going to their own top managers. The managers are becoming owners, deriving an ever-larger proportion of their income not from their managerial skills but from the stock they own in their own corporations.

You don't give a damn if he never come around. You never want to see him again. Fuck his round face and blond hair and his five feet ten inches lean body. Fuck him in shit. Fuck his screwed-up mouth and his skinny legs. Fuck him in piss. Fuck his broad shoulders fuck his "good-guy" manner fuck his 155 pounds fuck him with a needle fuck his filthy toes and his feet and his red nose fuck his hicksville manner and fuck that lousy cynicism that covers his naivete that's totally fake fuck his sexual uptightness fuck his scaredness fuck his egotism fuck everything he's ever done fuck everything he's ever said everything he's ever said is false stick it in a barrel and send it to me. I'll stick dynamite in it and up his ass and light 'em all. *KERPOW!* Fuck him in my blood.

Marcia woke up one morning and realized that Scott no longer loved her. I'm free. Singing and dancing on the streets in the bars they don't make me pay to get into, get as drunk as I want whenever I want. If I pass out someone will pick me up, or I'll just lay there I won't know the difference. Fuck everyone alive cause I'm so high: I'm zooming with the winds. Do ya' see me? I'm the wind cause I just go by what I feel. That's all I care about. And what other people feel. I can sense their feelings more and more strongly it's like my skin touches different kinds of air and knows what these kinds of air are. I'm always sensing and shaking and shivering and knowing the future. Long as I don't get too near anyone. I want to get too close.

She realized that Scott was no longer satisfied with a bum's life. What I wanna do is fuck every man in sight. Fuck every man who comes near me and fuck every man who looks at me like he wants to fuck me. Go into some bar, fuck three men in the bathroom, then lie down on the dance floor and wiggle out of my rags. Let every man do to me what he wants. Men will spit on me and piss on me. Women will shoot liquids up my cunt. People become shadows. Then I'll stand up and walk over to these famous businessmen, the Duponts, and put my arms around one of their necks. He'll lift me up and fuck me while I'm naked on the street. Someone else will take me home. I won't even look to see his face. I'll walk into a bum's bar, slowly take off my clothes. Slowly they'll notice me. They won't believe what's happening. I'll love watching the drool and vomit dribble out of their mouths. I turn on watching them remember they have cocks. Their hands slowly reach into their bums' clothing. Their hands are shaking so hard they can't even get it together to touch themselves. As soon as I see this happening, I'll begin to moan. I'll sleep with some bum, with some bum who graduated from the Sorbonne and who made $700,000 a week as a Marseilles gigolo, just to find out how it feels.

Scott wanted to get his own work known. Turn your head toward me gently. That's right. I'm looking at your face. It's almost touching mine. It's right next to me on the pillow. I feel very, soft. As if something's just touching me, beginning to smooth away the rough edges and granite boulders in my skin. Do you want to touch me? I'm always amazed anyone wants to touch me cause I'm always feeling these granite blocks and roughnesses and my ugliness. I have to be able to touch you and keep my distance from you. You're lying partly on top of me and you're falling asleep in my arms. You must've come. I feel you like me and I like you. I'm not thinking about Scott now. For the first time I've calmed down cause I know what to expect with you.

Scott wanted fame and fortune. I live totally by my emotions. That's who I am. Today someone told me I move like a little animal. She doesn't know how I survive. Yesterday someone told me I'm conventionally moral because I'm not fucking three guys at the same time. The same person who

told me I'm conventionally moral told me I need endless
shots of valium. Today this old lady told my closest friend
that I'm getting more and more violent. She's worried about
my work. I don't know what my work is. All this stuff passes
over my head. I feel a lot of pain most of the time because
I act on my feelings and I barge into other people's feelings,
opinions, beliefs, whatever they act on, and I scare and hurt
them.

Scott wanted beautiful Parisian women to drool over him
because he was the guy who was making the most powerful
architecture in Paris. If someone doesn't kiss me goodbye, I
think the person hates me. If someone I'm fucking doesn't
tell me he loves me, I'm sure he hates me. If someone I
want doesn't show me constant physical attention, I'm sure
that person wants nothing to do with me. If I'm living with
someone and he goes away, I refuse to speak to him when
he returns. If he goes away again and again, I leave him.
Once a man's fallen in love with me, I tell him I don't want
to fuck him anymore. I insult my friends to their faces and
to other friends. Sometimes I refuse to see the people I'm
closest to and I feel I hate them.

Marcia realized she was a bum and didn't belong in this
picture of Scott's success. Please tell me whether you love
me or not. WHY DO YOU WANT TO KNOW? I can't fuck
anyone else cause I'm always thinking about you and I'm
getting too horny. I'M NOT IN LOVE WITH YOU AND I
DON'T WANT A HEAVY RELATIONSHIP. I'M MORE
OFF THAN ON. I understand what's going on. THIS IS
CRAZY. WHY SHOULD I DEFINE MY FEELINGS FOR
YOU? I DON'T HAVE TO TELL YOU WHAT I FEEL.
YOU'RE SO CONVENTIONALLY MORAL: YOU CAN
ONLY FUCK ONE GUY AT A TIME. All I said what that
I was stuck on you. HOW CAN YOU BE IN LOVE WITH
ME? YOU'VE ONLY KNOWN ME FOR A FEW MONTHS

AND YOU'RE JUST A KID. I DON'T BELIEVE YOU
WHEN YOU TELL ME YOU LOVE ME.

She began to go crazy. A glance at the annual earnings of
220 men in charge of some of America's largest corporations
(there are no women) shows them to be at the very top of
the income pyramid.

Even though we no longer experience a laissez-faire, or
even a free market, economy, the multinational conglomerate
corporations that control the world's wealth need, as did the
capitalists of nineteenth century Britain, markets for their
products. Due to increasing inflation unemployment and
tightening of money, even the corporations are experiencing
increasing stagnation. The state can counteract stagnation by
suitably large expenditures on welfare and/or warfare, both
of which are indispensable to monopoly capitalism for other
reasons: welfare as a way of placating the masses and dissu-
ading them from turning to revolutionary politics, and warfare
as a means used by each leading capitalist power to maximize
its economic "living space" and to control undeveloped and
potentially rebellious dependent countries.

Since ours isn't a welfare economy, America is not going
socialist god forbid, it has become a war economy. The military market supports the largest single industry in the country
today, providing more than 40 billion dollars in sales each
year and involving in total over 20,000 firms. The industry
is remarkably concentrated, with the 100 largest contractors
receiving two-thirds of the total contract funds, and the top
25 receiving half these funds.

Negotiated contracts are the rule rather than the exception
in the defense industry, accounting for 58% of all military
contracts in 1968, with advertised competitive bidding
accounting for only 11.5% of the total procurement dollars.
This industry is one of our least competitive. Firms seldom
if ever suffer a financial loss in their defense business. The
Defense Department acts to insure that the firms which do

business with it remain financially healthy. In fact, the large defense firms often win and/or maintain goverment contracts by suggesting new systems and new systems improvements and establishing in the minds of the government the special competence of their firms to carry out the job. Peter Schenck, an official of the Raytheon Corporation and former president of the Air Force Corporation, put it in this way: "Today it is more likely that the military requirement is the result of joint participation of military and industrial personnel, and it is not unusual for industry's contribution to be the key factor. Indeed, there are highly-placed military men who sincerely feel that industry is currently setting the pace in the research and development of new weapons systems."

What are the economic results of this dependence upon arms production and maintenance? That wars are engines of inflation is well known: in fact, every substantial war in U.S. history has been accompanied by inflation. And the wildest inflationary periods in other countries have been associated with wars. For 30 years the United States has had a permanently militarized economy. The same applies, in a lesser degree, to other major capitalist powers and, to an even greater degree, to certain small capitalist states.

Militarization provides corporations with a cushion of high-profit business, enabling them to set and maintain higher profit margins in civilian markets. Fantastic markups of four or five times factory cost are applied to the sale of products originally developed for military use, for example, electronics. Efficiency in production for the military is a fraction of that in civilian production, and the corresponding multiplication of costs inevitably is transmitted, at least in part, to civilian sales of armament manufactures.

How does the rising inflation affect the large American, if they can still be called American, corporations and the United States government?

The multinational corporations are more and more, as has

been said, depending upon bank loans. The U.S. is the Debt Economy without peer. One trillion dollars in corporate debt. Six hundred billion dollars in mortgage debt. Five hundred billion in U.S. government debt. Two hundred billion in consumer debt. To fuel nearly three decades of postwar economic boom at home and export it abroad, this nation has borrowed an average net two hundred million dollars a day, each and every day, since the close of the Second World War.

The American government and the huge corporations took on their enormous burden of debt with the expectation that personal income (buying power) and corporate profits would continue to grow year after year and that government economic policy would remain essentially expansionary. But inflation, while adding greatly to the need to borrow, has slashed the share of income—corporate and personal—available to pay off debts, and an expansionary government economic policy would only add to the inflationary pressures.

So now the nation's burden of debt is like a string drawn very taut: 2.5 trillion dollars in debt outstanding and more money needed to keep the economy growing, while the ability of borrowers to repay what they owe and to find more money is very much in question. The string has not broken, and it may not. The energies of every economist, of every government official, of every lender and borrower will be directed in the weeks and months ahead to keeping that string from breaking. Yet no one knows the precise breaking point and, while there are schemes and theories galore, no one really knows how to ease the tension either.

As unwilling as economists are to admit it, the string has to break.

Keynesian economics, as a system of pushbutton monetary and fiscal policies designed to finely tune the economy and create full or near-full employment with zero or mild inflation, has seen its day (if it ever had a day). Economists can no longer describe what's happening. Economically we're going through a period of transformation.

So what are we to expect?

Capitalism has always been based on a certain relation between two living entities. There are the dominant exploiting countries. These two groups are indissolubly linked together, and nothing that happens in either part can be understood if it is considered in abstraction from the system as a whole. The principal contradiction in the system, at least in the present historical period, is not within the developed part but between the developed and the underdeveloped parts. The relations of the one to the other (and the policies which grow out of these relations) are fundamentally exploitative: they perpetuate and deepen the development/underdevelopment pattern. Keynesian economics had failed because of its policies and not its techniques—in broadest terms, because it attempted to paper over the class conflicts present in a capitalist society.

The transformation of American capitalism is now becoming manifest. The reversal in the historical (Keynesian) belief that profits are the outcome of high volume or mass production spells disruption for the ordinary processes of production and consumption. There will be frequent manipulated shortages of almost everything that is bought and sold. The notion that inflation can be stemmed by government action has one central defect: the government is subject to the political domination of the large corporations. The penetration by corporations of government agencies charged with regulating business activity vitiates the idea that the state is separate from the marketplace and independent of ruling class control.

There are no effective mechanisms for controling inflation within a highly centralized and monopolistic economy. Corporate and government decision makers will be constrained to find some solution to the crisis. The chance of stemming inflation depends on finding ways to expand war industries and other forms of public expenditures. The worsening economic situation within the U.S. will probably result in the widening of military influence.

There are substantial problems in implementing this option. First, the United States lacks an available external enemy. Second, the outcome of the Vietnam War has certainly dampened popular enthusiasm for military action.

Which raises the distinct probability of the emergence of new forms of authoritarian rule at home. We are on the road to what Bertram Gross has called "friendly fascism". Unlike its European predecessors, American fascism may not be marked by an "open terroristic dictatorship." The foundation of fascism has already been laid in the consolidation of political and economic power in incredibly few hands.

One night, as she was lying on the street, Marcia dreamt that she returned home. It seemed to her she stood by the iron gate leading to the drive, and for a while she couldn't enter for the way was barred to her. There was a padlock and a chain upon the gate. She called in her dream to her parents, and had no answer, and peering closer through the rusted spokes of the gate, she saw that the house seemed uninhabited.

No smoke came from the chimney, and the little lattice windows gaped forlorn. Then, like all dreamers, she was suddenly possessed with supernatural powers and passed like a spirit through the barrier before her. The drive wound around in front of her, twisting and turning as it had always done, but as she advanced she was aware that a change had come upon it: it was narrow and unkept, not the drive that she had known. At first she was puzzled and did not understand, and it was only when she bent her head to avoid the low swinging branch of a tree that she realized what had happened. Nature had come into her own again and, little by little, in her stealthy, insidious way had encroached upon the drive with long tenacious fingers. The woods, always a menace even in the past, had triumphed in the end. They crowded, dark and uncontrolled, to the borders of the drive. The beeches with white, naked limbs leant close to one another, their branches intermingled in a strange embrace, making a vault above her head like the archway of a church. And there were other trees as well, trees that she did not recognize, squat oaks and tortured elms that straggled cheek by jowl with the beeches, and had thrust themselves out of the quiet earth, along with monster shrubs and plants, none of which she remembered.

The drive was a ribbon now, a thread of its former self, with gravel surface gone, and choked with grass and moss. The trees had thrown out low branches, making an impediment to progress; the gnarled roots looked like skeleton claws. Scattered here and again amongst this jungle growth she could recognize shrubs that had been landmarks of her childhood, hydrangeas she had touched and seen as her friends. No hand had checked their progress, and they had gone native now, rearing to monster height without a bloom, black and ugly as the nameless parasites that grew besides them.

On and on, now east now west, wound the poor thread that had once been the drive. Sometimes she thought it lost, but it appeared again, beneath a fallen tree perhaps, or struggling on the other side of a muddied ditch created by the winter rains. She hadn't thought the way home was so long. Surely the miles had multiplied, even as the trees had done, and this path led but to a labyrinth, some choked wilderness, and not to the house at all. She came upon it suddenly; the approach masked by the unnatural growth of a vast shrub that spread in all directions, and she stood, her heart thumping in her breast, tears behind her eyes.

This was her home, secretive and silent as it had always been, the grey stone shining in the moonlight of her dream, the mullioned windows relecting the green lawns and the terrace.

Feeling lonely. Feeling lonely, and crazy all the time cause so lonely. Always wanting and wanting and the wanting's never satisfied. Hate myself for wanting so much and for feeling lonely cause it's disgusting and lowering to need someone else and to feel lonely. Hate everyone in the world cause they're all potential lovers and they don't love me. I hate them cause they hate me. Feeling envy and resentment and fear.

If no one bothers me I'll be O.K. As long as I don't have to see anyone and deal with their feelings. Walk the streets alone. Don't let anyone touch me, cause if someone touches me I might want him or her to touch me again.

Don't want anything to do with anyone anymore. Them coming too close to me, wanting to touch me, my skin's gone, wanting something from me, can't figure out what they want. They want me to smile and touch them, but not to smile and touch them too hard. Can't do that cause want affection so desperately. Am not in control.

Feeling almost cut to the bone. Part of me hates, snaps, wants to destroy, wants to cut out the part of other people that hurts me. This part's out of control. This part frightens me. Hurt other people and quiver and shake cause hurt them and run away. Two parts running away from each other. The string has to break. Feeling gentle and soft (the second part). Feeling incapable of doing anything except reaching in this totally soft way. Feeling big large eyes opening wider and wider. This part is all defense. Feeling can have power over my life. Can prevent myself from being hurt by snapping and by being defensive. Feeling I'm so special if I'm hurt I should stop being hurt.

Feeling like a thing rather than living. Knowing that wanting a lover, wanting Scott back, is wanting to be dead again, wanting one feeling so much that feeling becomes a thing, my possession. Knowing this but not feeling it all throughout my body.

CHAPTER SEVEN

THE LIFE OF JOHNNY ROCCO

SHE couldn't take it anymore.

She was just a cheap gun moll. He approached her sexually. But she was too scared of him and she didn't come through. He didn't want anything to do with her anymore. Sexually. He was punishing her.

He told her he was fucking a lot of women and he didn't want to fuck her. All the women he was fucking were taking away his energy. He needed energy for his business. He wanted to establish a relation with her that wouldn't sap his energy. She agreed with him.

In the beginning it was murder for the woman because he wouldn't show her any love. One day she slashed her wrists, not seriously, to make him notice her. A few days later she got seriously sick; her body had taken over her search for love.

The man told her she should look into herself for love.

The moll made a decision: This was the first man she had ever met in her 28 years of living to whom she was completely opening herself. She told the businessman she'd do anything for him. Would he just let her in. She'd be his secretary, his gun boy, his cook, anything despite her 28 years of increasing independence. He told her he didn't need anything from her.

Nonetheless the woman and the man were becoming closer and closer. They were slowly beginning to tell each other everything.

One day, over breakfast, they reached the height of their friendship. They both agreed that they weren't in love with anyone. The woman told the man who (she knew) tended to be dishonest, that he shouldn't pretend he was in love with the women he was fucking when he wasn't. The man told the woman she needed to be loved. She trusted him so much she openly agreed with him.

The next day the businessman said to the moll, "My love, I want to take you places you've never been . . ." The moll made her third mistake.

First mistake: fucking with the guy that one time he approached her.

Second mistake: thinking the guy might be falling in love with her when he said "My love . . ."

Third mistake: she said to the man, "Do you love me? I want to know because I could fall in love with you very deeply."

"I don't love you," the businessman replied. "However, I feel affectionately toward you. Right now you matter more to me than all the other women I know. Why don't you call me tomorrow?"

The next day she called him and he told her that he was exhausted because he had been fucking around. Then he lied to her, like she was another of those women who were chasing him only she was lower because he wouldn't even fuck her, she was no longer his friend because she had admitted to him she could fall in love with him, about his plans for that night.

When she got off the phone, she felt a lot of pain. She wrote him the following letter: I'VE GOT TO SPLIT. HERE'S THE OPIUM I OWE YOU AND A GOING-AWAY PRESENT. GOOD KNOWING YOU. Then she realized that she had cut off, purposely, willingly, the only person she had ever been able to talk to completely and learn from. She was more and more in pain. She didn't want to stay where people could reach her so she went outside. It was snowing, snowing so hard you couldn't see the hand you stuck out in front of your body. She was being even more stupid when she threw herself in front of a moving car.

The name of the businessman was Johnny Rocco.

What does being a man mean? The only thing you trust is the edge your own loneliness makes. You make your decisions according to this edge. You trust other perceptions and other people only partially. No matter how deeply you may love some man or how closely you may be working with some man, you'd cut that person dead if your loneliness demanded it.

"Have you got the guns?"

"Just got the shipment in from Vito. I don't trust that guy."

"Nobody cares whether you trust him or not."

"I care whether I live or die."

"Sure. Get the crates open. We've got to get the guns out of here soon."

"What about the dame?"

"What d'ya mean: 'What about the dame'?"

"The last time I saw the crates, there was a dame sitting on them."

"You're seeing things. No dame's ever come into this warehouse. Dames aren't part of the business.

"I said, 'Dames aren't part of our business.' "

"You said, 'Dames aren't part of the business.' "

"All we've got are ourselves and our blood. Dames, dope, ideas—they don't matter."

"The dame she wants to talk with you."

"Get rid of her."

"How should I do that?"

"Try killing her."

Johnny and I were children together. I can remember running around with him on the Brooklyn streets. Looking up to him like he was God. When I got old enough to go into business, he helped me open my first business. Gave me money and never questioned me. I try to keep my life clean, American; Johnny's the only person I'm friends with.

I went into my office to talk to her to see what kind of trouble she was bringing.

Her back was sticking in my eyes. She must have heard footsteps cause she turned round.

"I don't like women," I told her. "You don't concern me and you don't belong here. Tell me your business and then get out of here as quickly as possible."

"I'm not a woman," she replied.

"You look like a woman to me."

"That's your problem." She told me that the guns she was sitting on, the ones my brother had just sent me, were hot. The minute my boys used the guns, the cops would be on to me. I asked her why Vito had sent me hot rods. She said she didn't know anything else.

I stopped looking at her. "Get out of here."

She walked away like she was walking down Park Avenue. She wasn't running and she wasn't looking. I couldn't tell if she had been lying to me or not.

The years of pretense in my soul are nothing compared to the years the business for which they had hired me had been going on.

The Dominican Republic was going to hell. The economy was at an all-time low, for their President, Rafael Trujillo, was fleecing all of the industries and making treaties according to his personal needs. Censorship was absolute. No one in the country had any personal rights. Not that the United States minded any of this.

Unfortunately in March of 1960 President Romulo Betancourt of Venezuela asked the Organization of American States to censure Trujillo for "flagrant violations of human rights." Trujillo blew his cool and decided to off Betancourt. The assassination didn't work and the United States got worried that Trujillo was losing his touch.

Thirty-one years of Trujillo's fleecing and now the United States decided they needed a new fleecer. Trujillo had gotten so paranoid that he was controlling the Dominican military bases and weaponry. The United States decided they had to import some guns into the Dominican Republic.

On December 28, 1960, a man named Plato Cox told me he needed my trucks to ship some groceries to the supermarkets in the Dominican Republic. The Dominican Republic was having trouble getting food because Trujillo was appropriating all of the food. The groceries would consist of specially marked and packed food cans. Once the trucks reached the Dominican Republic, a man named Lorenzo Berry would meet each truck and show each truck where to go.

I wasn't sure these were the facts and I wasn't sure who was fleecing whom. All I knew was I was legitimate becase I was powerful and power causes legitimacy in this country.

"The guns're packed."

"What're you bothering me for? Did you put a tail on that dame?"

"The dame disappeared."

"She disappeared? Who'd you put on her?"

"She knew what she was doing."

"Then she must have had a reason for telling me what she did."

"Dames never do anything for reasons. You can never tell why they do what they do."

"I mean that she must working for someone. Someone who has a business of his own."

"I tell you you can never tell why dames do what they do. Forget whatever she told you, boss: she was probably halucinating like all dames do. I never should have let her in here. You can never trust what they say."

"Oh yeah?" There was ice in my soul. "The dame doesn't matter. Nobody matters to me."

All my consciousness has ever been is I love and adore Johnny. One man shouldn't feel this way about another man. But Johnny's my brother. I don't feel like I've given myself away to Johnny. I don't feel I've tried to escape my own loneliness. My business is the outpouring, the continuation of my loneliness, and my business is separate from Johnny's business. I supply guns and other tools to business in need. This isn't the truth. The truth is I exist according to the blood, the strength of the blood, I was born in. Johnny's the only family I have left. To the extent he'll stick to me, I'll doubly and triply try to give him what he wants, his muscle, because that's where one of my centers is.

The trouble's always been that Johnny isn't as simple as I am and doesn't support me the way I support him. Johnny says to me: "You're my brother. The only relations between people that can possibly exist in this world are blood relations. If it wasn't for blood, it'd be every man for himself."

"Yeah, Johnny," I say. He looks at me and walks away. He's forgotten when he's been saying. Johnny offers me 40 grand if I ever want it. A month later I'm in a jam. Johnny can't lend me the money cause he just bought too many racing horses. I figure Johnny hates me. Johnny calls me up, almost crying: Why am I acting so paranoid? Won't I have dinner with him at Teddy's? He's got a business engagement. He has to go now.

Johnny's ambivalence affects everything. His ambivalence makes him charming. I don't know whether to trust him or not.

Johnny doesn't kill because he's ambivalent and I'm a killer.

I had forgotten about the dame and, by chance, I met her again. It was a dimly lit street, the polluted air was so thick you could see it at the edge of the lights. Somewhere below Houston on the Bowery. I'm not usually found in such a filthy neighborhood.

The dame was walking up the street, slightly ahead of me. I increased my pace and caught up with her.

"Hello," I said to her.

"Hello," she murmured. She increased her walking pace.

The light from a bum bar sign cast a diagonal of purple light across her face. "I want to find out why you told me Vito's guns are hot."

"Why do you want to know?"

By now the purple light had left her face. "Either Vito sent me hot guns and someone wants me to know that. In that case I'd like to find out who my unknown friend is. In this business friends don't exist for no reason. Or else someone sent you with a phony story to break up Vito and me. So tell me who you're working for."

She didn't look she minded my questions. "I won't even try the story that Vito loved me, discarded me, and I'm trying to get revenge. Let's just say I decided to squelch on Vito for personal reasons."

"Meaning you have a business of your own. That's the only personal reason I know of. That won't help you. Dames don't have businesses of their own."

"Do you want to hear lies?"

I was getting sick of her toughness. It was a stupid toughness because it didn't make sense. "Listen, honey. You're going to tell me who you're working for whether you like it or not. So you might as well start telling me now before I start giving you trouble."

She had started walking again, as fast as she could. There was no one on the streets. There was no one she could run to. There was no where she could run to. "Get out of my life before I call the cops."

It was dark. I put my arms around her and pinned her to

the building. My hands held her wrists and my legs were stuck between her legs. The typical rapist's position. "Tell me who you work for, why he hired you, why he sent you over to me. I'm sick of fooling around."

"I told you already. I don't work for any man. I work for myself."

"I'll try again. Tell me who you work for, why he hired you, and why he sent you over to me. If you don't tell me, I'm going to beat you to a pulp."

She didn't say anything. I slapped her face a few times.

"I told you: I'm in business for myself. I went with Vito for a while. I learned the ropes, and when he dumped me, I decided to use what I'd learned.

"I thought you'd be nicer to me than Vito."

I almost puked. What did she want me to do? Make love to her like I was Daddy with his new little girl? I hit at her again and again. Then I realized how tough she was. She didn't even try to give me a believable lie. She just told me the stupidist thing she could think of, the sex line, and I fell for it. She was never going to tell me anything. I beat her up some more and left her there. I didn't know whether she was alive or dead.

I guess I didn't kill outright cause I was hoping she'd remember who I was.

I got back to the office. It looked like nothing had changed. A big empty warehouse with a few dollies shoved against the wall to my left. I walked into my office in the back of the warehouse. It was pitch black.

"Mr. Rocco,"

I didn't move. The lights were on all around me.

"I hope you don't mind I let myself into your office. I don't like to stand on the street. I can cause unnecessary attention."

"I'm a private man, Mr. Cox, and I get nervous easily. Why d'you break into my office?"

"Mr. Rocco, you're one of the most intelligent men it's

been my privilege to deal with. Our business is almost over with. I'm sure you're going to understand what I'm going to tell you."

His voice sounded like it was coming out of a machine. I looked at his pig face and held my breath.

"Because we live in a complex world, unfortunately we're forced to act one way and say we're acting another. Let me give you an example: A few months ago Castro allowed the Russkies to enter Cuba, build missile sites on the island, flood Havana with technicians. Naturally we couldn't allow this. We acted directly. We invaded Cuba and, when that failed, threatened to bomb Cuba. Castro successfully called our bluff."

"You wanted Batista back so you could keep splitting the profits with him and Mayer Lansky. Who're you kidding?"

He brushed my words off him with his fingertips.

"Of course the world no longer accepts our credibility. We're no longer able to act directly. But we still have to get rid of Castro."

"So why don't you hire Lansky to off Castro? Lansky's a better businessman than you are."

"Let's take another example:

"The horrendous situation of the people of the Dominican Republic. We'd like to help certain Dominican Republic patriots recover."

"Their beloved homeland. Your business is democracy. You want to ask Trujillo to resign."

"You don't understand, Mr. Rocco. Because of the Bay of Pigs fiasco, we can't risk another assassination at this time. We have to abandon our plans for Rafael Trujillo.

"We'd like you to remain quiet, Mr. Rocco. Very very quiet about your dealings with us."

"I don't care what your fuckin' plans are as long as you pay me for the business I've done for you. But if you ever break into my office again or in any way disturb my business operations, I'll blast this secret wide open."

"Of course we'll do you any favors you need. Because we're friends, Mr. Rocco. Let's both observe each other's privacy." I picked up my hat and left.

I dreamed I was in this plane. The earth was turning away from me as if it were running away from itself at 100 miles per hour. The sky's getting darker and darker. The winds are howling around me. When I come down to earth, I learn that two new mailplane pilots, Les and Joe, have entered the Dutchman's premises. Joe's girlfriend is Bonnie Lee. As head pilot of the Dutchman service successful landings and continuing flying are my business. Joe's up in a plane. The air changes to fog. I try to bring Joe down but I can't. The fog's too thick. Joe insists on landing, against his own rational knowledge, because he's supposed to have dinner with Bonnie. Grey haze. I'm sitting in the restaurant with some other flyers and Bonnie. Bonnie asks me if Joe's death is her fault.

"Sure it was your fault. You were going to have dinner with him, the Dutchman hired him, I sent him up on schedule, the fog came in, a tree got in the way. All your fault." The steaks Bonnie ordered for her and Joe arrive. I take Joe's steak. Bonnie says, "Are you going to eat it?" I say, "What do you want me to do, have it stuffed?" Bonnie says, "It was Joe's steak." "Who's Joe?" I look at the steak. Then Bonnie and I sing the 'Peanut Vendor' to signal her initiation into the acceptance of our living on the edge of death. We haven't forgotten Joe's death. We're shouting our defiance of the face of darkness surrounding human life and the chaos of the universe. Then Kid, my closest friend whose eyesight's been failing but who won't stop flying, fatally crashes his plane. I go crazy. In my craziness I realize I love Bonnie: I need her world of out-of-control feelings and personal commitment.

"Johnny"

"Huh?"

"What are you doing here?"

"I'm having this bad dream. Do you ever get worried?"

"Huh? I trust you boss. You run a powerful family. I came back to clean up."

"You came back to clean up. I think I'm going to die soon."

"You worried about Vito business, boss? Why don't you just give him a vacation?"

"I'm not worried about anyone. The dame. Vito. That lousy gun-running business that just fell through. I just think that things are over. I think Johnny Rocco has no more use."

"My brother-in-law told me this great joke. There's this lady, see, who lives in Brooklyn. Her backyard's been smelling worse and worse. She sees a skunk run into her kitchen so she captures the skunk in a brown paper bag and takes the paper bag to the nearest bus stop. She says to the bus driver of the first bus which comes along, 'Listen driver. Tell me when we get to the end of the line. In this bag I've got a skunk who's been smelling up everything so I want to get him as far away from my house as possible.' The driver tells the lady to sit in the back of the bus. She sits in the back of the bus. Some time goes by. The bus driver yells out, 'Will the lady with the stinkin' pussy please get off the bus?' All the women on the bus cross their legs as tightly as they can. Six women run out the rear door."

"I think that I'm dead. I don't care who I beat up anymore. I don't care if I beat anyone up anymore. I can sit on my ass and I can do nothing, I can destroy the world, and I don't know the difference. I'm a ghost wandering about in a ghost land that's made up of my own garbage."

"You don't look dead to me boss. We're gonna have two new trucks coming tomorrow."

"I've got guns and knives. I can do anything. I've got all the money I need. I planned it this way. I figured out the steps. I can make any move I want cause I've got the know-how to create reality the way I want it so all the others accept it as reality."

"The trucks're gonna be the biggest we've every had. The boys'll want to celebrate."

"How can I fight myself? How the hell can I start the real death battle of all time? I'm sick of the pretense. Maybe I'm going crazy like Joey Gallo went crazy when he took Profaci's four top men."

I was standing at the doorway to my private office. I saw a line of bullets rip through the windows. Bits of glass flying. A body throws me down to the floor.

"You wanna get killed?"

"Stay still." I watch the line of bullets go back and forth until the windows are wide open. I see a gun on the floor.

After a long quiet I walk to the gun. A note around the gun tells me I have to watch how I act: I'm forgetting my manners. I shouldn't have beat up the girl.

I guess the girl's still alive and has protectors.

"Looks like you've been asking for trouble Johnny."

I had to find the girl. I figured she was with Vito or she was with those thugs who had hired me for the Dominican Republic job. When I had gotten about three blocks from the warehouse, I saw her lurking next to the corner of a building.

"I've been waiting for you."

I looked at her. Bandages practically covered her face. I liked what I saw. "I don't want to be seen with you in public. We'll go to my place."

"I have to tell you something important," she said. "I'm scared."

I let her into my place and motioned her to sit down on the rickety armchair facing the leather sofa. Then I went to get us coffee.

"I've decided to tell you who I'm working for."

I brought out the coffee. "What happened after I beat you up?"

"One of my bosses had been following me. He picked me up and asked why you had been knocking into me."

"You mean he didn't try to stop me."

"Don't be a fool. I told him you were trying to find out who I was working for. Since I didn't tell you, you beat me up. He didn't believe me."

"Uh-huh. So now you're scared. You come running to me." There was something strange in her eyes.

"He said he was going to murder you cause you weren't obeying orders and he was going to murder me."

"I'm not obeying orders? You must be working for those government guys who hired me to run guns to the Dominican Republic. They sent you with that story about Vito to try to bust up me and Vito so they could get a tighter hold on me."

"I just did what they told me. I was working for them."

"You seemed so tough. And now you come running to me just cause your boss threatens to kill you. Even with all your bandages on, I still don't like you."

"You've got to believe me. We're up against people who are much stronger than us. After I told the boss my story, he left me. I was lying there in the dark. I overheard two men talking about Giancana. Giancana was the top Chicago boss no one had been able to do in for 30 years. The bosses hired him to help them assassinate Castro. When he didn't succeed, cause they couldn't trust him, they shot him in the throat, mouth, and back of the head.

"I came here."

I didn't like the parallel she was drawing between me and Salvatore Giancana.

"You can't fight them, Johnny. The only thing you can do is run. You must have enough friends who'll help you take a semi-permanent vacation."

"And you'll go with me cause you need protection." I

started talking to myself out loud. "And what about Vito? I need Vito's help." I looked at her bandaged face. "Were your bosses trying to break up Vito and me, or were they working in collusion with Vito?"

"I don't know. I never even saw Vito."

"I have to find out about that. I have to know if I can use Vito's help."

I turned to her. "Now I'm putting myself in your hands. I want you to return to your bosses and learn if they're working with Vito." I thought for a minute. "That'll show me I can trust you and take you with me."

"I don't have a choice."

"You can sleep here. I have to speak to Vito now." I threw her a blanket. "As soon as you wake up, go back to your bosses."

"Mommy always loved you more than she did me."

I was startled a grown man would speak to me this honestly. "I don't think that's true. She used me as a whipping post to get you to do what she wanted."

"She wanted me to be exactly like you. You were smart and tough and handsome. You knew what you were doing. I was stupid."

"She was just using who you thought I was to control you. You were so stupid you accepted whatever she said."

"She cared more about you than she did about me."

"The truth is she hated me. You don't know any of this. When she was 19, she was a wild kid. She used to escape from her strict parents at night, secretly, and fuck every guy in sight. She fell madly in love with this one guy. Maybe they got married. When she was three months pregnant, he split."

"You were the kid?"

"According to her, he split because she was pregnant. He

never sent her any money or wanted to see me. So when I was a year old, she married a guy she despised."

"She must have loved you too. You were all she had left of the guy she loved. I was the son of that good-for-nothing lazy vegetable she had to support. No wonder she despised me."

"She might have loved me when I was a kid. Remember I look exactly like her 'cept I'm a man, and you look like your stupid father. But once I started fucking around, she hated me."

"I don't understand, Johnny."

"She actually tried to kill me. I had run away from her to be with another woman."

"I thought you hated women."

"That was before I decided women were so stupid, they were only interested in their own comforts. She hired some class-C private dick, gave him some knock-out drops to give me so he could stick me in his car and bring me home. I tested those drops. They were poison."

"She's crazy cause she's always wanted a man and never got one. You can't blame her for the ways she's acted."

"You still adore her. I do too. She's a totally beautiful woman."

I was surprised to hear Johnny say that. I've always known my brother's a bit cold and has trouble feeling things. Whereas I'm stupid, but I feel strongly.

"Vito, I came to ask you about the guns you sent me."

"Huh? Didn't you get them yet?"

"Yeah. A dame came with them."

"I didn't know you had girlfriends, Johnny."

"The dame told me that guns you sent me were cop-registered. Then I found out the dame was working for the feds."

"You think I'm working for the feds? I wouldn't do that."

I saw the hurt in his eyes. "You're my brother. I don't

think you'd work against me unless you thought you'd become Capo di Tutti Capi. I'm in trouble, Vito. I've got to get out of town tonight and no one can know about it."

"You know I'll help you Johnny. Meet me at the store tonight at 8:00. Everything'll be set up. I'll be at my warehouse all day if you need me."

I put my hand on his cheek and kissed him.

When I got outside, the sun was coming up.

Most of my men were already in the warehouse when I entered it.

"Johnny, there's some guy here from the United Fruit Company."

"Tell him to wait. Did the new trucks come in?"

"Yeah, and they're beauts. We've never had bigger and they handle like happy prostitutes."

"The bigger they are, the bigger I am." I was feeling good. "And now the United Fruit Company, the only banana company who's been using free labor, comes to me.

"You know why they come to me? I know how to make the moves. I started off with nothing. I was a creep on the street like all of you are still creeps on the street. When I was still a kid, I saw everything clearly: If I didn't go ahead and make it for myself, no one would make it for me. It was black, nothing, a hole. I just made some moves. I wasn't smarter than you guys, I just had more guts. I saw it didn't even matter what moves I made, because everyone else was so stupid, they were just sitting on their asses and gawking.

"I'm the real bourgeoisie cause I'm one of the people who makes the paths everyone in this society follows."

"The United Fruit guy says he'd like to speak with you soon, if it's O.K with you, cause he has to get back to the docks . . ."

"Sure there are other guys who know enough to make paths that work. Their paths aren't my paths cause they aren't me. Their paths aren't my paths cause they aren't me. But no one and no family's ever crossed me and won. My territory works and remains untouched cause I know how to deal with the world. I'm a complex guy and I work as complexly as I see. That's what power really is."

"Hey boss go talk to that banana guy. He thinks you're offending him cause his prick's not long enough."

"You can't impose your will on the world. You can't go out and shoot some people and expect to get what you want. That's being a muscle-man. The only reason Anastasia lasted so long is cause Frankie backed him. I've studied all this. You've got to know how the world works. You've got to know exactly what the forces are you're dealing with so you know when to bend a little, even when to hide, and when to kill. The feds are a strong group so I have to take a little vacation. I know when to bend. I also know that in the long run the Reds are dependent on me cause I can do the work they can't do.

"A conscious man can absolutely make his way in the world."

"Boss, someone on the phone says he's sending over a present for you."

"Why d'ya have to tell me about crank phone calls, stupe?" I slapped him across the face. "I'm getting everything I ever wanted. Now the big importers are coming to me."

"The banana guy's waiting in your private office."

As I reached the office door, I heard a crash. I saw one window paneless and the broken glass scattered on the floor. A round object, partly white and partly red lay on the floor.

I knew what it was before I saw it close. It was the dame's head. The one who had worked for the feds. Better her head than my head.

I heard a voice behind me. It sounded like Cox.

"It looks like you were stupid. We asked you to keep your mouth shut and you went in search of that girl. Maybe you had crush on her and couldn't resist your manly ardour."

"So she told you she was working for me."

I guess you were just a little stupid Johnny and we're more powerful than you."

I heard some shots behind me and some thuds.

Screams of agony.

"You've been a good businessman, Johnny. You're getting sloppy taking care of business so we have to take care of your business for you."

I turned around. Now blood, flesh, and guts covered the floor instead of broken glass. I didn't see any of my men who were alive.

"We're going to do our own shipping instead of hiring people like you. Strong individualism is the American ideal."

"Have you killed Vito?"

"Let's clean up this mess." I threw down my gun and walked over to the nearest dead body. I ordered one of my men to pick up a broom and begin to sweep.

They weren't even going to kill me. I ran out of that warehouse. I had no idea where to go. I kept on running.

FLORIDA

MAYBE you're dying and you don't care anymore.

In the nothingness, the gray, islands almost disappear into the water. Black ovals the shape of leaves hide the crumbling of the universe. Key West Islands disappearing into the ocean.

You don't have anything more to say. You don't know what to do. Your whole life has been a mess. Grabbing on to whatever romance came along and holding on to it for dear life until it went so sour you had to vomit and leave. Then you'd recover, just like you recover from a hangover, by grabbing the next piece of tail who came along and wasn't so helpless or so demanding she'd force you to perceive reality.

One cunt's like every other cunt. One ideal's like every other ideal. When one dream goes, another takes its place. You're sick of standing in this shit and so you step out.

At the end of the world. Almost no one living in this perpetual Florida grayness. It may not be paradise, but it doesn't stink of the shit of your dreams. Not much to set you dreaming in this grayness.

There's an old dilapidated hotel on the island. Some old croaker who wheezes instead of talking runs the spa. As far as you know, the croaker won't bother you, no one else's staying at the hotel, and room-and-board are cheap. You decide to stay for a night.

There's nothing else to say. You're a piece of meat among other pieces of meat. It's like when you were at the hospital. The doctor couldn't get the needle in your vein to extract blood. Every time he stuck the needle in your arm, the vein rolled away. You felt like a piece of meat and you didn't care. You saw that the doctor saw living and dying and screaming people and the doctor didn't care if you were dying or screaming. So you didn't care if you were dying or screaming.

You can't tell what matters anymore. Every day you look out

at the ocean and you see a tiny boat going down that grayness.
One dark tiny boat going down the turbulent waters.

You're gonna stick with him, not cause you love him, but you've
gone this far. You've opened yourself to trusting him so deeply
if you turn back now, you'll be throwing everything you've got
away. The only thing you can call your life. You'll be left with
a rotting carcass. Besides, he's not so bad even if he is a gangster.
The dimple in his double chin.

He knows how to handle you. He's cruel to you just up to a
certain point. He knows that point and he knows if he was one
bit crueler to you, you'd leave him. He knows when to press you,
when to be a little bit crueler, and when to leave you alone. He
really cares about you because he bothers to know you so well.
Other people he doesn't bother about, he just kills them. He's
gotten into you and he knows how to manipulate your limbs with
his big naked hands.

He's a killer. O my God, he kills people. You know you've
got to get away from him.

You look up in the car, and there he is. Driving the car, as
usual. Never looking at you.

Johnny's running away from trouble again. He's always more
trouble than the trouble from which he's running away.

You're the big one. The big dingbat. The winner. You're in this
little hick town, this island, and you're gonna take it over until
the boat comes. As usual you've got everything arranged and
under control. You know how to move the little people around
so you can get everything you want.

It's quiet here, and gray. Layers of gray and layers of gray. Like
a numbness you can slice with your hand. When the numbness
separates, there's nothing. This's what you want.

The ocean waves're moving regularly up and down the beach. They leave lines of shells on the beach and sometimes large jellyfish. You can see the shells and the jellyfish only when the light manages to squeeze through the gray layers. Otherwise the shells and jellyfish look like darker gray blobs, then rows, on the gray.

The day gets darker. You see that the beach isn't the sea. The crummy wood boards that lead to the sea look wet. The whole joint's crumbling apart. How many more years does this hotel have? Three? One? One more hurricane? Maybe tomorrow. You can see the bones of the world.

Somewhere behind you, you hear a car stop and voices. You don't believe that you're hearing anything.

So now shitface is gonna take out his little gun. Order everyone around with his little gun, the old fuddy-duddy who doesn't keep up this palsied outhouse, probably pisses in his pants, and the doddering old man who's been the only hotel guest for the last twenty years. Phooey. Isn't Johnny tough? Johnny and his gun. You hope the hotel's got a bar cause you're gonna have to stick with Johnny until you can get out of this grayness.

You need another man. In this grayness it's easier to find a bottle of booze.

What man's gonna want you now? Once upon a time you were really hot stuff. With your blonde hair and big child's eyes, eyes so big and wide they denied the way your nipples got hard under your sweater, men were drooling after you. You could get anyone you wanted. For nothing. Now you get beaten up and shoved around. Every now and then you get a gun shoved in your mouth.

"OK. Everyone get your hands up. I'm taking over here."

You walk into the dark inner space of the hotel. You're gonna show them who's boss. A trembling white-haired guy appears with his hands held up.

You're dreaming that you're wearing your white Givenchy dress and your white and brown shoes. You're wading through about two feet of mud and water. Your dress is getting filthy, but you don't mind. You're trying to reach an old deserted house. Your fiancé's waiting for you there. You lift your eyes and see a large dark structure.

"We're almost there, dear." Your red fingernails carefully flick a cake-crumb off your summer dress.

You're still alone and with the grace of God you'll die alone.

Maybe you'll die soon and it'll all be over. No more fakes.

The ocean's calm. It's almost evening and it looks like dawn with that strange yellow sun, under the dark gray sky, making the lower third of the sky white-yellow-gray. Sending a triangle of yellow-white light out over the ocean.

The air's still and stinks of fish. You realize a storm's coming. One storm more or less don't make any difference to you. You walk into the dark interior of the hotel and see a gun pointed at your face.

"Back against the wall."

I moved back against the wall. I didn't feel frightened, yet.

"All of you, back against the wall."

The geezer who ran the hotel was already rubbing his back so hard against the wall, the wallpaper was crumbling. A dame with booze in her hand who was standing against the hotel register didn't move.

The guy with the gun walked over and slashed her face open with the point of his gun. She looked at him and walked over to the wall.

Lightning.

The hotel door flies open.

"OK Johnny. Men are for fucking and women for friendship. When I'm not fucking you, I'm your enemy."

I ignored what she said. The storm was coming up hard and fast and there was nothing I could do about that. The boat wouldn't come and I'd be stuck with these pawns for days.

"I want you to understand I'm boss here. This storm"

"It's a hurricane."

I gave the old guy a dirty look. "Hurricane. It's gonna be a while and I don't want trouble. As far as I'm concerned, you're pieces on a checkerboard that I'm moving around so everything's easiest for me. You're either on the board or you're off the board." I moved my gun.

The hotel door swung open and shut. When the door swung open again, an old guy in a wheelchair and a tall woman dressed in a lightish dress were standing in the doorway.

I thought I was hallucinating.

"Excuse me. I need help for my grandfather, Senator . . ."

"We're . . ."

You'd think this was Palm Springs at Christmas. "Both of you. Get over here. No, you," I pointed my gun at the hotel clerk. He should be doing his job. "Shove the wheelchair against the wall. No funny business."

I looked at the girl. "You can use your own legs, I presume?"

The girl was a looker. Legs and class. I wouldn't go near her if she was coated with hundred dollar bills. I didn't have to go near her. Johnny, as his drunk girlfriend called him, would be doing all our movements for us.

Hotel lights go out.

Old geezer takes advantage of blackness to try to shove wheel-chair with guy in it at me. I laugh and shoot geezer in arm.

"Looks like someone else is going to have to be hotel clerk for a while."

There're no lights and there's this storm, a hurricane I think, and there's this gangster and I'm totally confused. This isn't the way things are back home. Mummy and poppa always kept a quiet home, and now that they're dead,—they must not have loved me as much as I thought cause they died,—grandpa, the senator, takes care of me. I wish we were back home.

Grandpa said that politics was getting so crooked, he had to get away for awhile. He's not running from anyone; he's just trying to figure out how he can fight the crookedness more successfully. I want to be like grandpa: I want to fight for a better world.

I wonder if there are any more men in the world like grandpa.

"All of you. Get to your rooms. Remember that people die when they go out in hurricanes. The phone lines are dead. There's no way you can escape.

"Don't get any funny ideas. Brave pigeons become dead pigeons. Remember: to me you're just pieces of meat."

We were pieces of meat who were still bleeding. The worst was: we might stop bleeding soon.

"In two hours you'll all come down here for dinner. If we can't find any food, we'll live on the booze. I like giving parties. I'll wheel the senator to his room."

"Get upstairs like he says." She looked like an outraged mother hen, only her baby was an old man in a wheelchair and she was probably a virgin. I put my hand on her arm. I didn't want her making more trouble for all of us.

"Wait a second."

"Uh-huh."

"You look like . . . a reasonable man. Is that monster going to hurt my grandfather?"

"I doubt it. Your grandfather's probably too important a person."

"I didn't ask you to be smart. We're in a terrible situation and we have to help each other."

"The kind of help I could give you honey you wouldn't want."

"How do you know what I want?"

"I can tell by looking at your fingers. Your left hand pinky's shorter than the finger next to it. Now will you be a good girl and get upstairs?"

"You're a man! You could overpower this gangster. You wouldn't have to kill him. Just knock him cold."

    "A woman friend once told me the only thing men are good for is fucking. I'm afraid that's true."

"You're not a man. A man would realize that his and other people's lives are in danger. Even if he didn't care about the other people, he'd try to save himself. You're a flea, or some kind of . . . amoeba who just accepts things."

"Listen. I'm not going to do anything. I don't care how I die, honey." I started walking up the stairs.

    I began remembering her long legs and regretting I was walking away from her.

I wanted to kill him. The only thought in my mind was that I wanted to kill him.

I must have fallen asleep, for the next thing I know, I'm hearing these screamings and sounds of beating that make the old hotel seem like a flea-studded whorehouse:

". . . keep your mouth shut."

"Why don't cha beat me up again? Hurting me takes the place of sex these days."
   "I'm a businessman. I want you to remember. I'm a quiet businessman and I like my friends to be quiet about me."

"The only friends you have are dead men.
   "You're just a cheap dice man, Johnny. A cheap dice man who's running from the real crooks, the big crooks, and you think you can be a big guy to these crummy people in this crummy hotel."

"I suppose the takeover of The Flamingo and Virginia Hill's 'suicide' are small-time bits to you?
   "I shouldn't ever talk to you. I weaken myself when I talk to you."

"Johnny, straighten out. You're nothing Johnny, like me."

"You stinkin' whore. I'm gonna kill you one of these days."

"You're nothing like me.
   "Get me another drink, please Johnny"

I wanted to find my grandfather. I left the little room at the end of the hall against which the wild wind was beating and the trees and the telephone poles, the only bit of safety I had left, and I started down the hall. I knew my grandfather was somewhere downstairs.

The hotel was dark, almost black. Walls seemed to drift into more and more corners and walls. Finally I reached the stairs.

Large dark shapes moved in and out of the corners of my eyes. As I walked down the stairs, I saw the walls move, bend and almost crack, as if they were bowing to me. I was walking down the endless stairs in my long white dress. The train of my dress was slowly draped upward behind me. I felt so tall and proud my head was almost touching the ceiling. Soon I would be a new woman.

All the people I had ever known were waiting for me at the bottom of the stairs. My mother was crying and even my father had tears in his eyes. I was so happy I was almost crying. Somewhere in that mass of people, my fiancé, soon: my husband, was waiting for me.

What was I thinking? I had to find my grandfather. I was in a hotel which was being, for some reason, run by a gangster and I had to find my grandfather before the gangster killed him.

I was standing at the bottom of that endless flight of stairs. I could see the hotel door flying open and closed, almost flying off its hinges but not quite, and I could see the winds wiping the panes of glass out of the windows and I could hear the palm trees break and fall against the old hotel. I wanted to run, but I didn't know where I could go.

I realized that I've always wanted to run and never have anywhere to run to. I had to find my grandfather quickly. There were rooms and rooms and most of the rooms were empty and my grandfather was in one room and the gangster was in another room. I could hardly tell the rooms from the doors cause the large dark shapes were moving in front of and away from my eyes.

I couldn't see but I had to keep going. I stuck my hands out in front of me.

I kept on moving. Something clattered to the floor, and I almost tumbled.

A hand grabbed my wrist.

I didn't want to, but I couldn't get those legs out of my mind. I looked outside my room and saw those legs again. I didn't want to, I must have stopped thinking, but I began to follow them.

Long white legs.

They led me through the hall, down the stairs, and into some large room.

I found myself looking into that man's eyes. The one who wouldn't help me. "What do you want with me?"

"I want to talk to you."

"We've done all our talking. I don't want anything to do with men who are cowards.

"Excuse me, I have to find my grandfather."

"You've done all your talking. I still want to talk to you."

She tried to brush by me. I put my two arms around the sides of her body.

"What d'you want?"

"I want to find out who you are."

"I'm in trouble. Or do you want the irrelevant details?"

"Let's say I want the irrelevant details."

"When I was two years old, I refused to drink milk. My parents, they were still alive then, were scared I was going to die. My father started to take a camera apart. Only when he started to break the camera, would I drink the milk."

"That's certainly irrelevant."
   "Is it? I want to stay alive, Mr. Coward. I'm only interested in people who are going to help me stay alive."

"Aren't you being self-centered? Tell me about mom and pops. When did they die on you?"

"When I was eight. Just old enough to start feeling insecure and not old enough to know how to ask someone for help. My grandfather took me into his house and gave me what attention he could."

"Could? You mean you were a lonely child who spent lonely days making up fantasies and living in them?"

"My personal history concerns only those people who love me. Excuse me please."

"Tell me more about your parents. Did they love you a lot when you were a child?"

"I want to find my grandfather." I was begging him to help me. "If you care at all about me, you'll help me find him."

"I didn't know I cared about you."

"Help me."

For some reason I wanted to hear the rest of her words, but I couldn't. I kept hearing that stupid popular song, bits of it, that everyone was singing back where everyone was still living and burning each other out.

Baby don't give, baby don't get.
When it's cold, baby gets wet.
When baby gets wet, baby gets weak.
Baby don't find, baby don't seek.

You want to know the story of this song
It's about a woman who loves to go wrong.
She gets contented like a big fat cat
Only when she's lying flat on her back.

Well, this woman fell in love with a man
Just like some women unfortunately can.

This man had nuts but was nuts in the head
He refused to take this hot babe to bed.

Baby don't give, baby don't get.
When it's cold, baby gets wet.
When baby gets wet, baby gets weak.
Baby don't find, baby don't seek.

He told her he loved her; he told her he'd give
Anything to her so she'd continue to live.
He'd buy her minks and he'd buy her pearls
He just wouldn't give her cunt a swirl.
Too many women were pursuing him
And he was fucking too many girls.

So she sang him this sad sad song
About how the world was always wrong:
DIE IF I DO, DIE IF I DON'T:
DIE IF I WRITE, DIE IF I DON'T
DIE IF I FALL IN LOVE AND DIE IF I WON'T

He didn't give a shit, he didn't care.
She shouted to the cold winter air;
She slashed her wrists; she shaved her head;
She refused to eat so she'd almost drop dead.

He didn't run to her, he told her he
Was sick of people and their needs.
All he wanted to do was sit alone
In his country house by his telephone.

Baby don't give, baby don't get.
When it's cold, baby gets wet.
When baby gets wet, baby gets weak.
Baby don't find, baby don't seek.

So listen girls, do what you can
To find a horny loving man.
Give him all you've got to give,
Give him more so you can live.